FREE TO BE HUMAN

DAVID EDWARDS was born in Maidstone, Kent in 1962. After taking a degree in Politics at the University of Leicester, he worked in sales and marketing management for several large corporations. In 1991 he left the business world, to concentrate on writing and teaching. He is co-editor of Media Lens, which he set up with author and journalist David Cromwell in 2001 to counterbalance the distorted vision of the corporate media. Media Lens has become a major force in questioning the bias of the British media (free Media Alerts are available from www.medialens.org). David is a frequent contributor to the *New Statesman* and a monthly *ZNet* commentator (see www.zmag.org). He is also the author of *The Compassionate Revolution: Radical Politics and Buddhism* (Green Books, 1998).

Free
to be
Human

Intellectual Self-Defence in an Age of Illusions

David Edwards

green books

Re-printed in 2017 by
Green Books,
an imprint of UIT Cambridge Ltd
www.greenbooks.co.uk

PO Box 145, Cambridge CB4 1GQ, England
+44 (0)1223 302 041

First published by Green Books Ltd. in 1995, new introduction
included in 2002.

Cover design by Rick Lawrence

Cover illustration by Paul Carpenter

Typeset by Chris Fayers

ISBN: 978 1 870098 88 5 (paperback)

Disclaimer: the author and publisher accept no liability for actions
inspired by this book

10 9 8

CONTENTS

THE SKY IS A ROOF!
Preface for the third printing

There is a wonderful moment in the film 'The Truman Show' when Truman's 'friend' of more than thirty years, Marlon, responds to Truman's growing sense that his entire reality is somehow being fabricated as part of some great conspiracy:

> "The last thing that I would do is lie to you. If everybody was in on it, I'd have to be in on it too. I'm not in on it, Truman, because there is no 'in'."

The beauty of the scene is that Marlon's passionately sincere assurances that he would not lie, that he is not in on any conspiracy, are in fact being relayed to him through a microphone by a director watching the entire scene from atop the vast dome that covers the mock town and which doubles as the sky.

Truman, it turns out, has guessed right. He is the first child to be "legally adopted by a corporation" and has spent his entire life on a giant theatrical set modelled on small-town America, Sea Haven, observed through 5,000 pinhole cameras. His mother and father, his friends, his wife, are all actors in the ultimate docu-soap: 'The Truman Show'. Only the unwitting Truman is real. His society, of course, has programmed him to view all speculation on such a conspiracy as utter madness: he is controlled by fears, hopes, the need to belong, just like you are. Just like I am.

The Truman Show is a perfect metaphor for our time. It is exactly this level of deception to which we are subjected: unadulterated lie presented as absolute truth. As the historian Howard Zinn notes:

> "The truth is so often the reverse of what has been told us by our culture that we cannot turn our heads far enough around to see it."

You and I, nice people that we are, normally do not expect human beings to say the exact opposite of what is true. We know that people twist the truth, squash it a little, stretch it, but they generally don't reverse it. This is why it is important to remember that when we are listening to corporate and state spokespeople disseminating "the truth" of our culture, we are not listening to the independent human beings of ordinary, day-to-day experience; we are listening to human beings radically constrained by the structural requirements of their institutions. As John Steinbeck had a tractor driver declare in *The Grapes of Wrath*: "The bank isn't like a man."

More to the point is the fact that, very often, the spokesperson representing the bank also "isn't like a man".

'Oh come on, people aren't that dishonest!', I hear you cry. But they *are*—especially with themselves. Upton Sinclair explained the problem:

> "It is difficult to get a man to understand something when his salary depends upon his not understanding it."

Women too! People have a capacity for saying and believing whatever they have to say and believe in order to keep their jobs—history suggests that there are few if any limits to this self-deception.

A Snowflake Conspiracy?

Alas, seeing through the illusions of society is far harder for us than for Truman. A conspiracy can always be betrayed, exposed. The deceptions in our society, however, are not the product of a conspiracy; they are the product of market forces. Nobody conspires to build a snowflake; it is in the nature of water, ice, air and cold temperatures for snowflakes—which look for all the world like they have been painstakingly designed—to be perfectly symmetrical.

Likewise, nobody conspires to prevent the media telling the truth: a profit-seeking media system operating within a capitalist society dominated by corporate and state power just comes to report in a way that reflects the values, interests and goals of that power. Editors and journalists just come to believe that what they write is the unadulterated, unexpurgated truth. People who challenge the notion that a corporate press could be a free press, are odd, Truman-like figures shouting 'The sky is a roof! The sky is a roof! There is more!' Kalle Lasn of Adbusters describes how editors received his attempts to place his anti-consumerist TV adverts:

> "They laughed me out of the building ... They just giggled and laughed and said 'Hey, this isn't a commercial, we don't play this kind of thing'."

When environmentalist George Monbiot raised the issue of resource use and global warming with the Society of Motor Manufacturers and Traders, "they burst into gales of laughter. They found these concepts funny, I think because ... anyone who could compare them in importance to the growth of their industry had to be either joking or insane".

As Truman's wife pleads, "Let me get you some help, Truman, you're not well."

In Sea Haven, the local paper's headline reads: "Sea Haven: The Best Place on Earth". When Truman tells his teacher he wants "to be an explorer, like Magellan", she replies: "You're too late, there's really nothing left to explore." In the town's tourist office, a poster shows an airliner being struck by lightning: "It Could Happen To You!" it warns. Everything is designed to work against Truman's wanderlust.

In our corporate capitalist society, talk shows ask: "Shopping or sex: which is better?" Education ministers openly declare that "The end-users of education are the employers." Our news broadcasters announce: "And the main headline this lunchtime: Prince Charles and Camilla Parker-Bowles have appeared as a couple, in public, for the first time." Everything is designed to work against our *wonder*lust.

As Norman Mailer has written, all of this comes at a certain cost to the editors and journalists:

> "There is an odour to any Press Headquarters that is unmistakable ... the unavoidable smell of flesh burning quietly and slowly in the service of a machine."

Many of the ideas in our heads—the notion that we live in a free democracy, that the West supports human rights in the Third World, there is nothing more to life than fun, status is success, life is meaningless, romantic love is 'the answer', anger is empowering—are what comes out of the end of this machine. It's not pretty.

Few of us question the version of reality with which we are presented. But, as happens to Truman, glitches in the programme can wake us from our slumber. In the film, Truman begins to wake up when an object crashes down from the 'sky'. It is clearly a light from a TV studio, and is labelled 'Sirius'—it's the light used to represent that star on the roof of the dome. In the same way, climate change, ozone depletion, the mass death of species, are all waking us up to the fact that 'normal' is in fact pathological—the devastation of the environment may well prove to be the best thing that ever happened to freedom of thought!

Personal Is Political

I hope you enjoy *Free to be Human*. Most of it was written in a couple of months in the autumn of 1993, when I was unemployed during what was one of the happiest and most exhilarating times of my life. A frustration since then has been the difficulty of discussing these ideas outside the book format. Mainstream newspapers and magazines are out, for obvious reasons. But left-wing, anarchist and green magazines will also not include these issues because they are not purely 'hard-nosed' political/economic pieces. Since writing this book, I have written any number of articles on environmental, media and human rights issues, but have almost always felt constrained and have almost never been writing about what seems to me to be the most important—the kind of synthesis of personal and political realities contained in this book. There appears to be a strange belief amongst many radicals that personal issues and experiences—what we feel, what motivates us, hurts us, helps us—are not suitable for discussion. There is an almost technocratic obsession with facts and figures—radical writers are happy to act as fact-conduits, nothing more. We can talk endlessly about global warming, emissions trading and GMOs, but not about what motivates us to do this in the first place, why it's rewarding, why conformity isn't, what first made us question the sanity of the world around us. This seems to be considered soft-headed, embarrassing, a waste of time. Facts and figures are all assembled and communicated in the hope that they will motivate people to act—and yet, all the while, issues of personal motivation are off the agenda.

I suspect that this tendency is in part the result of the fact that our technology-obsessed society has discouraged the capacity for self-awareness in many people, dissidents included. It has also over-emphasised respect for the machine-like, the technical, intellectual, and inhuman, and diminished respect for the personal, subjective, emotional, human—'soft' human emotions are deemed a kind of poor relation to 'hard science' and 'hard' facts. I have to say that this view appals me. The equating of 'hard' with 'powerful', in this way, belongs to arms manufacturers and pornographers, not humanitarian dissidents.

As discussed in this book, the thing that finally persuaded me to abandon my own business career was my decidedly 'soft' human perception that conformist success was turning my blood to treacle, killing me with boredom; that working for the benefit and freedom of others would also benefit and liberate me. These were all very personal ideas, a matter of quite subtle psychological experience and awareness—facts and figures were a side issue.

The proper subject of dissident debate should include, for example, why a young person leafing through the jobs pages on his or her parents' lounge floor, feels utterly bored and depressed by every last one of the jobs on offer. Our task should be to take this very real, very important personal reaction, explain why it is absolutely valid, and link it to the very real destructive psychological, political, economic and environmental consequences of not accepting it as such. Personal is political—to ignore one is always to diminish the other.

David Edwards
February 2000

INTRODUCTION
The Limits of the Possible

This is a book about freedom, and above all about the idea that there is often no greater obstacle to freedom than the assumption that it has already been attained. What prison, after all, could be more secure than that deemed to be 'the world', where the boundaries of action and thought were assumed to define not the limits of the permissible, but the limits of the possible?

It seems to me that the struggle for human freedom is all too prone to illusory 'ends of history' of this kind. When we think we have arrived, when we think battles have been won, we have often simply arrived at more sophisticated forms of control, so that our 'triumph' is actually the obstacle we need to overcome.

Today we are living in a society that creates the powerful impression that, barring a few issues of inequality and distribution of wealth, freedom has been more or less fully attained for the majority of people (the chaos of the Third World being someone else's problem, a result of self-inflicted overpopulation, natural disasters, or whatever else serves to avoid the responsibility of five hundred years of European exploitation). As a result, the majority of us feel little urgent need to strive for freedom.

What will be suggested here, however, is that the battle for freedom from the control of earlier church-based and autocratic regimes has been, at best, only partially successful; that many of the devices used to maintain our conformity and passivity in the past have not been overcome at all but remain (often unconsciously) as servants of the powerful in new guises. Today, the same Emperor can be seen striding unashamedly across our TV screens, resplendent in the various guises of 'democracy', 'the free world', 'the free press', 'Third World aid', 'human rights concerns', 'normality', 'just the way world is', appearing to be noble and moral as a matter of 'self-evident' 'common sense'. We have merely come full circle to a new version of the old illusions that clothe the same naked ambition and greed.

While it is true that we in the West (though certainly not in the Third World) have largely escaped the physical chains and violence of state control, these have been replaced by psychological chains which are, in many ways, even more effective if only because they are invisible and thus far more difficult to perceive. Because we are talking here about manipulation of thought, we find that these chains come in an almost endless variety of forms.

We can of course be controlled by simply not being informed, by limiting our access to the facts so that we perceive no need to be concerned or take action; but we can also be pacified by the framework of presupposed ideas into which we are born, by the assumption, for example, that the search for truth is the business of 'experts', that understanding the world is not possible or important for that mythical creature 'the average man in the street' (women can be pacified by not even being mentioned in this regard!).

Similarly, we can be made to defer to our leaders by the spectre of awesome enemies bent on our destruction (devils, Evil Empires, New Hitlers); by exploiting our tendency to idolise some all-powerful father-figure (either declaiming from heaven or chatting by the fireside); by using scapegoats to play on our need to belong with the herd (one of 'us'—moderates, liberals, freedom fighters) and to not be an outsider (one of 'them'—terrorists, communists, extremists); by obscuring the ugly truth beneath the camouflage of opposites beloved of all tyrants and deceivers (as in the Department of Defence, the Ministry of Truth, the People's Revolution, Green consumerism). The result is that we are persuaded to applaud the forces of exploitation as they march forward under the flag of equality and justice.

In short, we can be manipulated in any number of subtle ways—through what we know and don't know, through what we desire, through what we fear, through what we assume to be the truth about ourselves, human nature and the world generally. The consequence of this is that it is not enough simply to succeed in unearthing the facts about, say, our government's complicity in human rights atrocities abroad, because fundamental areas of our belief system may have been subject to the same influences which made the recovery of those facts so difficult. We may have gained the facts, but not the belief that is up to us to do anything about them; either because we are not 'experts', or because truth, compassion and understanding seem a side issue and even a hindrance in our lives devoted to improving our 'standard of living' and 'having fun'. The world is full of examples of individuals who have glimpsed the horror of what is being done in their name in the Third World, or who have collided with the limits of justice and freedom in their own lives, but have turned away for exactly this reason.

As a consequence, we will not be content here to restrict ourselves to a political analysis. Instead, we will begin with such an analysis and move on, or rather down, to examine some of the fundamental issues of the human situation to seek out areas in which we may have been manipulated at the most basic levels of thought. The problematic nature of this strategy is clear—some readers may be drawn to factual political analyses (media studies, human rights, the environment, and so on), others may be drawn to more philosophical (dare I use the word 'spiritual'?) interests (mythology, psychology, humanistic religious speculation) with some deeming the other to be irrelevant in comparison. Indeed from my own experience, I would argue that it is possible to see both areas of interest as irrelevant from the perspective of 'the other side'. For example, an understanding of the messages of mythology can seem academic in the extreme when set alongside the terrible and urgent facts of the latest Western-backed massacre in East Timor. On the other hand, the importance of individual cases can seem to diminish when set beside the assertion in endless mythological tales that genuine motivation to act on such horrors with any conviction and hope of real change is gained only through understanding that the 'wasteland' 'out there' is reflected in the 'wasteland' in our minds and hearts, which have been desolated by the same web of necessary illusions supporting the same mindless greed that have destroyed—and obscured the destruction of—the people of East Timor. Only when we make that link of understanding can we be fundamentally transformed and so truly willing and able to act.

It is my belief that neither perspective is unimportant, that both are absolutely vital and, in fact, mutually reinforcing and illuminating. If you and I are to truly master the arts of intellectual self-defence, if we are to gain the freedom to be human as independent, critically thinking individuals able to fight for the life, liberty and happiness of ourselves, each other and all life against those who would use us for their own ends, then we need to gain as rational an understanding of the facts as possible—of the world of politics but also of the underlying framework of modern beliefs and values.

Above all, if we are to escape from the prison as 'the world', we need to be wary of our own presumptions, in the understanding that what we thought were the limits of the relevant, of the useful, and of the possible, may indeed turn out to be simply the (subtly imposed) limits of the permissible.

Chapter 1

BEYOND TOTALITARIANISM
Noam Chomsky and the Propaganda Model of Media Control

'Our whole social system rests upon the fictitious belief that nobody is forced to do what he does, but that he likes to do. This replacement of overt by anonymous authority finds its expression in all areas of life: Force is camouflaged by consent; the consent is brought about by methods of mass suggestion.' Erich Fromm, *The Art of Being*[1]

Proceed With Caution! The Pitfalls of 'Common Sense'
Psychologists advise caution in situations where we find either ourselves or other people dismissing an argument out-of-hand as absurd or incomprehensible. It seems that several very different motives may account for our response.

First, rejection may of course be a rational response to the nonsense of a demonstrably irrational argument. Secondly, however, it may be triggered by the accurate but uncomfortable nature of an argument— we may reject an idea as 'nonsense' precisely because we recognize (perhaps unconsciously) that it raises a profoundly unpleasant truth we would rather not confront. Thirdly, the argument may be so contrary to our common sense view of the world that it strikes us as being simply ridiculous (the word derives from the Latin *ridere* meaning 'to laugh'; we tend to find ridiculous, or funny, that which dramatically contradicts our usual conception of the world). Fourthly, we may simply be lying when we dismiss an argument that we perceive as damaging to our interests.

In short, immediate rejection of an argument may be based on rational, emotional, or self-interested motives. While it may often be difficult to establish which motivation, or mixture of motivations, is involved at any given time, rejections based on emotional discomfort, intellectual sloth and/or self-interest will tend to claim a greater level of certainty than those based on reason; reason, after all, is not in the business of absolute certainty, while emotion and self-interest often tolerate nothing less.

Unfortunately it is when we claim to be most certain about what is or is not a 'common sense' argument, that our judgement is most suspect. In the face of this all-too-human predicament, our only realistic strategy would appear to be to rely on our powers of doubt and reason, to put aside our (perhaps) irrationally-motivated knee-jerk response and take as careful a look as possible at *the facts*.

This, I would like to suggest, is the course of action demanded of anyone encountering for the first time the dissident political writings of linguist Noam Chomsky. For, in his criticism of the abuse of contemporary economic, political and military power in the United States and beyond, Chomsky presents a view of the world that is in extreme conflict with the 'common sense' version held by the majority of people. In fact, his argument is at such odds with the view of the world presented, for example, by the mass media, that an emotionally-motivated dismissal seems almost guaranteed. Similarly, the nature of his attacks on vested interests are such that responses motivated by self-interest also seem extremely likely.

In short, Chomsky's views are so contrary to what most people believe and to what some people would *like* most people to believe, that it is easy to imagine that he rarely receives a fair intellectual hearing. The factual record does not disappoint us. A typical example of the sort of out-of-hand dismissal he generally receives was provided by the New York Times:

> 'Arguably the greatest intellectual alive, [Chomsky's political writing is]... maddeningly simple-minded.'[2]

According to this view, immediate rejection is demanded by the self-evidently absurd nature of Chomsky's arguments. Yet the reader will agree that the statement itself presents us with a bewildering problem for, the author of these 'simple-minded' political views is indeed one of the truly great intellectuals of our time. We might feel inclined to pose the question differently, then, and ask how it might be that a thinker with Chomsky's spectacular intellectual track-record could come to be adjudged to be simple-minded when he chooses to criticize the powerful?

Thus we come to the crux of the matter: is it Chomsky's intellectual competence which deserts him when he criticizes the powerful, or is it the willingness of Chomsky's critics to perceive that competence which deserts *them*? Is this great mind so fatally flawed by an eccentric, irrational, anti-authoritarian bent that his political arguments can be dismissed out-of-hand? Or is it possible that critics are in some way influenced by emotional, and/or self-interested prejudices, thus ensuring that Chomsky's work is met with ridicule and silence in such a way that they suppress the dissident criticisms of one of the clearest thinking, most rational intellects of this, or any other, age? Intellectual responsibility surely requires—no matter how absurd or pointless we might initially consider the task—that we look at the facts of the argument in a rational manner.

Tools of the trade: Chomsky as man of the Enlightenment

Intellectually, Chomsky is a man of the Enlightenment. As such, his revolutionary work in linguistics has been founded on a simple, rigorous application of the basic tools of scientific method. Chomsky argues that all intellectual problems should be approached in the same way—by gathering all the available facts, constructing provisional hypotheses to account for them and by then testing and refining, or rejecting and replacing those hypotheses in the light of the available facts. This is a simple restatement of Popper's process of 'conjecture and refutation' and while it does not claim to deliver absolute certainty, it does seek to advance the most plausible hypotheses in the light of the available data. There is no room (or ability) here to detail Chomsky's success in applying this method within the field of linguistics; suffice it to say that the history of linguistics is commonly divided into two ages—BC (Before Chomsky) and AD (After his Discoveries).

This, of course, proves nothing about the rationality of Chomsky's political writings, but it does provide significant circumstantial evidence for Chomsky's capacity for rational thought. However, in accordance with the method favoured by Chomsky himself, let us turn to the facts of some of the simple-minded political ideas he is proposing.

Manufacturing consent: media as propaganda

In their book *Manufacturing Consent*, Chomsky and Edward Herman propose a hypothesis which they call *a Propaganda Model*. (Although we are focusing on Chomsky's political writing, it should be noted that much of this model was actually formulated by Edward Herman.) This model:

> '…reflects our belief, based on many years of study of the workings of the media, that they serve to mobilize support for the special interests that dominate the state and private activity, and that their

choices, emphases, and omissions can often be understood best, and sometimes with striking clarity and insight, by analyzing them in such terms.' Chomsky and Herman, *Manufacturing Consent*[3]

It is important to be clear that this propaganda model of media performance is not merely intended to account for the capacity of dominant interests to loosely influence the general direction of mass media. Rather, it is intended to account for a dramatically effective system of control by which dominant interests are able to manipulate media behaviour from the broadest direction of strategy down to the minutest detail of stress and intonation in individual journalistic reporting. In fact, this model is intended to account for a system of control far tighter than anything imagined by Orwell, or practised by totalitarian governments. The achievement of this extreme level of control, it is argued, is ultimately facilitated precisely by the fact that it is almost completely invisible. The ultimately secure system of control, after all, would be one presenting every appearance of complete freedom—for who, then, would perceive any need to challenge it? This would represent a system of control far beyond any based on totalitarian force.

It is here that we confront what has been described (by Chomsky himself) as the 'Neptune factor' when considering Chomsky's ideas. For at first sight the notion that even the tiniest detail of journalistic reporting might somehow be controlled by the powerful institutions of society, may indeed give the impression that Chomsky is 'fresh in from Neptune'. The reasons for this reaction are clear enough.

Whilst we might be prepared to admit the possibility that the higher echelons of state and business power exert influence over what does or does not appear in our media, we find it frankly ridiculous to suggest that everyone—from the editor down to the most junior hack on the street in all the newspapers, magazines, TV and radio studios around the world—is involved in some kind of global conspiracy to advance the interests of the élites by which they are employed. This, we know, is simply not realistic. As a matter of common sense, we know that such a conspiracy would have been exposed: we would have heard about it from close friends or family members, and anyway, we may in fact know some journalists and they find the whole notion utterly risible. As an English commentator, whilst discussing the issue of freedom, recently asked: 'Who are these people controlling us, restricting our freedom? I just don't see them!'

And yet is not some sort of active conspiracy of precisely this type implied, even demanded, by the suggestion that modern democracies are in thrall to a system of control so complete that it surpasses anything achieved by totalitarianism? Chomsky and Herman's reply to this suggestion is a disconcerting one:

'We do not use any kind of 'conspiracy' hypothesis to explain mass-media performance. In fact, our treatment is much closer to a 'free market' analysis, with the results largely an outcome of the workings of market forces.'[4]

Chomsky and Herman argue that maintenance of control over the media (and society generally) does not even necessarily require conscious planning (although this does take place), but simply 'happens' as the result of 'free market' forces operating to meet the needs of the day. Their theory as to how this works is reminiscent of the old school chemistry experiment designed to demonstrate the formation of crystalline structures.

Framing conditions and 'accidental' necessity

At first sight, it seems extraordinary that snowflakes and other crystalline structures are able to form almost perfect, symmetrical shapes in the complete absence of conscious control or design. The mechanism by which this occurs can easily be demonstrated by setting-out a flat, box-like framework on a table. By pouring a stream of tiny balls over this frame, we find that we eventually, and inevitably, end up with a more or less perfect pyramid shape. Because the most stable resting position in the structure (given the square framework and the spherical shape of the balls) is always one that contributes to the construction of a perfect pyramid, any ball that settles inevitably builds, while all others in less stable positions are moved into more stable positions or bounce out. No one is designing the pyramid, or forcing the balls into place; the pyramid is simply an inevitable product of the framing conditions of round objects falling onto a square wooden frame.

In an analogous way, I would suggest, Chomsky and Herman argue that powerful state and business élites seek to determine the basic framework of modern social goals: maximum economic growth generated by maximized corporate profit, fuelled by mass production, fuelled by mass consumerism. By 'pouring' news, information and ideas into this basic economic framework, a version of reality progressively suited to the requirements of the framework is inevitably produced. As with the crystal model, conscious design is not at all required beyond the initial framing of conditions (which Chomsky and Herman argue business élites *do* consciously try to maintain: any threat to compromise the basic, unchallengeable goal of maximum economic growth from maximum corporate profit is vigorously and consciously opposed at home and abroad). So long as the basic framework is maintained, the pyramid will simply 'build itself'. Thus supportive media, editors and journalists will find a stable place in the economic pyramid, while their unsupportive counterparts will either be moved, or will bounce out (of business).

If we accept the basic plausibility of this model, we have to at least admit the theoretical possibility of extreme levels of control without coercion or planning (beyond that required for the maintenance of the framework). Similarly, we must admit the possibility that a state of extreme lack of freedom might be able to exist in an ostensibly 'free', 'non-totalitarian', 'democracy'.

Let us now look at some of the framing conditions which, according to the propaganda model, provide the basis for a system of media control of near-crystalline and extra-totalitarian perfection.

The Five Reality Filters

Chomsky and Herman argue for the existence of 'filters' by which money and power are able to filter out news 'fit to print', marginalize dissent, and allow government and dominant private interests to get their message across to the public. (The details here refer to state and business control of the US media).

The First Filter: the size, concentrated ownership, owner wealth, and profit-orientation of the dominant mass-media firms.
Media ownership is limited by the substantial cost involved in running even small media entities. With the industrialization of newspapers, for example, the cost of machinery required for even very small newspapers has for many years run into the hundreds of thousands of dollars. As has been ironically suggested, anyone is free to open their own newspaper, so long as they have a couple of million dollars to spare. Thus the first filter is the limitation on ownership, by the large amount of investment required, of media with any significant influence.

In 1986, there were some 25,000 media entities (daily newspapers, magazines, radio and TV stations, book publishers and movie studios) in the United States. Of these, many were small, local news dispensers heavily dependent on the large national companies for all but local news. Also, despite the large numbers of media, the twenty-nine largest media systems accounted for over half the output of newspapers and for most of the sales and audiences in magazines, broadcasting, books and films.

These top companies are of course all large, profit-seeking corporations, owned and controlled by wealthy people. Many of them are fully integrated into the stock market and, consequently, face powerful pressures from stockholders, directors and bankers to focus on profitability. Despite often being in competition, all have a basic framework of identical interests:

> 'These control groups obviously have a special stake in the status quo by virtue of their wealth and their strategic position in one of the great institutions of society [the stock market]. And they exercise the power of this strategic position, if only by establishing the general aims of the company and choosing its top management.'[5]

Mark Hertsgaard has commented (in conversation with David Barsamian) on how this commitment to the status quo means that major media corporations tend to avoid reporting that seeks out root causes of the problems that afflict our world:

> '...that's the kind of reporting that raises very serious and pointed questions about the way our society is organized, about power relations in our society, about the advantages of and problems with a capitalist system. It raises real questions about the status quo. Those questions are not going to be asked on a consistent basis within news organisations that are owned by corporations that have every interest in maintaining the status quo. Those corporations are not going to hire individuals to run those organisations who care about that kind of reporting. Therefore, those individuals are not going to hire reporters who do that kind of reporting, and so you're not going to see it.... Generally, if you start as a reporter early in your career you pick up the messages and it becomes almost instinctive. You don't even realize all of what you've given up, all of the small compromises that you've made along the way.'[6]

The control groups of the media giants are brought into close relationship with the mainstream of the corporate community through boards of directors and social links. This relationship is intensified by the fact that the corporate parents of media giants like NBC, Group W television and cable systems are themselves corporate giants dominated by corporate and banking executives (here General Electric and Westinghouse respectively).

The Second Filter: advertising

Before advertising became prominent, the price of a newspaper had to cover the costs of production. With the growth of advertising, however, newspapers attractive to advertisers were able to lower their copy price below the production cost. This put newspapers which attracted less advertising at a serious disadvantage—their prices would tend to be higher, which reduced sales, and they would also have less profit to invest in improving saleability through quality, format, promotions and so on. For this reason, an advertising-based system will tend to drive into the margins, or out of existence all together, media entities that depend on revenue from sales alone.

'From the time of the introduction of press advertising, therefore, working-class and radical papers have been at a serious disadvantage. Their readers have tended to be of modest means, a factor that has always affected advertiser interest.'[7]

Chomsky and Herman cite several examples of media that have failed for this reason. The British *Daily Herald* newspaper, for example, failed despite having double the readership of *The Times*, the *Financial Times* and *The Guardian* put together. A significant reason was the fact that, whilst the *Herald* had 8.1 percent of national daily circulation, it received only 3.5 percent of net advertising revenue. Apart from the lower disposable income of its readers, an additional reason the *Herald* received so little advertising was clearly the fact that it promoted:

'...an alternative framework of analysis and understanding that contested the dominant systems of representation in both broadcasting and the mainstream press.' James Curran, *Advertising And The Press*[8]

That is, the *Herald* challenged the status quo and was not as business-friendly as other newspapers competing for advertising revenue. Chomsky and Herman go on to cite several examples of advertisers and corporate sponsors clearly (and quite naturally) supporting periodicals and television programmes which support their interests, while withdrawing support from media deemed 'anti-business'.

In 1985, the public television station WNET lost its corporate funding from Gulf & Western after the station showed the documentary 'Hungry for Profit', which contained material critical of multinational corporate activities in the Third World. Even before the programme was shown, station officials 'did all we could to get the program sanitized' (according to a station source). The Chief Executive of Gulf & Western complained to the station that the programme was 'virulently anti-business if not anti-American,' and that by carrying the programme the station was clearly not a 'friend' of the corporation. *The Economist* reported that WNET is unlikely to make the same mistake again.

In similar vein, Proctor & Gamble instructed their advertising agency that 'There will be no material on any of our programmes which could in any way further the concept of business as cold, ruthless and lacking in all sentiment or spiritual motivation.' The manager of corporate communication for General Electric (which, as we have discussed, own NBC-TV) has said: 'We insist on a program environment that reinforces our corporate messages.'[9]

If advertisers, and corporate sponsors generally, tend to support media which boost their message, and these media consequently tend to flourish relative to those not so supported, then we have one example of a tight system of control that does not at all require a conspiracy theory but simply the operation of market forces. For advertiser control clearly extends to the detail of the contents and tone of media. This influence can be extremely subtle and far-reaching (the beginnings, perhaps, of the invisible hand of total control implied by the pyramid model above). A truly advertiser-friendly TV station, for example, will be supportive of the advertiser's desire for the maintenance of a 'buying environment' in between commercials.

> 'Advertisers will want, more generally, to avoid programs with serious complexities and disturbing controversies that interfere with the "buying mood". They seek programs that will lightly entertain and thus fit in with the spirit of the primary purpose of program purchases—the dissemination of a selling message.'[10]

Editors are well aware that a failure to maintain advertiser-friendly content and tone will result in the loss of critical advertising revenue to the competition—a double blow. According to Lewis Lapham, former editor of *Harper's* magazine, New York editors 'advise discretion when approaching topics likely to alarm the buyers of large advertising space.' He goes on:

> 'The American press is, and always has been, a booster press, its editorial pages characteristically advancing the same arguments as the paid advertising copy.'[11]

The Third Filter: the sourcing of mass media news

The mass media, Chomsky and Herman suggest, are inevitably drawn into symbiotic relationship with powerful sources of information by economic necessity and mutual interest. As we know, the media must have a steady, reliable supply of news. For obvious economic reasons, they cannot have reporters everywhere around the globe, so resources are concentrated where significant news is likely to occur. The White House, the Pentagon, and State Department are central news terminals of this type. Similarly, business corporations and trade groups also act as significant, regular news terminals. Their importance as news sources is a direct result of the fact that both corporate and state sectors have enormous resources dedicated to public relations and the dissemination of promotional material.

The US Air Force, alone, for example, publishes 140 newspapers every week and issues 45,000 headquarters and unit news releases a year. Similarly, in 1983 the US Chamber of Commerce had a budget for research, communications and political activities of $65 million. Among many other things, it produced its own weekly panel discussion programme carried by 128 commercial television stations. The scale of this influence dwarfs anything that might be mounted by the combined effort of, say, human rights, church and environmental groups, who might attempt to present a view of reality less in harmony with state and/or corporate goals (the leading dissident magazine currently publishing in the US—*Z Magazine*— is run by a grand total of three people. By comparison, even as far back as 1968 the US Air Force PR effort involved 1,305 full-time staff, as well as countless thousands of staff with public relations duties).

The huge volume of state and business communications not only swamps dissenting voices, but provides the media with cheap and readily available news. This effective subsidising of the media is another important factor in determining what tends to become news.

'To consolidate their pre-eminent position as sources, government and business-news promoters go to great pains to make things easy for news organisations... In effect, the large bureaucracies of the powerful *subsidize* the mass media, and gain special access by their contribution to reducing the media's costs of acquiring the raw materials of, and producing, news. The large entities that provide this subsidy become 'routine' news sources and have privileged access to the gates. Non-routine sources must struggle for access,

and may be ignored by the arbitrary decision of the gatekeepers.'
Chomsky and Herman[12]

The Fourth Filter: 'flak'

The term 'flak' refers to negative responses to a media statement or programme, which may take the form of letters, telegrams, phone calls, petitions, law-suits, speeches and bills before Congress as well as other modes of complaint, threat and punishment. One form of flak mentioned above is the threat of withdrawal of advertising revenue; this threat alone is often sufficient to persuade editors to review the contents of their product. Business organisations regularly come together to form flak machines. One such machine formed by a collection of corporate giants is *Accuracy In Media (AIM)*, whose income rose from $5,000 in 1971 to $1.5 million in the early 1980s. At least eight oil companies were *AIM* contributors in the early eighties. The function of *AIM* is to generate flak and put pressure on the media to follow a corporate-friendly agenda.

Just as state and corporate communications power naturally tend to assist supportive media, so state and corporate flak machines tend to attack and undermine unsupportive media. These are both powerful factors tending to bias the viewpoint of media that are able to flourish. For example, it will be far safer for media to opt for uncontroversial, advertiser-friendly news proffered by state and corporate information machines which will not draw flak, than news proffered by isolated dissident sources which may draw intense flak from state and corporate institutions.

The Fifth Filter: anti-communism

Until recently, this has been especially useful for justifying corporate behaviour abroad and controlling critics of corporate behaviour at home. The creation of an 'evil empire' of one sort or another, Chomsky and Herman suggest, has long been a standard device for terrifying the population into supporting arms production and economic/military adventurism abroad (both important revenue-generators for the corporate community).

Before Communism, the role of 'evil empire' was played by the 'devilish' Spaniards, the 'savage' American Indians, the 'treacherous' British, or the 'baby-eating' Hun. More recently, since the collapse in credibility of any communist 'threat', the war against 'international drugs trafficking and terrorism' as well as skirmishes against various 'new Hitlers' and 'mad dogs' in the Middle East, have served to mobilize the populace around and against threats to élite interests in a similar way.

'This ideology helps mobilize the populace against an enemy, and because the concept is fuzzy it can be used against anybody advocating policies that threaten property interests or support accommodation with Communist states and radicalism.'[13]

Testing the Hypothesis

Chomsky evaluates the propaganda model against the available facts in books like *Manufacturing Consent, The Political Economy of Human Rights* (both with Edward Herman), *Deterring Democracy, Necessary Illusions* and *Year 501*. His method is to compare the type and extent of media attention given to reasonably closely-paralleled examples taken from contemporary history. According to the propaganda model, the media will tend to emphasize and ignore news according to its appropriateness for state and above all corporate ends. Thus, for example, human rights offences committed by clients of the United States supporting US corporate aims will tend to be downplayed or overlooked, while offences by states deemed to be unsupportive—or enemies—of US corporate interests will tend to be vigorously emphasized.

In *Manufacturing Consent*, Chomsky and Herman go to undeniably impressive lengths to establish their case. They compare, for example, media attention given to the murder of Polish priest Jerzy Popieluszko by Polish police on Oct 19, 1984, with media attention given to the murder of 72 religious victims in Latin America in the years 1964-78 (they also compare the Polish murder with the assassination of Archbishop Oscar Romero in El Salvador on March 18, 1980, with similar results). In the New York Times, for example, we find that the Polish murder received 1183 column inches of coverage, while the 72 Latin American victims received just 117.5 inches (9.9% of the Polish total). Even wider discrepancies are found in *Time* and *Newsweek* (313 column inches combined against 16 column inches combined respectively) and *CBS* news (23 programmes against 0 programmes). Chomsky and Herman suggest that these discrepancies can be explained in terms of a propaganda model.

The Polish murder came at a time when the Reagan administration was eagerly soliciting support for increased arms production against the threat of the 'evil empire' of communism; publicising the murder provided an ideal mechanism for generating that support.

Arms production is, of course, an extremely significant source of corporate revenue. (Chomsky and Herman argue that élite state managers are essentially drawn from—and/or controlled by—the same pool of élite managers controlling the major corporations and, for this reason, state interests are often indistinguishable from corporate interests, though differently termed; thus the term 'strategic importance' is generally interchangeable with 'economic importance'.)

Thus reports of atrocities committed by the communist Polish 'enemy' would be expected to pass easily through the filters and be boosted by the flak machines exploiting the ideology of anti-communism. On the other hand, because the 72 Latin American victims were murdered by regimes of client states (often directly installed through US economic and military support and pressure, and closely pursuing US corporate goals), we would expect their fate to pass less easily through the filters and be downplayed by flak machines. It is interesting to note that the propaganda model predicts that any mention of 'friendly' human rights offences which do manage to slip through the filters will draw considerable flak, insisting that the media is far too vigorous in emphasising violations by US-supported regimes and far too lenient on 'enemy' violations. Thus, the famous rumour of an anti-business, left-leaning tendency in the media is actually predicted by the propaganda model.

Drugs and Terror

Another example of truth-filtration is, according to Chomsky, the emphasis in recent years on the need for an 'international defence against drugs and terrorism'. Chomsky argues that, beyond the media and state versions of reality, 'international', 'defence' and 'terrorism' are not what they seem. He cites the American invasion of Panama—ostensibly to arrest General Noriega on drugs and human rights charges on December 20th 1989—as a case in point.

It is well understood that Noriega was closely supported and protected by the US government up until 1986. Yet, during his trial in Miami subsequent to arrest, he was indicted on only one charge relating to events *after* 1984. In other words, Noriega was indicted as part of the 'war against international drugs and terrorism' on charges relating to a time when he was actually supported by the United States in that 'terror'. Chomsky surmises that it was not drug trafficking or terrorism that turned the US against Noriega (drug trafficking has more than doubled since the invasion) but the fact that he grew over-confident, began to compromize American corporate interests in the region and so had to be replaced. This, together with the fact that, in accordance with the Canal Treaty, the Panama canal was due to pass largely under Panamanian control on New Year's day 1990, suggests that the United States decided it needed someone better disposed to its requirements.

Significantly, just as US troops were attacking Panama as part of the 'yearning for democracy and human rights', the US government eliminated trade sanctions against China (only weeks after the Tiannamen Square massacre), having authorized the sale of $300 million of high technology equipment (for military and other uses), whilst the Agriculture Department announced its resumption of subsidized food sales. The US media saw nothing ironic in Senate minority leader Robert Dole's declaration that the capture of Noriega 'proves America won't give up or cave in to anyone, no matter how powerful or corrupt.' [14] Compared to America's friends in Beijing, Chomsky suggests, Noriega could 'pass for a choirboy'.[15] Chomsky explains (in conversation) the mechanism by which the US government consistently manipulates the media to act as a propaganda support machine to prepare the ground for an attack on a previous ally.

'They start getting too independent or interfere with US investors. That happens often. At that point we suddenly start hearing about human rights violations and our yearning for democracy immediately becomes dominant and all sorts of elevated remarks about American ideals, etc. Then there's a period of some ambivalence. After all, you can't flip instantaneously. There's a period in which you try to decide what to do about this.' [16]

In the case of Panama, this propaganda process was hugely successful.

'Noriega remained a very minor thug, exactly what he had been when he was on the CIA payroll, but the US government attitude toward him changed. So therefore automatically the media attitude toward him changed. By the time the invasion took place, you could get Ted Koppel talking about how Noriega is one of that small group of monsters like Stalin and Hitler and Qaddafi and Khomeini who Americans just love to hate and so we have to destroy him.... Dan Rather and Peter Jennings described him as one of the most odious creatures of modern times. The mood was set, and it's true that Americans hated Noriega by 1989. They've been inundated with this totalitarian-style propaganda for several years, and yeah, they hate Noriega… and it created the propaganda framework for the invasion.' [17]

Similarly, the bombing of Libya was justified on the pretext that Colonel Qaddafi was the 'King of International Terrorism'. While Chomsky certainly agrees that Qaddafi is a terrorist, he also points out that Qaddafi is an extremely small-time terrorist. In *Amnesty International's Political Killings By Governments*, Qaddafi is listed as having killed 14 people (mostly Libyans) during the 1980s. Over the same period, the government of El Salvador—with an army supplied, organized, trained and directed by US forces—was responsible for the often extremely sadistic slaughter of approximately 50,000 people. While Qaddafi is labelled 'The Mad Dog of The Middle East', nowhere in the US media has its US-backed activity been described as terrorism for the simple reason that, as Chomsky says, 'it is done by us.'

Elsewhere Chomsky discusses US media behaviour prior to March 1986, when there was to be a major congressional vote relating to the supply of aid to US-backed Contras fighting the Sandinistas in Nicaragua. The administration then in office was keen to reverse congressional backing for the restriction of Contra aid. This is what Chomsky has to say of the three months leading up to the vote:

'I took the two national newspapers, the *Washington Post* and the *New York Times*, and I went through all their opinion pieces, every column written by one of their own columnists, every authored submitted opinion piece and so on for January, February and March. There were 85. Of the 85, all were anti-Sandinista. On that issue, no discussion was even tolerable. So, 85 out of 85 followed the party line: Sandinistas are bad guys… On the major issue, Are we against the Sandinistas?: 100 percent control. Not a whisper of debate.' [18]

Invisible Genocide: The Silent Death of East Timor

Chomsky and Herman seek to explain not only distorted reporting of events, but also massive media black holes into which 'unsuitable' truths somehow fall out of sight. Thus they use the propaganda model to explain the essentially non-existent media coverage of the Indonesian massacre of 200,000 people in East Timor which, as a consequence, has long been a non-event for the general public. (John Pilger's excellent documentary *Death of a Nation* has recently succeeded in generating some media attention.) Contemporaneous massacres on a similar scale carried out by the communist 'enemy' in Cambodia, on the other hand, have become Hollywood material and are rightly infamous. The disparity in media coverage is revealing— a study of the *New York Times Index* 1975-79 shows that East Timor received only 70 column inches of entries over this period, while Cambodia received 1,175 column inches. An explanation is clearly required—the Timor massacre was no less real, criminal and bloody.

Despite having no historical or ethnic claims to East Timor, Indonesia invaded the former Portuguese colony on December 7, 1975. Five days after the invasion, the United Nations General Assembly 'strongly deplore[d]' the aggression, calling on Indonesia to withdraw its troops 'without delay'. Yet, in contrast to the dramatic reaction which resulted in the repulsion of Saddam Hussein's invasion of Kuwait, the governments of the US, Britain, Australia, Germany and France actually abstained from taking any action. This is less surprising when we understand that the United States had given the Indonesian regime its secret approval to the invasion, with President Ford and Henry Kissinger visiting Jakarta only hours before the launch. As former CIA operations officer Philip Liechty recently told John Pilger:

> '[The Indonesian President] Suharto was given the green light [by the US] to do what he did. There was discussion in the Embassy and in traffic with the State Department about the problems that would be created for us if the public and Congress became aware of the level and type of military assistance that was going to Indonesia at that time [approximately 90% of its arms]. It was covered under the justification that it was "for training purposes".'
> John Pilger, *Distant Voices*[19]

In his autobiography, Senator Daniel Patrick Moynihan (US ambassador to the United Nations at the time of the invasion) was equally candid about his role:

> 'The Department of State desired that the United Nations prove utterly ineffective in whatever measures it undertook. This task was given to me, and I carried it forward with no inconsiderable success.'[20]

The result of Moynihan's 'success' has been nothing less than the century's greatest genocide by proportion of population, with 200,000 people, or one-third of the East Timorese population, slaughtered. By all accounts, the savagery of the violence has been awesome.

At the time of the invasion, a lone radio voice from Timor was picked up 300 miles away in Darwin, Australia making a desperate call for help:

> 'The soldiers are killing indiscriminately,' it said. 'Women and children are being shot in the streets. We are all going to be killed. I repeat, we are all going to be killed.'[21]

Since then, the genocide has continued apace, with mass starvation, concentration camps, forced birth control, torture, random imprisonment and murder becoming routine facts of life. Large scale episodes of slaughter also continue. In November 1991, the massacre of 273 and wounding of 160 unarmed Timorese demonstrators in Santa Cruz was witnessed by Alain Nairn, a writer with *New Yorker* magazine:

> 'What I saw was a cold-blooded execution and the facts are very simple and very clear. Indonesian soldiers marched up in massed formation and opened fire in unison into a peaceful, defenceless crowd... People fell, stunned and shivering, bleeding in the road, and the Indonesian soldiers kept on shooting. I saw the soldiers aiming and shooting people in the back, leaping bodies to hunt down those who were still standing. They executed school girls, young men, old Timorese, the street was wet with blood and the bodies were everywhere.' [22]

General Try Sutrisno, Indonesian Armed Forces Commander, was quick to explain the massacre, insisting that 'These ill-bred people have to be shot... and we will shoot them.'[23]

Chomsky and Herman argue that the almost universal ignorance of these facts is a direct result of the performance of the propaganda system which has long preferred to focus on the 'unspeakable evil' of the Cambodian communists. The *Wall Street Journal*'s reaction, for example, was to report that Indonesia's President Suharto had 'moved boldly in defeating the coup makers [in fact, the democratically-elected government of East Timor] and consolidating his power', using 'strength and finesse'.[24] A subsequent headline described the Indonesian leader as 'a Figure of Stability'.[25] The same dictator was described by the London *Economist* as 'at heart benign'[26] (doubtless referring, Chomsky suggests, to his compassion for transnational corporations). In 1991, former Australian prime minister Gough Whitlam felt able to write in the *Sydney Morning Herald* that Indonesia's President Suharto 'is a reasonable and honourable man'.[27]

An editorial in *The Australian* reassured its public that the Jakarta regime 'can be declared moderate',[28] although not by Amnesty International, which recently described Indonesia as a country 'ruled with an iron rod, where any dissent is punished by torture, imprisonment or death.'[29] Indeed, it is interesting to consider that this is the same regime fronted by the same man who, quite apart from the Timorese genocide, presided over the murder of some 500,000 people in Indonesia following the CIA-backed military coup of 1965. Suharto's philosophy is there for all to see in his memoirs (1989) where he writes of the Indonesian massacres:

> 'Some of the corpses were left in public places... This was done so that the general public would understand that there was someone capable of taking action to tackle criminality.'[30]

The rationale behind the otherwise incomprehensible reaction to one of the century's worst atrocities is not difficult to ascertain, and accords well with the predictions of the propaganda model. Quite simply, Indonesia is a major client state subservient to Western business interests. The US Department of Commerce recently reported that Indonesia offers 'excellent trade and investment opportunities for US companies that are too good to be ignored.'[31] True enough—not only do poverty wages and violent suppression of workers' rights guarantee a 'good investment climate' (for companies like Reebok) but—and this is the key to understanding the fate of both the Timorese and news about them—huge reserves of natural gas and up to seven billion barrels of oil have been located off the coast of East Timor in the Timor Gap. In 1989, Australian Foreign Minister Gareth Evans signed a treaty with Indonesia dividing up Timor's plundered wealth, estimated by Evans to be worth 'zillions' of dollars.[32] By 1990, Australia had received $A31 million from sales of permits to oil companies for exploration. As Evans explained: 'The world is a pretty unfair place, littered with examples of acquisition by force..'[33] —sentiments which, be sure, do not extend to the subsequent Iraqi invasion of Kuwait, the crucial difference being that the latter challenged, rather than enhanced, Western control of Third World resources.

Another causative factor which brought about the media blind spot over one of the century's greatest holocausts is that Britain is now the world's largest supplier of arms to Indonesia, selling £290 million worth of equipment in the 1986-90 period alone (arms which have been used in the East Timor genocide, as eye-witnesses have testified. See John Pilger's *Distant Voices* pp303-4). By the end of 1994,

British companies will have sold, or agreed to sell, a further forty Hawk ground-attack aircraft worth £25 million each. These are in addition to Wasp helicopters, Sea Wolf and Rapier SAM missiles, Tribal Class frigates, battlefield communications systems, seabed mine disposal equipment, Saladin, Saracen and Ferret armoured vehicles, a fully-equipped Institute of Technology for the Indonesian army and training for Indonesian officers in Britain. As former prime minister Margaret Thatcher, who also understands that the world is 'an unfair place', told the assembled chiefs of Indonesia's weapons industry in 1992, 'I am proud to be one of you.'[34]

In similarly 'pragmatic' vein, while Britain was heaping praise on the film *Schindler's List*, documenting the Nazi holocaust, Alan Clark, defence procurement minister under Thatcher, responded to the question of any personal remorse he might feel over the consequences of his arms deals for the Timorese people, saying 'I don't really fill my mind much with what one set of foreigners is doing to another.'[35]

Massive arms sales, vast oil reserves, a client dictatorship willing to enforce a 'good investment climate'—all these combine to ensure the efficient functioning of the filter system so that the general public remains unaware of one of the century's greatest crimes against humanity. With so much profit at stake for major corporate groupings like the energy industry, the owners of the media (such as arms manufacturers General Electric, who, as we have discussed, own NBC) and major advertisers like British Aerospace, the propaganda model predicts that awkward truths are extremely unlikely to surface. Instead, intense concentrations of flak will rise to meet any attempt to even discuss the facts, whilst anti-communism and other devices of demonization will be used to justify military action. Thus we find that the Timorese Fretilin party has indeed been depicted as a terrorist 'Marxist' organisation by the Western media (New York Times and Newsweek, for example),[36] although it was actually a moderately reformist national front, headed by a Catholic seminarian, enjoying widespread support among the people. Another device, as we have seen, has been to insist that the billions of dollars worth of arms sold to Indonesia are for training purposes only.

Beyond these fictions, the simple and tragic truth was probably best expressed by Professor Forman of the University of Michigan, who assured us that we are here discussing nothing less than the 'annihilation of a simple mountain people'.[37]

It remains a matter of conjecture whether the facts will be allowed to surface so that history may one day accord with the sentiments of

Portugal's President Soares, who spoke recently of Britain's role in supporting dictators in his own country as well as in its former colony:

> 'I was in England recently and spoke to John Major and Douglas Hurd about Timor... I said "We can never forgive you for this. It's also possible the Timorese will never forgive you, either." ' [38]

'It Doesn't Take A Hero!' War Crimes in the Gulf

Silence in the media and general ignorance surrounding Western-backed crimes against humanity that benefit Western business are in themselves powerful evidence of the operation of systematic filtering of what we come to receive as news. Somehow it just comes to seem irresponsible to focus on crimes supportive of, and facilitated by, Western state and business interests—events are discussed within a different framework, or not at all, so that issues of Western criminality do not arise, or come to seem unbelievable. Kurt Vonnegut has likened the reality hidden beneath this type of 'respectable' discourse to a nauseating smell which refuses to go away. Let us take as a further illustration of the operation of the propaganda system, the destruction of Iraq during the Gulf War.

The standard media version of events is familiar enough. Kuwait was invaded by a Hitlerian dictator bent on stealing its oil and perhaps moving on to conquer Saudi Arabia, thus threatening to eliminate not only Kuwaiti freedom but also key Western interests. In response, the United Nations—freed from the constraints of the Cold War—was able to fulfil the promise of the new world order and stand up for the freedom and human rights of Kuwait even in a region as sensitive as the Gulf (where military intervention might previously have been expected to initiate a nuclear holocaust).

In response, a grand alliance devoted to the cause of freedom was formed and a massive military force prepared to encourage and, if necessary, compel Iraqi withdrawal. When the stubbornness and foolishness of the Iraqi tyrant obliged the use of force (despite all diplomatic efforts), an efficient, almost 'surgical', strike was launched to disable the Iraqi war machine. With the aid of 'smart' technology, casualties were kept to a minimum—certainly on the Allied side—and if the Iraqis suffered rather more, then that is the nature of war. According to former US Attorney General Ramsey Clark, this is the conventional state and media version of events and, as such, is a great lie obscuring major war crimes for which—by the rules of our own Nuremberg Charter—you and I, as democratic citizens, are ultimately responsible.

In his book *The Fire This Time: US War Crimes In The Gulf*, Clark dismantles the standard media version of events piece by piece. Firstly, he suggests, the last thing Iraq wanted, or could afford, in the aftermath of the crippling eight year war with Iran (fought during 1980-88 at a cost of hundreds of thousands of lives), was a military showdown with history's premier military power—the United States. Clark argues that even US Army reports prior to the crisis confirm this:

'...it is our belief that Iraq is basically committed to a non-aggressive strategy, and that it will, over the course of the next few years, considerably reduce the size of its military. Economic conditions practically mandate such action... There seems no doubt that Iraq would like to demobilize now that the war has ended.'[39]

Yet between 1988 and 1990, the same war-related economic problems making any new conflict so undesirable for Iraq were also the source of escalating antagonism with Kuwait. By over-producing oil, Kuwait was acting to force down oil prices so that Iraq's attempts to recover from the war with Iran were being severely hampered (to such an extent that, by 1990, the Iraqi economy was in worse condition than during the war, with inflation at 40 percent and its currency plummeting). Worse, Iraqi attempts to negotiate with Kuwait on this issue were firmly rebuffed. A senior Bush administration official told *New York Newsday*:

'Kuwait was overproducing, and when the Iraqis came and said, "Can't you do something about it?" the Kuwaitis said, "Sit on it." And they didn't even say it nicely. They were nasty about it. They were stupid. They were arrogant. They were terrible.'[40]

King Hussein of Jordan expressed his confusion about the Kuwaiti response to the San Francisco Chronicle in March 1991:

'He [Saddam Hussein] told me how anxious he was to ensure that the situation be resolved as soon as possible. So he initiated contact with the Kuwaitis... this didn't work from the beginning. There were meetings but nothing happened... To my way of thinking, this was really puzzling. It was in the Kuwaitis' interest to solve the problem. I know how there wasn't a definite border, how there was a feeling that Kuwait was part of Iraq.' [In 1921, the British Colonial Office had arbitrarily drawn a border separating Kuwait, originally part of Basra province, from Iraq, prohibiting Iraq's access to the Persian Gulf.[41]

Was this intransigence in the face of the struggling Iraqi economy simply a coincidence? Clark argues that, in fact, it was part of a long-standing policy designed to seek confrontation with Iraq. Dr Mussama al-Mubarak, a political science professor at Kuwait University has this to say:

'I don't know what the [Kuwaiti] government was thinking, but it adopted an extremely hard line, which makes me think that the decisions were not Kuwait's alone.'[42]

Interestingly, just as Kuwait was at its most intransigent, the United States reassured Iraq that it had no interest in a local dispute of this nature—a surprising declaration, given the subsequent immediate and massive response to the invasion. (By August 11, eight days after the invasion, 40,000 US troops were in the Gulf. By September 4, 100,000 were in position.) US Ambassador Glaspie told Saddam Hussein: 'We have no opinion on Arab-Arab conflicts, like your border disagreement with Kuwait... [Secretary of State] James Baker has directed our official spokesmen to emphasize this instruction.'[43] Indeed, on July 24, Glaspie had received a cable from the State Department explicitly directing her to reiterate that the United States had 'no position' on 'Arab-Arab' conflicts. [44]

Clark says that this combination of Kuwaiti provocation and US reassurance was a trap designed to lure Iraq into committing a crime that would permit it to be destroyed:

'The evidence that this assault was planned for years before Iraq invaded Kuwait cannot be doubted. That a decision to provoke Iraq into an act that would justify the execution of those plans is clear beyond a reasonable doubt.' [45]

The rationale behind these plans, Clark argues, lies in the perceived need to control the strongly nationalistic Iraqi regime bent on controlling its own oil. US policy makers had long understood that this type of independence raised the threat of Arab oil revenues being invested in Arab countries with correspondingly higher oil prices—something the United States was not prepared to tolerate.

'It was not Iraq but powerful forces in the United States that wanted a new war in the Middle East: the Pentagon, to maintain its tremendous budget; the military-industrial complex, with its dependence on Middle East arms sales and domestic military contracts; the oil companies, which wanted more control over the price of crude oil and greater profits; and the Bush administration, which saw in the Soviet Union's disintegration its chance to establish a permanent military presence in the Middle East, securing the region and achieving vast geopolitical power into the next century through control of its oil resources.'[46]

Having invaded Kuwait, Clark argues that Iraq was not at all intent on staying. He quotes a democratic staff member for intelligence oversight:

'The Iraqis apparently believed that having invaded Kuwait, they would get everyone's attention, negotiate improvements to their economic situation, and pull out... [A] diplomatic solution satisfactory to the interests of the United States may well have been possible since the earliest days of the invasion.' (quoted Robert Parry, 'The Peace Feeler That Was', *The Nation*)[47]

Yet the possibility that Iraq might withdraw before the country could be devastated by a massive attack was a threat carefully avoided by the Bush administration. As readers will recall, from the very beginning, the President announced that there would be no negotiation. Clark suggests that this stance was designed to frustrate a peaceful solution and was therefore, by the rules of the United Nation Charter, a war crime:

'The parties to any dispute, the continuance of which is likely to endanger the maintenance of international peace and security, shall, first of all, *seek a solution by negotiation*, enquiry, mediation, conciliation, arbitration, judicial settlement, resort to regional agencies or arrangements, or other peaceful means of their own choice.' (The Charter of the United Nations, Chapter VI, Article 33—my emphasis)[48]

Evidence indicating that the Gulf crisis was an excuse to remove a nationalist obstruction to Western economic interests in the region is provided by the massive, entirely disproportionate (and largely unknown) levels of destruction visited on Iraq. Under the 88,500 tons of bombs that followed the launch of the air campaign on January 17, 1991 (the equivalent of no less than seven Hiroshimas), and the subsequent ground attack, fully 150,000 Iraqi troops and 50,000 civilians were slaughtered. By contrast, the allies lost 148 troops (many to 'friendly fire'). Not one B52 was hit, nor a single Abrams tank. This disparity, Clark suggests, indicates that this was less a war than a war crime—the criminal and indefensible massacre of people with no means of defending themselves.

Despite the impression given by media reporting, this was no 'surgical' military strike—only 8% of the bombs used were so-called 'smart' bombs, the rest being free-fall bombs of the type used in the second world war. Indeed, Iraq's second city of Basra was actually carpet-bombed by B52s. Beyond even this though, it is clear that Iraq's entire civilian economic infrastructure was targeted and largely destroyed by bombing. A few examples suffice. All of Iraq's eleven major electrical power plants as well as 119 substations were destroyed—90 percent of electricity generation was taken out of service within hours, within days all power generation in the country had ceased. Eight multi-purpose dams were repeatedly hit and destroyed. This immediately wrecked flood control, municipal and industrial water storage, irrigation and hydroelectric power. Four of Iraq's seven major water pumping stations were destroyed. Fourteen central telephone exchanges were irreparably damaged with 400,000 of the 900,000 telephone lines being destroyed. Twenty-eight civilian hospitals and 52 community health centres were hit. Allied bombs damaged 676 schools, with 38 being totally destroyed. Historic sites were not immune—25 mosques were damaged in Baghdad alone and 31 more around the country. Seven textile factories sustained damage, as did five engineering plants, five construction facilities, four car assembly plants and three chlorine plants. A major hypodermic syringe facility was destroyed. All major cement plants were hit along with various clothes and cosmetic factories, and so on. Bus and train stations and depots were hit, civilian cars, buses and lorries were regularly strafed on roads across Iraq—the list goes on. What emerges from this picture, is that, contrary to the media version of events, the primary Western goal was not in fact the removal of Iraq from Kuwait:

> 'The bombing of Iraq's cities and infrastructure had nothing to do with driving Iraq from Kuwait. It was intended to cripple a developing Third World country that was a politically independent military power in the region; and that was rich in oil and committed to its own economic development.'[49]

This intent, Clark argues, is confirmed by subsequent sanctions which have had devastating consequences for the Iraqi population. At least 100,000 people have died since the end of the war, many from diseases and malnutrition exacerbated by the sanctions which have prevented the generation of oil revenue to pay for medical and food supplies.

By April 1992, sanctions were killing children under five at the rate of 300 per day. In September 1992, a special report by the *New England Journal of Medicine* based on research by an international group of researchers independent of the Iraqi government showed that:

'The Gulf War and trade sanctions caused a threefold increase in mortality among Iraqi children. We estimate that an excess of more than 46,900 children under five years of age died between January and August 1991.' [50]

The requirements for lifting these sanctions continuously change but essentially involve massive war reparations, which Iraq, devastated and impoverished by two major wars, is unable to pay, if only because the same sanctions do not allow it to raise revenues by exporting its oil (a classic *Catch-22* situation). Lifting the sanctions has, anyway, not been a realistic consideration, Clark suggests, because their actual purpose is not payment but the destabilisation of Iraq so that a client regime favourable to Western goals can be installed, a common strategy in many other Third World nations such as Iran, Nicaragua, Guatemala, Indonesia, etc. In essence, Clark suggests, the people of Iraq are being held hostage—do as we want with your oil or we will let you die.

What has been the media reaction to the spectacle of a wrecked country strewn with the corpses of 250,000 men, women and children (for the loss of 148 allied lives)? Ted Koppel, presenter of ABC's 'Nightline', described the 'efficiency and humanity' of Operation Desert Storm, being 'in military terms, a work of art'—a version repeated endlessly around the world. The truth about the extent of the allied destruction of a country unable to defend itself against far superior air and ground forces has not yet been reported by our media.

'Nothing I had experienced prepared me for the conduct of the media during the Gulf crisis... What occurred was not merely the presentation of a false picture or the failure to adequately inform the public. Instead, there was a massive media campaign to persuade the public of the righteousness of the American cause and conduct, including an intense promotion of U.S. military actions. It required justifying violence by creating hatred toward and dehumanising Iraq, and concealing or misrepresenting anything that conflicted with that purpose.' [51]

Significantly, one reason that Ramsey Clark became so involved in the issue of war crimes in the Gulf is that he and a small television team took the extraordinary step of travelling 2,000 miles through

Iraq at the height of the allied bombing in February 1991, so that they were able to record six hours of uncensored film depicting the effects of that bombing on the civilian population. The media's reaction to this obviously major 'scoop' is itself revealing. Quite simply, the film has never been shown by the mass media in the United States. First CBS, and then every major US TV organisation rejected the footage. Clark's explanation of this uniform rejection, along with the submissiveness of the media to the government version of events (with which we began this section), accords closely with Chomsky's:

'Its intimate financial relationships with the military and weapons industries, its dependence on major corporate advertising, its political campaign contributions, its close alliances with political parties and leaders, the celebrity status and huge salaries of the major TV news readers identified as friends of the famous, made the American media virtually one with the government... Many times American correspondents abroad and reporters in the United States have turned off their cameras, laid down their pens, and frankly said that their networks or newspapers would not use the story. More often they have admitted they stayed away from interviews or press conferences of people who criticize U.S. actions and policies. Some reporters have said they would be fired if they submitted a story based on such critical reports. Thus the American people are deprived of information and opinions that are necessary for democratic institutions to be meaningful.'[52]

Like Chomsky, Clark goes further in suggesting that the media plays an important part in maintaining our ignorance and passivity:

'The media, owned by the wealthy, speaking for the plutocracy, has the dual role of anaesthetizing the public to prevent serious consideration or debate of such staggering human issues as world hunger, AIDS, regional civil wars, environmental destruction, and social anarchy, and emotionalizing the people for aggression, all without a serious military threat in sight.'[53]

The basic pattern, then, is surely clear from these few examples (Chomsky's, Herman's, Pilger's and Clark's books provide an extremely large number of supporting cases): regimes, facts and events which facilitate profitable Western corporate exploitation of local resources will tend to receive a favourable press, while regimes, facts and events compromising Western corporate goals will tend to be ignored, downplayed or attacked.

For those concerned with environmental issues, the general lack of media interest in investigating the true causes, solutions and scale of seriousness of issues like ozone depletion, global warming, general air and sea pollution, and so on, is explained by the propaganda model in the same way. For example, at an October 1990 UN conference, an international panel of scientists reached virtual unanimity on the conclusion that global warming had occurred over the past century and that the risk of further warming is serious, ranging from significant to near-catastrophic. Yet not a single member of the panel agreed with sceptical views expressed in the US press, gaining such headlines as 'US Data Fail To Show Warming Trend' (*New York Times*) and 'The Global Warming Panic: A Classic Case of Over-Reaction' (cover of *Forbes*)[54]. One American scientist on the conference panel told *Science* magazine that 'The US press has focused on the outlying views [that question the consensus] without pressing hard on justifying them.'[55]

The key point is that the facts of this issue represent a serious threat to corporate goals. Stephen Schneider, head of Interdisciplinary Climate Systems at the US National Centre For Atmospheric Research, has estimated that conversion to a post-greenhouse economy would cost 'hundreds of billions of dollars every year for many decades, both at home and in financial and technical assistance to developing nations'.[56] Consequently, like inconvenient human rights atrocities and costly facts more generally, the global warming issue—and certainly the idea of a need for immediate and drastic action—will tend not to pass through the filter system. Instead, as Sherwood Rowland, whose laboratory first discovered the ozone-depleting properties of CFCs, has said:

> 'It is quite common on the scientific side of industry to believe that there aren't any real environmental problems, that there are just public relations problems.'[57]

All Aboard the Neptune Express! Chomsky as Latter-Day 'Ass'

My aim in this chapter has not been to prove Chomsky's hypothesis (the reader will quite rightly require a far greater wealth of evidence in support of the argument) but to indicate that it quite clearly merits urgent and detailed discussion, especially in the light of the fact that it is so often declared absurd and irrelevant for no apparently rational reason. In the following chapters, however, we will be less tentative and proceed under the assumption that the propaganda model *does* indeed provide a useful tool for understanding modern society.

It may be that some will find that reading Chomsky really is a bit like listening to someone 'fresh in from Neptune'. On the other hand, others may find that the experience is more like travelling oneself to a new planet, to a new world that in fact is none other than our old world seen from a new perspective dramatically freed from the distortions, omissions and outright lies of those who have vested interests in controlling what we believe—including the belief that what we believe is not controlled. We may find that there are layers of double- and treble-think here that make Orwell's *Newspeak* seem positively benign by comparison.

Perhaps one day we will come to view the scorn heaped on Chomsky's supposed lapses from rational excellence into 'simple-mindedness' in the same way that we now view the ridicule visited on earlier iconoclasts who were impudent enough to challenge the self-evident goodness and righteousness of the powerful. After all, it was not so very long ago that a lone proponent of the heliocentric theory of our solar system elicited great hoots of laughter and abuse. Then it was Copernicus who was derided by Luther for talking nonsense and for being:

> '…an ass who wants to pervert the whole art of astronomy and deny what is said in the book of Joshua, only to make a show of ingenuity and attract attention.'[58]

It is all too possible that dissidents like Chomsky, who today argue that modern 'democracies' most certainly *do not* revolve around the twin suns of freedom and democracy, may one day prove to be 'asses' in precisely this way!

Chapter 2

EXTENDING THE SCOPE OF THE PROPAGANDA MODEL

Freedom to Conform

In the previous chapter we saw how a propaganda model seeks to account for a tight system of state and corporate control over the functioning of the mass media. We saw that this level of control does not at all require a conspiracy theory but relies only on the initial framing of conditions followed by the operation of market forces. Thus once it has been accepted that industrial society should be dedicated to economic growth through corporate profit generated by mass production and consumption, these framing conditions can be expected to produce a version of social reality progressively reflecting their requirements in an almost automatic way.

It comes as no surprise that the giant corporations controlling and funding the various media entities influence their performance (it would be extraordinary if they did not) but, equally, it should come as no surprise that the framing goals of business influence the minutiae of our behaviour and thought at work. The uncomfortable truth is that what we believe to be voluntary behaviour at work is very often behaviour demanded by the corporate goal, from which even the smallest departure may result in our being censured for having 'a bad attitude', for being 'uncooperative'; a collapse in career prospects, or simple dismissal, can follow. No matter what we might prefer to believe, the rule is simple:

> 'The chairman of the board may sincerely believe that his every waking moment is dedicated to serving human needs. Were he to act on these delusions instead of pursuing profit and market share, he would no longer be chairman of the board.' Noam Chomsky, *Necessary Illusions*[1]

The more general point being, as Erich Fromm said:

> 'From the fight against the authority of Church, State, and family which characterize the last centuries, we have come back full circle to a new obedience; but this obedience is not one to autocratic

persons, but to the organization. The 'organization man' is not aware that he obeys; he believes that he only conforms with what is rational and practical.'[2]

The real choice is between obedience and expulsion. For this reason, there is a powerful tendency for people to want to believe that their thoughts and behaviour at work are voluntary—the alternative, of perceiving the actual conflict, is simply too painful. Indeed, this struggle with conformity will be painful to the extent to which individuals are aware that it is real, to the extent to which they are aware of their own conflicting inner needs, thoughts and desires. A person will suffer more intensely the more he or she is strong and independent. Given the apparent hopelessness of resistance, there is a powerful and continuous incentive for individuals to become less aware of their own feelings, beliefs and needs. Indeed, the only rational solution for an individual may often be to become dead inside, to become alienated from his or her feelings and desires. And it is exactly this internal deadness which has been declared the great sickness of modern man, the great *mal du siecle* (see the writings of Kierkegaard, Marx, Nietzsche, Tillich, Jung, Laing, Fromm, Campbell, and others).

Thus when modern men and women insist that they feel completely free in their work, they are in a sense telling the truth, for the triumph of conformity lies in the crushing of all resistance, all experience of conflict.

Success As Obedience

The realities of this situation, as Chomsky and Herman have indicated, are particularly apparent within the media. Here the requirements of advertising revenue combine with the realities of flak, media ownership and reliance on state and corporate news sources to pressurise journalists, editors and directors into toeing a very particular line. Many (though by no means all) media people apparently experience no conflict in this situation and thus deride any notion that they are being controlled. In *Chronicles of Dissent*, Chomsky explains (in conversation with David Barsamian) how the pressure to conform has its effect, often without being consciously perceived:

'In order to progress you have to say certain things; what the copy editor wants, what the top editor is giving back to you. You can try saying it and not believing it, but that's not going to work, people just aren't that dishonest, you can't live with that, it's a very rare person who can do that. So you start saying it and pretty soon you're believing it because you're saying it, and pretty soon you're inside the system. Furthermore, there are plenty of rewards if you stay inside. For people who play the game by the rules in a rich society like this, there are ample rewards. You're well off, you're privileged, you're rich, you have prestige, you have a share of power if you want. If you like this kind of stuff you can go off and become the State Department spokesman on something or other, you're right near the centre of at least privilege, sometimes power, in the richest, most powerful country in the world. You can go far, as long as you're very obedient and subservient and disciplined.'[3]

For those who are not obedient, subservient and disciplined in this way it is a different story. Erwin Knoll, editor of *The Progressive*, tells of how, as the White House correspondent for the *Newhouse Newspapers* in the mid-1960s, he made the mistake of asking Lyndon Johnson some questions about his policy in Indochina. The result was that his career as a Washington correspondent was effectively ended.

Similarly, in *The Sponsor*, Erik Barnouw recounts the history of a proposed NBC documentary series on environmental problems at a time of great interest in these issues. Barnouw notes that although at that time a great many large companies were spending money on 'green' commercials and other environmental publicity, the series failed for lack of sponsors. The problem was that the series included suggestions of systemic or corporate failure, whereas the corporate message 'was one of reassurance'.

The last example is particularly disturbing, as it suggests that vested interests are extremely able to suppress in-depth analyses of 'sensitive' issues. This means that analyses deemed to be in conflict with corporate interests are likely to be replaced by superficial and trivial alternatives. For example, the emphasis on green consumerism, corporate responsibility and sustainable growth in the late 1980s and early 1990s can be seen, in this light, to be corporate-friendly surrogates for a true analysis of the causes of, and solutions to, environmental problems. These slogans are powerfully promoted by corporate interests *precisely because* they do not impinge upon profit-orientation; they actually assist the on-going destruction of the environment for short-term corporate gain by camouflaging inaction as action (inaction is almost always far more cost-efficient than action, at least in the short-term to which businesses address themselves). Thus any attempt to discuss the *genuine* causes of environmental degradation—including, above all, the short-term profit motive of global business—will tend *not* to be funded by corporate sponsors and advertisers and tend *not* to get through the filters, so suffering the same fate as 'unfriendly' media generally. Corporate-supportive 'solutions', on the other hand, will be vigorously promoted by the PR and 'flak' machines discussed in the last section.

Who's Watching Big Brother? Filtering the Classics
Chomsky and Howard Zinn suggest that the same filtering process that determines what comes to be seen as important in current affairs, also accounts for which literature comes to be regarded as 'classic' and important. Once again, we find that we are completely free to write what we like so long as we do not threaten to interfere with state or corporate interests. Even when we do go beyond these limits, we will still be free to write such a challenge without being dragged from our beds in the middle of the night (the inefficient totalitarian way). Instead, we will simply *tend* not to find a publisher, will *tend* not to be supported by advertising, will *tend* not to have significant audience out-reach and so will *tend* to be ignored or drowned-out by those who *are* supported by major publishers and advertising. In *Political Shakespeare*, Dollimore and Sinfield have even dared to suggest that one reason why Shakespeare has been so popular for so long is because his writing promotes an essentially right-wing picture of the world suitable to the long-established requirements of the ruling élite. They quote Rachel Sharp, who has this to say:

> 'The power relations which are peculiar to market society are seen [in Shakespeare's writing] as how things have always been and ought to be. They acquire a timelessness which is powerfully legitimized by a theory of human nature… Political struggles to alter present-day social arrangements are seen as futile for 'things are as they are' because of man's basic attributes and nothing could ever be very different.'[4]

Certainly this was Tolstoy's view. He argued that Shakespeare's plays have continued to be admired for so long because they:

> '…correspond to the irreligious and immoral frame of mind of the upper classes of his time and ours.'[5]

Tolstoy did not only take issue with Shakespeare's reputation as a genius; he took issue with the notion that Shakespeare was even a good writer:

'I have felt with an even greater force… that the unquestionable glory of a great genius which Shakespeare enjoys, and which compels writers of our time to imitate him and readers and spectators to discover in him non-existent merits—thereby distorting their aesthetic and ethical understanding—is a great evil, as is every untruth.'[6]

In similarly controversial vein, historian Howard Zinn explains Plato's standing as one of the 'untouchables' of modern culture ('You don't criticize Plato without a risk of being called anti-intellectual', he warns) by the fact that he advocated blind obedience to government, and has thus long been in favour with governments and educational systems working to instil the 'right' attitudes in the young. In the *Crito*, for example, Plato has Socrates refuse to escape from prison on the following grounds, here paraphrased by Zinn:

> "No, I must obey the law. True, Athens has committed an injustice against me by ordering me to die for speaking my mind. But if I complained about this injustice, Athens could rightly say: "We brought you into the world, we raised you, we educated you, we gave you and every other citizen a share of all the good things we could." Socrates accepts this, saying: "By not leaving Athens, I agreed to obey its laws. And so I will go to my death."[7]

As Zinn says, it is important to be aware of the fundamentally anti-democratic nature of these arguments and of the high regard in which they are held by modern 'democratic' states, not for the purpose of judging Plato, but because:

> '…they are a way of thinking which every nation-state drums into the heads of its citizens from the time they are old enough to go to school. And because they show the perils of placing our trust, and the lives of our children, in the hands of the Experts, whether in politics or philosophy.'[8]

Likewise, Chomsky argues that Orwell's *Animal Farm* and *1984* (both standard school texts) are as highly-regarded as they are, not because they provide particularly astute insights into modern systems of tyranny (he describes *1984* as 'essentially a very shallow book'), but because they constituted suitable satirical attacks on our long-time Soviet enemy.

'Fame, Fortune, and Respect await those who reveal the crimes of official enemies; those who undertake the vastly more important task of raising a mirror to their own societies can expect quite different treatment. George Orwell is famous for *Animal Farm* and *1984*, which focus on the official enemy. Had he addressed the more interesting and significant question of thought control in relatively free and democratic societies, it would not have been appreciated, and instead of wide acclaim, he would have faced silent dismissal or obloquy.'[9]

Interestingly, Orwell himself rejected Tolstoy's criticism of Shakespeare, arguing (in a way that supports Chomsky's argument for the superficiality of his understanding of thought control) that it was 'impossible' that Tolstoy could seriously believe that:

'...for a century or more the entire civilized world had been taken in by a huge and palpable lie which he alone was able to see through'.[10]

Certainly, one 'huge and palpable lie' by which 'the entire civilized world' would appear to be regularly 'taken in' by, is the notion that 'the entire civilized world' could never be 'taken in' by a 'huge and palpable lie'. After all, it took two hundred years for the United States to recognize the genocide it committed against the native Indians of North America (a significant and rather obvious historical fact). As we know, until very recently, the Indians were considered to have been the 'merciless' aggressors. Similarly, one can only speculate on whether the idea that South Vietnam was defended, rather than attacked, by the United States (which dropped 3.9 million tons of bombs on its 'ally'—twice the total expended by the US during the second world war—often 'saving' highly populated areas by the use of B52 carpet-bombing) will survive a further 70 years and thus reach Orwell's 'impossible' target.

Orwell's relative blindness to the possibility of systems of thought control not reliant on brute force, is indicated by his own recognition of the apparent divide between the awed reverence associated with Shakespeare's name and his actual limitations as a writer:

'As Tolstoy justly complains, much rubbish has been written about Shakespeare as a philosopher, as a psychologist, as a 'great moral teacher', and what-not. Shakespeare was not a systematic thinker, his most serious thoughts are uttered irrelevantly or indirectly, and we do not know to what extent he wrote with a purpose... It is perfectly possible that he looked on at least half of his plays as mere pot-boilers and hardly bothered about purpose or probability so long as he could patch up something, usually from stolen material, which would more or less hang together on stage.'[11]

And Orwell even provides a convincing explanation for Shakespeare's success, without drawing any conclusions which seem too 'impossible' to him:

'[Shakespeare] liked to stand well with the rich and powerful, and was capable of flattering them in the most servile way. He is also noticeably cautious, not to say cowardly, in his manner of uttering unpopular opinions. Almost never does he put a subversive or sceptical remark into the mouth of a character likely to be identified with himself. Throughout his plays the acute social critics, the people who are not taken in by accepted fallacies, are buffoons, villains, lunatics or persons who are shamming insanity or are in a state of violent hysteria.'[12]

Here Orwell seems to have provided an explanation for Shakespeare's free passage through filter systems old and new in a way that accords well with the predictions of the propaganda model.

It is interesting to compare the reaction received by books like *Animal Farm* and Chomsky's own work. In the prefatory note to their book *The Washington Connection and Third World Fascism*, Chomsky and Herman describe efforts made to suppress its publication.

Originally the book was enthusiastically contracted for and produced as a monograph by Warner Modular Publications, a subsidiary of the Warner communications conglomerate. Just prior to publication, however, in the autumn of 1973, officials of the parent company looked the book over and were horrified by what they considered to be the 'unpatriotic' nature of the contents.

'Although 20,000 copies of the monograph were printed, and one (and the last) ad was placed in the *New York Review of Books*, Warner Publishing refused to allow distribution of the monograph at its scheduled publication date. Media advertising for the volume was cancelled and printed flyers that listed the monograph as one of the titles were destroyed. The officers of Warner Modular were warned that distribution of the document would result in their immediate dismissal.'[13]

For a time, it looked as though Warner would actually be prepared to violate a legally binding contract to prevent the book seeing the light of day. Instead, however, Warner eventually decided to close down Warner Modular, selling its stocks of publications and contracts to a small and quite unknown company loosely affiliated with the parent company, MSS Information Corporation. This company was not a commercial distributor and lacked distribution facilities. It did not promote its list and did not even list the monograph, adding it only after a considerable delay on an additions sheet.

This treatment is closer to the rule than the exception. Chomsky's work on international affairs has never been reviewed by any major professional journal in the United States (by contrast his books on Southeast Asia, for example, have all been reviewed by the Canadian professional journal on Asia—*Pacific Affairs*). The same is true of the media, where his books on contemporary issues are rarely reviewed. The book review editor of the *Boston Globe* (considered a liberal newspaper by the standards of US journalism) has gone so far as to publicly announce that she will not only not review Chomsky's books, but will not review any South End Press books so long as Chomsky remains on their list of authors. Martin Peretz, editor of the *New Republic*, has similarly declared Chomsky 'beyond the pale of intellectual responsibility'.[14] Chomsky has never been invited to write for the *New York Times* opinion page, or its *Book Review*, or for many other major magazines such as *Harper's*, *The Atlantic*, or *Village Voice*. Mass media TV and radio appearances are even less common; he has appeared only once on the influential Nightline programme, and has never been invited to appear on Face The Nation, the evening news, or on National Public Radio, despite being, as we have discussed, 'arguably the greatest living intellectual'.

Needless to say, this is all in accordance with the working of the five filters listed in the propaganda model. But how far can we go with this interpretation? If an institutionalized propaganda system really is able to dramatically distort the version of reality with which we are presented, to what extent is what we believe simply a necessary illusion?

Necessary Beliefs

Let us reiterate that our corporately-run economies rely on adherence to a specific framework of ideas for their functioning and survival.

First, it is important that the majority of people agree that corporate profit maximisation leading to economic growth is the primary goal of industrial society (we are allowed to talk in high terms of freedom, democracy, charity, religious ideals and so on, but the primary *functioning* goal must turn out to be that of maximizing corporate growth).

Secondly, we should believe (or be resigned to the idea) that our functioning as 'cogs' within this process of mass production is the best way of leading a worthwhile, fulfilled life. Ideally, we should believe that 'success' as defined by society is critical to our happiness. This 'success' should be defined in terms of status resulting from conspicuous consumption, which in turn should be made possible by conspicuous conformity to the economic system. Thus, 'success' through status, through conformity, should be the dominant goal.

Thirdly, we should believe that mass consumption is the most sensible, sane and realistic means for finding happiness. Because this consumption necessarily involves consumption beyond the necessities of life, mass consumption is required to emphasise the desirability of status products and luxury. Once again, it is important that we come to believe that status and luxury are important for our happiness.

Fourthly (and perhaps most importantly), this system has an interest in our believing that we *freely choose* these goals. The level of effort required to maintain a complex technological/industrial society will be forthcoming only where the mass of people firmly believe they are pursuing their own happiness (no one could believe they were pursuing their happiness under duress). The increased efficiency of this system over the totalitarian alternative (of the former Soviet Union, for example), resides precisely in this notion of voluntary participation in, and (ideally) dedication to, the system for personal gain. In the end, this system depends on the notion that freedom from coercion is commensurate with full freedom, that free decisions can meaningfully be made under conditions where the powerful institutions of society have the ability and motivation to manipulate what we think.

Because these beliefs are essential for the effective functioning of a corporate consumer system, the propaganda model predicts that the five filters will operate to boost these beliefs while rejecting all conflicting alternatives. Thus advertisers will boost consumption for status and corporate conformity as 'success' in life. Similarly, the flak systems will tend to support the notion that we freely choose these goals, while deriding the suggestion that we do not.

The overall implication is clear: the propaganda system will powerfully support versions of 'success', 'happiness' and 'freedom' that support corporate ends, regardless of their impact on people and the wider environment.

The Economic Expedience of Neurosis

Given the importance of the above beliefs to the efficient functioning of the corporate system, the propaganda model predicts that all competing conceptions of the problems of human life, and possible solutions to these problems, will tend to be marginalized, ridiculed or simply ignored. Indeed, in order to maximize the efficiency of the system, corporate consumerism will tend to discourage the capacity of people to imagine alternative ways of living.

'They (the public) ought to be sitting alone in front of the TV and having drilled into their heads the message, which says the only value in life is to have more commodities or live like that rich, middle class family you're watching and to have nice values like harmony and Americanism. That's all there is in life. You may think in your own head that there's got to be something more in life than this, but since you're watching the tube alone you assume, I must be crazy, because that's all that's going on over there. And since there is no organisation permitted—that's absolutely crucial—you never have a way of finding out whether you are crazy, and you just assume it, because it's the natural thing to assume.' [15]

One result of living according to a business-friendly set of values and being unable to consider and seek out alternative values is that large numbers of people are *necessarily* in various states of psychological ill-health—as demonstrated, for example, by British government figures indicating that one in four people suffer from mental illness at any given time. Similar figures for Sweden show that two out of three Swedish women and half of Swedish men visit a psychiatrist for help at some time in their lives—figures which are extraordinary given the general taboo against seeking such help (we can only speculate on the numbers of people who feel in need of such help but do not act on their despair). Figures from the United States, where 10 percent of all woman are either anorexic or bulimic (with the figure as high as 20 percent among the female student population), add to the impression that it would be more appropriate to talk in terms of the percentage of people not suffering from some form of mental ill health. Indeed, since its birth with Freud and Jung, the psychoanalytic movement has been concerned with understanding and curing an omnipresent modern sickness known variously as alienation, depression, malaise, or ennui, which appears to afflict corporately-controlled man and woman.

The attempt that psychoanalytic theory has made to understand and deal with this modern illness is itself illustrative of the supreme power of the propaganda system. This is significant because, as the science of revealing psychological delusion, we would expect psychotherapy to be supremely resistant to the lies and illusions of thought control, thus providing the propaganda model with its sternest possible test.

Cure or Conformity? The Sickness of Psychotherapy

The widespread dis-ease of the modern soul is said to consist of anxiety, guilt and emptiness linked to a stifling sense of meaninglessness, boredom and deadness. Some commentators have gone so far as to suggest that whereas the problem in the nineteenth century was that 'God is dead!', the problem in the twentieth is that 'Man is dead!'

Most psychotherapists (apart from isolated radicals like Erich Fromm, R.D. Laing and James Hillman) have approached this modern problem by attempting to alleviate symptoms of dis-ease on the basis of the Freudian hypothesis, suggesting that neurosis is primarily (if not always) a result of sexual repression. More recently, therapists have emphasized the need to re-live repressed childhood trauma, so relieving the symptoms of the repression that are their cause. Rarely have psychotherapists sought the cause of neurosis in the economic and political system within which we live. Instead, the underlying premise has always been that the neurotic individual is dysfunctional and the industrial system 'normal'; in other words that neurosis should be essentially defined by the inability of the individual to function 'normally' within that system.

> 'The aim of therapy is often that of helping the person to be better adjusted to existing circumstances, to 'reality' as it is frequently called; mental health is often considered to be nothing but this adjustment... [Thus] the psychologists, using the 'right' words from Socrates to Freud, become the priests of industrial society, helping to fulfil its aims by helping the individual to become *the perfectly adjusted organization man*.' Erich Fromm, *Beyond The Chains of Illusion*[16]

Yet clearly any system concerned with alteration of the personality that assumes as its premise that the requirements of society define the norm of sanity into which the personality should be fitted, is little more than a system of brainwashing.

Many psychotherapists are uncomfortable with the notion that there are norms by which sanity can be judged. Yet to take the requirement of effective functioning within society as the standard against which sanity can be measured, involves selecting a set of norms in just this way. Psychotherapy can never escape from the need for norms, because without such norms its task would be meaningless; how would we be able to say who was mentally ill, how they could be 'cured', and by what standard they could be adjudged to have been cured?

To suggest that there are no norms of human mental health is as sensible as suggesting that there are no norms by which human physical health can be judged. Similarly, the idea that the norm for mental health is whatever fits the requirement of society, is equivalent to suggesting that physical health can be judged by the capacity to lift a forefinger to push a factory button a thousand times a day, so that only when that forefinger breaks down can a person be said to be ill. Whilst it is of course difficult to define norms for both physical and mental health,

> '...this is no reason for a relativism which says that we cannot know what furthers life or what blocks it. We are not always sure which food is healthy and which is not, yet we do not conclude that we have no way whatsoever of recognising poison. In the same way we can know, if we want to, what is poisonous for mental life. We know that poverty, intimidation, isolation, are directed *against* life; that everything that serves freedom and furthers the courage and strength to be oneself is *for* life.' Erich Fromm, *The Fear of Freedom*[17]

The irrationality of trying to make a human being sane by emphasising his or her childhood and sexual experiences while largely excluding the impact of the requirements of the economic and political system has, apparently, only recently begun to strike a minority of psychotherapists.

In the light of the evidence of reality-distortion provided by the propaganda model, it seems reasonable to suggest that the vast majority of modern neuroses are not at all rooted in repression of childhood trauma or sexual drives, but in a violent individual/social conflict between the desire of human beings to live and think in reasonably sane and rational ways and the requirement of our society that we live and think in ways which are absurd. Given the extent to which reality is filtered to fit the corporate need, it seems hardly imaginable that *anyone* today could have the independence of mind to form a balanced, realistic, sane view of the world—on which human happiness and sanity surely depend.

James Hillman is one of a minority of psychotherapists now beginning to deal with the realities of a sick-making political and economic system:

> 'We're working on our relationships constantly, and our feelings and reflections, but look what's left out of that. What's left out is a deteriorating world. So why hasn't therapy noticed that? Because psychotherapy is only working on that "inside" soul. By removing the soul from the world and not recognizing that the soul is also *in* the world, psychotherapy can't do its job anymore. The buildings are sick, the institutions are sick, the banking system's sick, the schools, the streets—the sickness is out *there*.'[18]

Hillman provides a convincing description of the role psychotherapy has come to play in supporting the programme of corporate consumerism:

> '...And so the adult says, "Well, what can I do about the world? This thing's bigger than me." That's the child archetype talking. "All I can do is go into myself, work on my growth, my development, find good parenting, support groups." This is a disaster for our political world, for our democracy... we're disempowering ourselves through therapy.'[19]

What Hillman does not go on to say, as Chomsky and Fromm do, is that this 'disaster for our political world' is no act of God, but is actually required for the maintenance of the necessary illusions on which our entire system of 'democracy' depends. The point is that the corporate consumer system needs us to 'go into ourselves', it needs us to be obsessed with the apolitical, internal world of our psyche and relationships. Any identification of the *actual* source of our ill-being with the fundamental nature of our political and economic system is bound to be discouraged by that same political and economic system. Such concerns will be passed over and swamped by endless facts and ideas supporting the status quo on which all major corporations depend (thus the otherwise inexplicable contrast between the prime concerns in our heads and in the marginal media on the one hand, and the mass media with its quiz shows, sports specials and soaps, on the other). Quite simply, the vested interest in our remaining introverted and, in effect, stupid, is just too powerful.

'A properly functioning system of indoctrination has a variety of tasks, some rather delicate. One of its targets is the stupid and ignorant masses. They must be kept that way, diverted with emotionally potent oversimplifications, marginalized and isolated.' Noam Chomsky, *Deterring Democracy*[20]

This seems more or less to describe the function of psychotherapy today. Chomsky's understanding of the requirement that the masses be harmlessly diverted is based on long-established theories of the need for the containment of democracy. Rienhold Niebuhr, who was much revered by the Kennedy intellectuals, wrote that the powerful must recognize 'the stupidity of the average man' and provide the 'necessary illusions' to keep him on the right path.[21] Similarly, Walter Lippmann wrote of the need to 'manufacture consent' because:

'…the common interests very largely elude public opinion entirely, and can be managed only by a specialized class whose interests reach beyond the locality. This class is irresponsible, for it acts upon information that is not common property…'[22]

But these were only the latest reiterations of long-established views dating back to John Locke's contention that 'day-labourers and tradesmen, the spinsters and dairymaids… cannot know and therefore they must believe.'[23]

Hillman goes on to argue that our obsession with childhood, feelings and relationships in the absence of concern for the world around us leads us to place an impossible burden of expectation on our relationships, which consequently disintegrate under that weight. The most notable non-material obsession of our society is, after all, the dream of romantic love as an answer to all our troubles. When we listen to the endless stream of love songs, we hear continuous references to 'eternity', 'truth', 'dreaming', 'searching', 'the promised land' and so on, and this is surely the sound of the search for truth banished to the only permissible realm—the personal.

Unfortunately no romance can ever provide an adequate answer to a life lived in a society of dramatically limited freedom. 'All you need is love!', in fact, is an *economically* 'correct' fiction which, like green consumerism, corporate responsibility and the Western 'yearning for freedom and human rights', serves to divert genuine concern, genuine searching, into a harmless cul-de-sac while appearing to be a genuine message of hope for humanity.

Psychotherapy has been transformed into a similar mechanism for diversion, as Hillman seems to argue:

'Psychology, working with yourself, could that be part of the disease, not part of the cure?'[24]

Certainly, and we might suggest that the reason that psychotherapy has persisted with its irrational approach, rather than seeking rational norms for sanity, is because that search is in profound conflict with the propaganda system, which requires an essentially insane set of presupposed (but not explicitly stated—because absurd) norms for the successful functioning of corporate consumerism. And when we consider that psychology is intended to be the very science of ascertaining and promoting psychological reality and sanity, is meant to be about increasing consciousness, about escaping delusion, we can begin to appreciate just how powerful and all-pervasive the modern filter system really is. For we can see that the very science of raising consciousness has come to *prevent* the raising of consciousness, has dedicated itself to 'curing' people of symptoms of resistance to conformity. If this sounds like a scenario from *Invasion of The Body-Snatchers*, then we need only think back to the little experiment in chapter one, describing the process by which crystals are formed with almost total perfection.

Freudian Psychoanalysis, the Sexual Revolution and the Propaganda Model

In order to understand how psychotherapy has come to be so well-suited to the propaganda system, we need to understand how and why it came to be embraced by that system.

Freudian psychoanalysis was originally based on the notion that neuroses—such as anxiety, depression and compulsive behaviour—are the result of a conflict between instinctive sexual desires and conscious conceptions of right and wrong learned through socialization. Essentially, Freud argued that the moral 'police force' of our socially-conditioned conscious minds acts to block the powerful energy of our sexual drive. The consequence, according to Freud, is that this sexual energy is then diverted to find release in any number of ways, manifested as neurotic symptoms. By raising awareness of the obstacles responsible for sexual repression, the sexual energy can be naturally released so that the neurotic symptoms disappear.

Undoubtedly the most valuable aspect of Freud's theory was his demonstration of the existence of a conscious, aware side of the personality, and an unconscious side which functions beneath the level of individual awareness. Thus a person can feel pain, anger or happiness, without being consciously aware that he or she is doing so. Freud showed that we often remain unaware of certain emotions and ideas because our ability to perceive them is blocked by a sort of filter system that prevents them from coming to awareness. This filter system consists of a moral code, or value system—the sense of right and wrong, good and bad, worthy and worthless—operating in individuals. If, for example, we believe that sex is 'wicked', we will tend to become unaware of the fact that we have strong sexual desires. Although Freud believed that civilization was necessarily in conflict with man's sexual drive which, he argued, must always be repressed to some extent, his theories were generally taken to imply that mental health was possible through the free expression of sexuality.

Since Freud, radical psychotherapists have accepted his concepts of the conscious and unconscious, of repression leading to neurosis and of de-repression leading to removal of the symptoms of neurosis. Many of these psychotherapists, however, have strongly rejected Freud's belief that the cause of neurosis is *always* to be found in sexual repression. From the beginning, Jung, for example, never found the notion credible:

'Here I could not agree with Freud. He considered the cause of the repression to be a sexual trauma. From my practice, however, I was familiar with numerous cases of neurosis in which the question of sexuality played a subordinate part, other factors standing in the foreground—for example, the problem of social adaptation, of oppression by tragic circumstances of life, prestige considerations and so on.' [25]

Erich Fromm was more to the point:

'Both the 'economic' man and the 'sexual' man are convenient fabrications whose alleged nature—isolated, asocial, greedy and competitive—makes Capitalism appear as the system which corresponds perfectly to human nature, and places it beyond the reach of criticism.' [26]

Yet, having received an initially hostile reaction, Freud's hypothesis of sexual repression as the sole cause of neurosis was enthusiastically adopted by modern consumer society. Indeed, it is often said that Freud's theory of sexuality led directly to the sexual revolution. But, as Fromm has written, this is to confuse cause with effect:

'Had it not been for the needs of a consumer culture, Freud would not have become so popular. The popularization of Freud's theories was a handy, semiscientific rationalisation for the change in mores that would have happened anyway in the period after 1920.' [27]

It is interesting that the 'sexual revolution', which culminated in the 1960s, was seen as a *challenge* to the status quo (in the same way that the press are seen as a 'left-biased' 'challenge' to power). In reality, this explosion of sexuality suited the requirements of corporate power, for it facilitated a boom in consumerism. This fact is observable today in the monotonous use of sex in adverts to sell everything from clothes and soft drinks, to jewellery, cars and holidays. In the search for new sexual 'highs', people are encouraged to buy any number of products to increase their chances of success. Quite simply, it strongly suits modern consumer culture that people be obsessed with fleeting sexual encounters, rather than any concern with deeper, more spiritual love (and deeper thought more generally), because the former—to use the marketing term—'shifts product'.

Clearly one explanation for the fact that the practice of modern psychotherapy is so well accommodated to the requirements of the consumer system, is that it originally thrived precisely because the Freudian hypothesis served, rather than challenged, that consumer culture. In the same way that elements of our mass media (like the *Daily Herald*) tend to fail or flourish according to their suitability to the needs of advertisers, so the findings and practice of flawed psychotherapy, which emphasize sexual expression and the personal and relational factors in mental ill-health, have been powerfully boosted by the propaganda system, and have therefore prospered— albeit at the expense of the mental health of society. The more radical branch of psychotherapy, on the other hand, has met a very different response. Thus we find, for example, a complete discounting of the work of Erich Fromm (whose concept of 'social filters' bears a striking resemblance to Chomsky and Herman's propaganda 'filter system'). Fromm's fate has been summarized by Daniel Burston:

'American psychiatrists of the Freudian persuasion simply ignored Fromm, as the paucity of references and lack of a single substantive analysis in the orthodox American psychoanalytic literature demonstrate.' [28]

Those unfamiliar with the workings of the filter system might be forgiven for assuming that this dismissal is an indication that Fromm (like Chomsky) is simply unworthy of serious consideration, which is of course always a possibility. Yet Burston—writing without apparent awareness of, and certainly without reference to, Chomsky's and Herman's propaganda model—provides the following, by now familiar, explanation:

'They [Fromm's reviewers] could not relinquish their image of Fromm as a fuzzy-headed utopian lacking an appreciation for the irrational and tragic dimensions of human life... Given the extent and frequency of these errors it seems almost pointless to blame individual authors. Something of a more global character is obviously at work here. Indeed, the grotesque distortions by Fromm's American critics and would-be expositors attest to the validity of Fromm's theory of social filters, in which experience and information are screened according to cultural preconceptions. Thus, for someone who bothers to read Fromm carefully, there is a comic irony and, in a sense, vindication in this sad and deplorable state of affairs.'[29]

Like Chomsky, Fromm has the tragi-comic distinction of being sufficiently accurate in his analysis to know that he would be declared absurd and irrelevant. Thus he, too, has been consigned to the Lutheran 'zoo' along with Copernicus, Chomsky, and all the other 'asses' who dare to speak out against the limits of 'respectable' discourse. We spend our time well when we consider that this fate befell Fromm—an outstandingly clear and rational thinker—within the 'science' devoted to *exposing* lies!

Limiting the Debate: Ridicule

When Hillary Clinton stepped out of line early in 1993 by declaring that something needed to be done about the terrible 'emptiness' at the heart of modern work, her previously high public standing more or less disintegrated beneath a barrage of flak from the likes of the *New York Times*, *Time* and *Newsweek* magazines. which berated her for talking 'mystical psycho-babble'. (Note that words relating to the search for truth have become terms of abuse, just as we 'get' religion like a disease, and myth is used as a synonym for lie—indications of the extent to which our culture is hostile to such a search. On the other hand science, when in the service of power, is a source of 'certainty'; the exception being when it addresses inconvenient issues like ozone depletion or global warming. Then, a lack of complete 'scientific certainty' is invoked, in clear contradiction to the fact that scientific method is based on the *impossibility* of absolute certainty.

Thus the fundamental logic of science is obscured—no mean achievement.)

As discussed earlier, an inconvenient truth can be dismissed as incomprehensible if it is not possible to dismiss it as 'simple-minded'. In the above case, to suggest that there is *not* some kind of emptiness at the heart of modern work is itself a remarkable lie, as even government statistics on mental health testify. This mechanism of using ridicule for the suppression of truth and the prevention of meaningful discussion, is, I believe, deeply ingrained in each and every one of us. We have all, no doubt, been criticized for discussing something that is 'too deep', whether we are discussing matters psychological, philosophical, religious, environmental—anything that attempts to go to the root of problems. We all sense where the limit is. We know when we are stepping over the line and when we can expect a sarcastic aside, or groan, from someone around us. We may even make a self-deprecatory joke to pre-empt the disapproval. Similarly, when listening to other people, we immediately sense when the conversation has stepped over the mark and will elicit disapproval, when it has become too 'serious' or 'deep'. We might ask who, or what, is setting the tolerable limits of 'depth'?

The answer is that they are set by the same framing conditions on which our system depends; the same system which maintains the near-uniform frivolity on our magazine shelves and in our television schedules; the same system that depends on our commitment to light-hearted, frivolous consumption. The simple fact is that our culture needs to be infused with a 'buying environment', it needs to be swamped in 'muzak' encouraging us to have fun—and fun requires that we do not consider anything too seriously. For were we to do so, the version of common-sense reality to which we are continually encouraged to adhere (that fun, status and consumption are everything) would be revealed for the childish absurdity that it is.

Again, this is not the result of a conspiracy; it is simply that the framing goals of modern life are such that to suggest anything so contrary as the notion that life is 'empty' makes little sense within the parameters of the framing goals. After all, such a claim invites us to examine exactly what it is that might be missing; what we are really aiming for; and how we might live differently. In other words, it invites us to begin the search for norms of human sanity that transcend the norms of society and, as discussed above, this search is contrary to the requirements of the propaganda system. For this system must have us, noses down, producing and consuming, convinced that status and consumption produce happiness.

It does not matter that dedicating our lives to this level of absurdity drives us mad, makes us miserable and isolated. The collective, systemic power that requires us to live self-destructive lives is sufficient to make us suppress both our own doubt and that of those around us—an infinitely more effective system of control to totalitarian force, as Thoreau understood:

> 'It is hard to have a Southern overseer; it is worse to have a Northern one; but worst of all when you are the slave-driver of yourself.'[30]

Today most people declare themselves to be more or less comfortably happy in their alienation. In our culture it is considered a virtue to 'cheer up' even when we are clearly miserable, to hide our unhappiness rather than expose the truth. After all, it is only recently that those who maintain that the environment is being made sick by the modern version of progress have begun to escape this type of abuse (the evidence has simply been too overwhelming). Ridicule notwithstanding, informed observers present a different picture of 'cheery' modern man:

> 'The 'normally' alienated person, by reason of the fact that he acts more or less like everyone else, is taken to be sane… The condition of alienation, of being asleep, of being unconscious, of being out of one's mind, is the condition of the normal man. Society highly values its normal man. It educates children to lose themselves and to become absurd, and thus to be normal. Normal men have killed perhaps 100,000,000 of their fellow normal men in the last fifty years.' R.D. Laing, *The Politics of Experience*[31]

Limiting the Debate: Silence

E.F. Schumacher, the economist concerned with 'economics as if people mattered', drew our attention to the fate of any suggestion that cog-like conformity within corporate industry is a less than adequate answer to life in a little essay entitled *Insane work cannot produce a sane society*. He begins by quoting the following extract from an article appearing in *The Times*:

> 'Dante, when composing his visions of hell, might well have included the mindless, repetitive boredom of working on a factory assembly line. It destroys initiative and rots brains, yet millions of British workers are committed to it for most of their lives.'[32]

Schumacher goes on to comment on the interesting reaction to this article:

'The remarkable thing is that the above statement in *The Times*, like countless similar ones before it [sic], aroused no interest: there were no hot denials or anguished agreements; no reactions at all. The strong and terrible words—visions of hell; mindless, repetitive boredom, destroying initiative and rotting brains; millions of British workers, committed for most of their lives—attracted no reprimand that they were mis-statements or over-statements, that they were irresponsible or hysterical exaggerations or subversive propaganda. No, people read them, sighed and nodded, I suppose, and moved on.' [33]

This is in complete accordance with the propaganda model. As we saw with regard to East Timor, human rights violations by client states may be vigorously denied by state and corporate flak machines but often far more effective is simple, outright silence. After all, for every isolated article questioning work values, there will be a hundred which assume that scaling the ladder of corporate conformity is the self-evidently natural goal of school leavers, graduates, and so on. A direct response is unnecessary.

Limiting the Debate: The Relativity of Truth
If the propaganda model suggests that modern society will be flooded by a version of reality closely conforming to the requirements of state and corporate interests, then it is essentially suggesting that modern society will be flooded by a necessarily irrational version of reality. It comes as no surprise, then, to find that modern society takes a hostile position to the very existence of truth itself; if inconvenient ideas are dismissed as ridiculous, or ignored through an absence of comment, then so too will the search for truth itself. Today all truth is deemed to be relative. Any discussion of truth is made out to be a metaphysical concern, and the conventional wisdom is that anyone talking in terms of wanting to discover the truth is somewhat unsophisticated. This modern relativism is based on the extraordinary notion that all truth is somehow a matter of opinion and that it is not possible to determine, for example, what is good and bad for people, because everyone is different. Again, this involves a fantastic distortion of the scientific method (which accepts the impossibility of absolute certainty, but operates on the assumption that a good hypothesis is often adequate to the task).

The notion that there is no truth because all truth is relative seems deeply ingrained in modern individuals. No one would disagree that it is unquestionably bad to put a finger in an electric socket; yet when it comes to challenging the norms of society, an argument is presented which effectively *does* challenge the truth of this assertion.

Here we are presented with a profound contradiction, typically indicative of the presence of a powerful system of lies. Economic growth, status through success, corporate profit-maximisation, increasing wealth and comfort and so on are deemed to be unquestionably good and right; yet parallel to this and considered equally unquestionable (when required), is the notion that all good and right is relative and so essentially meaningless. The ability to alternate between these two completely incompatible ideologies is another impressive feat of the filter system (incidentally, the notion that all truth is relative is itself presented as an absolute certainty—a logical absurdity!).

The Invisible Tyrant

In the first chapter we tentatively suggested that the framing conditions of society (and the media industry in particular) might be operating to filter what does or does not come to be deemed newsworthy by the mass media. We end this chapter by raising the possibility that any number of areas of human life may be subject to the same distorting influence—our thoughts and behaviour at work, our attitudes towards success, literature, the study of psychology, what we ridicule or ignore, our understanding of basic scientific method and the search for truth, and even what is deemed admissible in everyday conversation.

However, in order that the necessary beliefs of corporate consumerism remain unchallenged, it is not enough for the propaganda system to restrict access to the truth, it must also restrict the desire and capacity to search for the truth—it must kill the dream of truth.

In the next two chapters, we will examine the extent to which the requirements of the goals of society have crippled our capacity to gain a coherent picture of the world by distorting and thus destroying our understanding of the two most fundamental areas of human thought—religion and morality.

The propaganda system has distorted our understanding of these foundations of human thought and action in such a way that we come to believe ideas (no matter how absurd) which support the corporate goal and to reject the possibility of seeking more adequate answers to life. We will see that only when we are able to escape the propaganda system as it operates at the very deepest levels of human belief, can we hope to find genuine alternatives. If the roots of our understanding remain caught in the required beliefs of that system, all our other political, psychological and philosophical beliefs must to some extent remain trapped within the required parameters of 'thinkable thoughts'.

Chapter 3

KILLING THE DREAM
OF RELIGIOUS TRUTH

Storms in the Propaganda Tea Cup

One of the most effective ways of preventing people from discovering the truth about a given issue is to make an unwelcome idea absurd through misinterpretation—and then vigorously challenge that misinterpretation. In this way, all discussion becomes a matter of rejecting or accepting the misinterpretation. Both of these positions are beside the point (and are in fact intellectual cul-de-sacs); nevertheless they effectively swamp any discussion of a genuine interpretation by which progress might be made (the stormier the argument the better, as this all the more convincingly creates the illusion of free debate). With regard to the argument under discussion, for example, this might involve vigorous disagreement between those said to be supporting a conspiracy theory and those ridiculing such theories as mere paranoia—with both completely missing the point of the argument, which is that no conspiracy theory is required.

During the Vietnam war, the hawks argued *for* using extra force to defend South Vietnam, on the grounds that the war was winnable; whilst the doves argued *against* using extra force to defend South Vietnam, on the grounds that the war was unwinnable. As long as these arguments defined the parameters of government and media debate, it was extremely difficult for anyone to raise the point that the United States was not at all defending, but was actually invading and destroying South Vietnam—regardless of whether the war was winnable or not. The limitation of the discussion in this way was ideal from the point of view of the US government and military (who, prior to the 1968 Tet Offensive, were determined not to withdraw without victory). For, as Chomsky has said of the doves:

> 'In a society in which that position is considered to be the dissenting, critical position, the capacity for thought has been destroyed. It means the entire spectrum of thinkable thoughts is now caught within the propaganda system.'[1]

This device of invisibly limiting the parameters of conceivable opposition is an infinitely more effective technique of thought control than that of forcibly censoring unsuitable ideas. For here the two false poles act like magnets attracting the iron filings of debate to either side, making it extremely difficult to pass through the middle to a more adequate argument beyond—which will tend to be dismissed as 'fresh in from Neptune', or the product of neurosis (later, in our discussion on mythology, we will see that the name of Parzival, the great truth-seeking hero of the Grail legend, derives from the Old French per-ce-val, meaning 'through the middle', in just this way).

This type of false debate is, I believe, responsible for our understanding (or misunderstanding) of religion today. In the following two chapters, I will argue that the orthodox version of religious understanding—as a matter of believing in an authoritarian, cosmic overlord—has long suited the requirements of the powerful institutions in our society, emphasising as it does that we should worship an all-powerful God precisely because He is all-powerful (with clear implications for our attitude towards His earthly representatives). But I will also argue that the commonly-held atheistic alternative to this view—that all religion is a lot of superstitious nonsense—is a false pole in exactly the way of the doves of the Vietnam war. I will argue that modern atheism is simply the latest version of what I will call *power religion* and, as such, performs a more or less identical function in support of the heirs of church-based power, namely the great corporate institutions of modern consumerism.

It seems to me that these misinterpretations of religion are a cornerstone of thought control because, beyond the distortions of church, state and other power, we find that religious speculation has always been concerned with the individual search for fundamental human freedom and truth, with understanding reality beyond superstition, common sense, duty and servility to power. And because the requirements of exploitative power have always (quite necessarily) been based on a set of necessary illusions, this real purpose of religion has long been understood to be ultimately threatening to all who would manipulate human beings for their own ends. Consequently it has long been an urgent requirement of propaganda systems, be they church-based, autocratic, totalitarian or democratic, that they distort religious understanding in such a way that either we come to accept a ridiculous version of religion or, in the case of modern consumerism, we reject serious concern for religious speculation altogether.

The point is that the truth is stifled and the lie maintained not merely by continuous promotion of factual lies, but by continuous promotion of underlying falsehoods, such as the idea that questioning and the pursuit of truth leads to absurdity, futility and pointlessness.

Our independence of thought is not destroyed primarily by our inability to learn the specific facts about, say, corporate collusion with violent dictatorships around the world; rather it is destroyed by far more subtle, barely perceived ideas or background philosophies of life, which suggest that: 'There are no answers', 'Nothing can be done about this tragic world', 'Life has no point anyway', in which case— 'So what! Why care!'. These types of unconscious, apparently apolitical, often unspoken ideas form, and always have formed, I believe, the real bedrock of thought control. It would, after all, be a surprise if specific facts turned out to be more important in restricting thought than the general, background framework of basic understanding into which those facts are assimilated.

In the first chapter we noted that rational decisions are best distinguished from the irrational by their relative lack of absolute certainty. Our way out of this trap must be to approach areas of unquestioned (and, above all, cherished!) 'certainty' and 'common sense' wherever we find them, and ask ourselves some basic questions—Why are they so unquestionably certain? What are the conceivable, rational objections? Are they being heard? If not, why not? Above all, we need to ask ourselves who might be benefiting—and in what ways—from our being so completely certain.

The extreme difficulty with this is that very often, even as we are going out on a limb to saw through various types of rotten 'certainty' and 'common sense', we find that we have all along been sitting on an absolutely fallacious 'certainty' of our own. We must therefore be prepared, not only to go out on a limb, but to saw through the very limb itself!

Clinging Religiously to Non-Belief: The Political Economy of Atheism

Most atheists are familiar with Nietzsche's great declaration that 'God is dead!' Few, however, are aware that, in the selfsame book, Nietzsche gave a dire warning:

> 'Yes, it divines you too, you conquerors of the old God! You grow weary in battle and now your weariness serves the *new* idol!'[2]

In connection with this, we may be reminded of an apparent natural law whereby, when taken to their extreme, all things become their opposite. This principle is neatly represented in the Taoist yin and yang symbol—in black and white spirals we find respectively white and black dots representing the seeds of the opposite qualities. These seeds are brought to fruition, as the symbol elegantly shows, when the spirals reach their extreme value. In other words, go far enough and day becomes night, night becomes day, pleasure becomes pain. This is what is so interesting about Nietzsche's warning, and so troubling about atheism. For whilst atheists so ardently castigate the religious for clinging to religion as a sort of crutch—arguing that all belief in a creator is a matter of mere wishful thinking and faith—atheism is itself just such a crutch, just such a faith clung to no less religiously than the belief in the great Cosmic Father Figure. Atheism, in propounding its extreme opposition to religion, reveals itself to be—a religion.

The point is, of course, that non-belief is also very much a belief. Ultimately, we have to *believe* there is no God; we have to *believe* that we (and those we criticize) have truly understood what is meant by this noun; we have to *believe* the universe has no meaning; we have to *believe* that this belief, in itself, is meaningful.

Security in Despair

We human beings are above all characterized by our escape from instinctual programming into self-awareness. As a result, we are obliged to involve ourselves in a lifelong inquiry into the nature of our relationship with the world around us. This process of replacing our instinctual ties with the world we call culture, myth and, above all, religion. For the word religion does not at all imply belief in a God or a devil, but derives from the Latin *re-ligare*, meaning to re-join the individual with the society, world and cosmos (*ligare* being the root of 'ligament', by which muscle is connected to bone). All answers supplied to the question of our relationship with the world are therefore essentially religious answers, whether they involve belief in a God, a devil, or nothing at all. For animals, no equivalent answers or solutions are required, as they face no such problem—their relationship with the world is largely pre-determined by instincts which guide them for the duration of their lives.

This, as we know all too well, is not the case for us human beings. The young human being indeed has little or no idea of what it means to live a happy and sane human life. This makes human life supremely difficult and challenging, for life is fired at us point-blank and, like it or not, we do have to make important decisions, whether we are ready or not, and whether we are certain or not. (In a sense, every time we do anything, the real world requires that we temporarily put aside our doubts, make a decision and act as though certain. This need to act with conviction, day-in day-out, often leads us to forget that our 'certainty' is purely provisional. In many mythological tales, the hero, the truth-seeker, is removed from the everyday world by some great crisis in order that he or she might remember his or her true uncertainty.)

It is easy to discuss this human problem without fully recognising the significance of the confusion implied for our actual lives. Yet, we need only think of the adolescent predicament, where a young person may quite literally sit on the side of his or her bed in the morning and wonder whether it would be best to fight or to forgive any hateful people he or she meets that day. What is the best way to deal with hate? Should we be forgiving, or vengeful? Is it better to respond to hate with hate, or with understanding?

This is a fundamental question. But where is the answer? For animals, it is written in their instinctive biological programming. For human beings, it is found only in our individual understanding of the nature of the world, of ourselves, and the relation between the two. Thus our teenager may consider that life in this world is a brutal matter of self-preservation and so decide to fight hate with hate. A moment later, he or she may decide that, whilst pain is inevitable in the world, much unnecessary pain and struggle could be avoided by maintaining a forgiving attitude, in the understanding that most hatred is caused by the absence of understanding and so, rather than re-fuel the cycles of hate, he or she should starve them and so bring a little peace to the world—and so on.

The point is that our teenager must choose; he or she must make a decision every time he or she interacts with other people. In reality, we rarely fight heroic battles with utter conviction for a definitely vital cause, for a certainly true love, for an assuredly heroic achieve-ment. More often, we fight for our lives not really knowing what is truly good or bad, what is right or wrong, what is surely worthwhile or worthless, whether we are defending true love or childish infatu-ation, a noble cause or a political lie, whether we are even being brave, or simply weak and foolish.

As we know, many individuals find this terrible human burden of uncertainty and doubt too much to bear. Many abandon their doubt at the foot of some convenient, reassuring certainty—a mother or father figure perhaps, an authoritarian leader, an ancient set of scrip-tures, a stone idol, a Cosmic Father Figure and, indeed, atheism. For atheism, as surely as so many other religions, tells us that there *are* certainties in life—there is certainly no significance to life, certainly no creator, we are certainly just machines, or animals, we will certainly never live again, so we should certainly gather rosebuds while we may. These are deemed to be certainties. Bertrand Russell famously insisted as much when he said:

'Only on the foundation of unyielding despair can the soul's habitation henceforth be safely built.' [3]

Religion has of course often served as a wish-fulfilling escape from the awesome uncertainty of the human condition. But atheism argues that, because religion is mere wishful-thinking, it must certainly be realistic to accept a 'desperate' alternative. Indeed, atheists seem seduced by the belief that an answer to the uncertainty and mystery of life is more likely to be certain and real the more appalling it is (the word 'reality', after all, is often used synonymously with 'painful'—we talk of 'facing reality', of 'facing painful reality', of the 'cold light of day'); and to not be certain is simply escapism.

But, whilst atheistic desperation might seem courageous, it is also too convenient. Atheism is no more certain for being founded on desperation. The universe is simply far too unknown to allow for this level of certainty—however despairing. Bertrand Russell had no right at all to designate desperation a 'foundation' on which to build some spurious certainty: the mystery of the universe undermines his unhappy construction work, which is no less shaky, no less naive, no less false, for being desperate. As R.D. Laing said so simply: 'Who are we to decide that it is hopeless!'

The mysteriousness of our lives in this universe is such that we must continually face and endure the remorseless terror/wonder of uncertainty/mystery.

Although the atheistic certainty regarding God, life and death is essentially another religious retreat from the awesome uncertainty, mystery and bewilderment of the human condition (and, today, as we shall see, from radical doubt of our conformity to the propaganda system) into false certainty, there is a difference that entirely separates it from all other religious ideas. For, as a belief, atheism is supremely resistant to iconoclastic criticism because it purports to be *not belief*, not religion, but—reality. However not only is atheism a belief, a religion, but it is one that declares itself to be the final reality, the final truth beyond all lies—and where have we heard that before? In the same way that 'The true fiend rules in God's name', so true delusion speaks in the name of true realism! True belief speaks in the name of non-belief.

The CFF is Dead: Long Live Religion!

It is easy to imagine that belief in a Cosmic Father Figure involves the projection of a biological father figure onto a screen of cosmic proportions. After all, as individuals we were created by our biological mother and father; thus it is easy to imagine how many people might come to assume that the universe must similarly be the work of a cosmic mother or father. In many cultures the Goddess—for example Gaia, Gula-Bau, Demeter, or Persephone—was originally worshipped as the fount of all life and revered as a source of unconditional love and life, as are our biological mothers. And, in the same way that children move on from the infantile, unconditional love of mother to seek the more demanding, conditional love of father, so many religions have moved on to worship the loving but angry God— Ahura Mazda, Yahweh, the Lord—who cares for us when we are good but punishes us when we are bad, just as our own fathers did.

Buddhism, on the other hand, has long insisted that belief in an actual, personal God always involves cosmic parental projection of this type, arguing that just as true maturity in an individual involves gaining independence from reliance on both mother and father, so mature understanding dispenses with the need to believe in a personal God or Goddess but looks for truth in the true nature of the self and the real world beyond our fantasies (which brings us back to the real meaning of the word religion, as defined earlier).

The Buddhist and Taoist conceptions of 'holiness', as well as the Roman 'numen' (as in numinous), are altogether different from that held by Western theists and attacked by atheists—that which embodies the law of a cosmic lawgiver. I wonder what atheists make, for example, of the story of the Buddhist monk who has his feet resting on a statue of the Buddha—when an unenlightened passer-by angrily demands that he remove his feet from the 'holy Buddha', the monk replies 'And where shall I put my feet that is not holy?' The idea that the universe is somehow holy does not necessarily involve believing that it must be governed by an external cosmic judge (nor, indeed, that it must be serving some great purpose), for the Buddha is here most certainly a symbol and not a supernatural person to be worshipped, as the monk makes clear. And yet the extraordinary truth, beyond the required distortions of power, is that virtually all religions the world over have always had this symbolic, rather than supernatural, emphasis at heart. In *The Hero With A Thousand Faces*, and in his great tetralogy *The Masks Of God*, Joseph Campbell showed that:

'Whether we listen with aloof amusement to the dreamlike mumbo jumbo of some red-eyed witch doctor of the Congo, or read with cultivated rapture thin translations from the sonnets of the mystic Lao-tse; now and again crack the hard nutshell of an argument of Aquinas, or catch suddenly the shining meaning of a bizarre Eskimo fairy tale: it will be always the one, shape-shifting *yet marvellously constant* story that we find, together with a challengingly persistent suggestion of more remaining to be experienced than will ever be known or told.'[4]

This 'marvellously constant story' treats of nothing less than the understanding and experience of the ultimate unity of all things— 'That art thou!'. Thus Campbell sought to show that the Tao, Buddha, Holy Ghost, God, Gaia, Zeus—along with all other mythological metaphors—should be read not as references to historical or supernatural fact, but as symbols or sign-posts pointing beyond themselves to a fundamental unity which, because it lies behind and beyond all aspects of the phenomenal world of separate 'things', must remain beyond all language used to describe those separate parts. The great tragedy, Campbell argued, is that humanity has all too often been deluded into worshipping, rather than following, these sign-posts—even fighting for 'this' sign-post against 'that' sign-post. For beyond this squabbling, the sign-posts all point the same way:

'It is amazing, but now undeniable, that the vocabulary of symbol is to such an extent constant through the world that it must be recognized to represent a single pictorial script, through which realizations of a *tremendum* experienced through life are given statement. Apparent also is the fact that not only in higher cultures, but also among many of the priests and visionaries of the folk cultures, these symbols—or, as we so often say, 'gods'—*are not thought to be powers in themselves* but are signs through which the powers of life and its revelations are recognized and released: powers of the soul as well as of the living world.'[5] (my emphasis)

Yet as we know, the great mass of critics and supporters of religion consistently mistake these 'signs' for 'powers in themselves' and so respectively attack and support their own error of misinterpretation. It is understandable that atheists deride the supernatural claims of some of these misinterpreters, but how often do they consider the fact that so many of the great religions of the world also dismiss these supernatural claims—with their notions of a supernatural God, a 'meaning' to life and divine intervention? How do they deal with the suggestion that we kill the Buddha if we see him walking along the road, or that we wash our mouth out if we use his 'filthy' name (both suggestions designed to make clear that idolatrous worship of some 'superior' being is the antithesis of the teaching)? There is obviously much more here than childish supernatural fantasy. Indeed, it is an extraordinary fantasy to believe that there is not.

But many atheists seem determined not to look beyond the superstitious corruption of religion. This is for good reasons. Many people are so appalled by the version of religious education that they were subjected to at school that they come to feel an almost phobic revulsion for all things religious (an example of the tremendous power of misinterpretation in regard to controlling thought). Religion was made to seem nothing more than a bludgeoning effort to make them believe something that made no sense at all. But do we loathe Nietzsche because Hitler used him to justify his banal ideology? We know Nietzsche would have found Hitler and his lies beneath contempt. Do we reject the genius of the great teachers of modern science because profit-hungry exploiters are laying waste to our world? Surely it has always been the fate of the great ideas of human culture to be abused and misinterpreted by the lesser, manipulative, power-seeking minds of the world. We should not judge the idea by its corruption, and surely it has always been the great intellectual task to separate the one from the other.

Atheism as Anaesthetic: The Great 'So What!'

That the false certainty of atheism is a powerful device for persuading us to attempt to escape from the truth of life can be appreciated when we understand the import of its great nihilistic phrase, 'So what!'. For when considering, for example, Yeats' sublime observation and question:

'Man is in love and loves what vanishes.
What more is there to say?'[6]

many modern atheists answer with complete assuredness 'So what! Nothing *really* matters anyway'. Now, this may or may not be true and important in the grand scheme of things, but to you and I as individuals it is a lie, because to lose the ones we love, to lose our friends, our lives, matters terribly to us.

Here we can see that atheism involves an attempt to escape from painful awareness by hiding behind a purported cosmic *pointlessness*, just as other religions have hidden behind a purported cosmic *meaningfulness*. After all, what does it matter that we lose everything if nothing matters? Where now is death's sting? If atheism is the philosophy of despair, as Russell claimed, then it is a despair conspicuously ameliorated by the anaesthetic properties of its great 'So what!'.

An extreme example of this atheistic attempt to avoid facing painful reality is provided by individuals who, when pressed, respond to the issue of environmental degradation by saying in effect, 'Okay, suppose we *are* destroying the life-support systems of planetary life—so what! There is not one scrap of evidence you can present to support the idea that this world is important, or unique—we may be only one of millions of inhabited planets.'

Again, this may or may not be cosmologically true, but, psychologically, it is a terrible lie. Why? Because we believe it to avoid facing the ultimate, devastating tragedy that such a loss would actually mean to us as living beings. We say 'So what!' to avoid facing the fact that we are talking about the ultimate painful possibility: *So everything! So, our world!* Such a statement is a rationalization of minds hell-bent on avoiding the pain of self-doubt. Can living creatures really talk this way about the fate of their own lives, their species, their world—the only world they know—and be considered sane? We are here in the presence of a grand religious delusion, a powerful, de-sensitizing, anaesthetizing rationalization whose function is to ensure that we do not consider the truth about our actions, the true significance of our conformity.

We all know that one of the permanent temptations in life is to flee from our pain, our doubt, and our responsibility to meet both where they must be met. Yet we sophisticated, cynical, certain 'postmoderns' believe our cynicism can shrug a shoulder at the stupidity, horror and tragedy of what we are doing, we believe that we have somehow matured beyond 'sentimental' caring. Nothing could be further from the truth. We, who think we are so strong, are hiding from our weakness, from our failure to face our moral and intellectual capitulation in the face of conformity. Our heroic cynicism is intellectual cowardice on a giant scale. Our courageous indifference in the face of despair is merely a form of mental leprosy by which our nerve-endings have been numbed and our sanity eaten away. Our lack of pain, our 'maturity', is our extreme sickness, our utter immaturity in our unwillingness to entertain radical doubt. We put our hand in the flame of global human and environmental devastation and, with a shrug and a 'So what!' leave it there and call ourselves 'post-modern', 'scientific', 'hard-headed', 'unsentimental', and 'rational'; actually, we are burning.

The Unholy Trinity: Atheism, Consumerism and 'Progress'

With its naive, unyielding emphasis on the empty, pointless nature of existence, on the lack of all meaning, on the lack of all intrinsic value in life, the world and the universe—atheism has provided the ideal religious dogma to fuel the infernal fires of consumerism and rampant industrial 'progress' over the last 150 years. As a consequence, atheism has been powerfully boosted by the propaganda system.

Of course, we like to imagine that the cold light of hard science and technology has shooed away all the shadows of earlier, primitive, superstitious thinking. No chance: the idea that we are really just machine-like containers, that we are essentially just animal lumps of meat, that the world is just a natural resource to be consumed, are superstitions clutched with fanatical conviction by all with an interest in promoting consumerism and 'progress'. For these social goals require maximum consumption, and maximum consumption requires maximum belief in ourselves as fleeting, uncomplicated 'lumps of meat' who might as well satisfy our physical needs, our mechanical lusts as soon as possible, for as long as possible, because beyond the neon-lit room of self-gratification, there lies only an abyss of dark despair. Like so many superstitious religions, the false religion of consumerism lures us with the promise of heaven through consumption and threatens us with the hell of desperate emptiness beyond.

The young today are quite literally warned not to think too much, not to go 'too deep', not to be too serious, not to place the cares of the world on their shoulders, because their parents and peers really have been persuaded to believe that, beyond consumerism, there lies a sort of dark hell of meaninglessness and desperation. Self-gratification through consumption is seen as a sort of existential life-jacket. It is commonly expected that any deep thought will end in depression, suicide or madness, that the devil of desperate reality will pounce on our sinful, non-consuming souls.

Progress—which has come to mean little more than the progressive satisfaction of desires—demands a zealous commitment to, and total faith in, the value of immediate self-gratification in the name of

the rhetorical question 'Is there more to life than fun?' Anyone who
has been condemned for being concerned with subjects deemed 'a
bit serious', or 'deep', knows what it is to be a heretic. Faith in fun as
the only answer to life is every bit as religious, every bit as irrationally
fanatical as any belief in a Cosmic Father Figure. Indeed, as we have
said, it is more fanatical, because it is utterly convinced that it is not
belief, but the final, unsentimental, rational truth beyond belief—we
are just machines, so we might as well get on with consuming.

By encouraging us to abandon all philosophical and religious speculation and get on with the day—that is, with gathering our corpo-
rately-grown rosebuds while we may—atheism creates the perfect
void into which the philosophical muzak of 'progressive' corporate
consumerism may enter. To hell with the possibility of expanding
human freedom through radical doubt, to hell with the possibilities
of fulfilment through simple living, loving, meditation, creativity,
abstinence and, above all, radical, unlimited questioning; to hell with
a sense of wonder at this universe—atheism gives us permission to
abandon this escapism and furiously seek the pleasure, fun and excitement of consumerism in the short time left to us.

Agnostics, quite reasonably, propose that we cannot know the truth
of life, but atheism goes much further—it demands meaninglessness,
and this, as formulated by modern society, turns out to be a simple
recommendation for irresponsible, immediate gratification. The
combination of atheism and consumerism was bound to lead to the
modern environmental crisis, because according to its credo, nothing
matters beyond the moment (actually, not even the moment matters,
but at least the experience of pleasure offers some distraction).

To be convinced of this can only be viewed as a sort of sickness,
a madness; it is impossible to imagine that any civilization, any species,
could survive for very long believing this *en masse*. To empty life to
this extent is to create a giant hollow centre in human culture that
must eventually collapse under its own weight; much as a star, having
spent its nuclear fuel, can collapse under the weight of its own gravity.
Assuredly this point will be reached when modern consumerism,
having eaten the heart out of the environment, will become a 'super-
nova', collapsing under the weight of its own *frivolity*.

We see all around us people who do not care about anything—
the great issues of religious, philosophical, political and economic life,
the present, the planet, the future, themselves, or others. This is not
merely passive indifference; it is a religious stance. Atheistic
consumerism, as espoused by the propaganda system (through endless

adverts, films, magazine articles, quiz shows, soap operas, love songs, etc) has convinced us it is sentimental *fantasy* and even dangerous to think too deeply, to care about the world. Today even love is deemed a sort of biological mutton dressed up as spiritual lamb. So, too, spiritual and poetic impulses bring forth hoots of delighted, certain, atheistic derision; if anything, the desire to understand is seen as frustrated sexuality gone wrong.

The only artistic endeavour deemed to have any real validity today is the cathartic expression of Russell's despair, which is seen at least as a valid biological release, a way of getting some of the bleak emptiness of life (which is often, in fact, the bleak emptiness of capitalist consumerism) out of the system. Gone are the courageous, life-affirming poets, philosophers and action-oriented individuals epitomised by the Greeks and Romans. Today, the artist is a brooding, desolate, despairing hermit who shuns light and life—all else is considered not art, but naïvety and wishful-thinking. Nowhere are there the likes of Socrates, with his life-affirming philosophy of the escalating appreciation of beauty:

'...Next he must grasp that the beauties of the body are as nothing to the beauties of the soul, so that wherever he meets with spiritual loveliness, even in the husk of an unlovely body, he will find it beautiful enough to fall in love with and to cherish—and beautiful enough to quicken in his heart a longing for such discourse as tends toward the building of a noble nature... And now... there bursts upon him that wondrous vision which is the very soul of the beauty he has toiled so long for. It is an everlasting loveliness which neither comes nor goes, which neither flows nor fades, for such beauty is the same one at every hand, the same then as now, here as there, this way as that way, the same to every worshipper as it is to every other'.[7]

Nowhere are there the likes of the lame slave Epictetus, who whispers to us with a great burst of human optimism:

'How can it be that one who has nothing, neither raiment, nor house nor home, nor bodily tendance, nor servant, nor city, should yet live tranquil and contented?...Behold me! I have neither city nor house, possessions nor servants: the ground is my couch; I have no wife, no children, no shelter—nothing but earth and sky, and one poor cloak. Yet, what do I lack? Am I not untouched by sorrow, by fear? Am I not free?[8]

'Always Winter, Never Christmas'

Consumerism needs a society of discontents. It must see to it that we are never satisfied, at peace. Naturally, therefore, it is opposed to any philosophy of acceptance of life, of affirmation of its pains—the last thing consumerism wants is for us to *accept* our pain. For, in conflict with the wisdom of Epictetus (and so many of the other great teachers of human culture), consumerism demands that, rather than learning to accept the pains of life, we consume in order to remove them. And it demands this with the massed might of the filter system driven by the giant, global corporations which push their propaganda over global telecommunications networks twenty-four hours a day, every day. These networks show us the ideal self, the ideal life, the good, happy, successful life, in order that we may feel inadequate—fat, old, ugly, stupid, poor, unsophisticated, lowly, insignificant, foolish, unhappy—that we may then alleviate our dissatisfaction, satisfy 'our' desires, which are in reality the desires of corporations for profit. But we can never find ultimate satisfaction because consumerism ensures that, like the Hydra of Greek mythology, for each desire that is satisfied, eight new ones will arise to ensure our profitable discontent!

Today, all around us, lame Epictetus is nailed to the cross of industrial growth, along with the legions of otherwise perfectly normal people: anorexic and bulimic girls (too 'fat'), the depressed and suicidal adolescents (too 'ugly', 'young', 'stupid'), the desolates of middle and old-age (too 'old', 'unattractive', 'unsuccessful'), and all the rest.

Together, then, atheism, consumerism and 'progress' form an unholy trinity that is a devastating enemy of humanity and life generally. While the Spanish Inquisition tortured and killed thousands in the name of religious certainty, today the atheists of industrial consumer 'progress' torture the entire world—from the ozone layer down—in the name of their certainties, their Gods: meaninglessness and self-gratification as the only answers to a desperate life.

Atheists have long savoured the cliché that religion is the root of all evil, ignoring the carnage wreaked by two of the truly monstrous and essentially atheistic regimes of the 20th century—Nazism (responsible for 6 million murdered directly and 50 million dead from the world war it instigated) and Stalinism (25 million murdered). Above all, they ignore the ultimate carnage of capitalist, atheistic 'progress', with its space-age capacity for transporting our generation to a new and alien world unsuitable for human life— Industrial Earth! In truth, the religion of 'progress' has already been far more   devastating than any mere God-worshipping religion. The naïvety of this cliché notwithstanding, there is a certain truth to it—for both Nazism and Stalinism were religions in the sense that they represented a framework of responses to the human condition (albeit pathologically deluded ones), as is the case for industrial 'progress', and even atheism. But to declare all religion evil achieves nothing at all, because whatever we offer in its place must in some way define our relationship with the cosmos, which is by definition a religious issue.

Milk and Sugar?

The only option lies not in rejecting religion, but in transcending false religion. As Tolstoy found, the solution to a problem often involves finding not a better answer, but a better question. Thoreau summed this up in his dryly humorous way, revealing that he changed from wondering how to get people to buy the baskets he made, to wondering how to avoid needing to sell baskets in the first place—so liberating himself from economic necessity by abandoning, rather than satisfying, gratuitous desire.

We need, not an end to the search for religious answers (which is itself a religious answer and, as we have seen, an entirely inadequate one), but a search for better, more sane, more human answers to life. Fortunately we are not alone—or in the dark—in this search. For we can still draw on the wisdom, courage and grace of individual men and women throughout history, if we can only open our minds to the reality of what they are trying to say, behind the symbols they use.

Our society has re-written history (as have all fanatically religious societies in the past), as having been a primitive, religious void prior to the enlightenment of the one true reality that is progress. But their 'superstition' is a reflection of our ignorance; their 'meaninglessness' is our confusion. Our problem is that of the Western professor who visited a Zen master to learn his wisdom. Pouring his guest a cup of tea, the Zen master filled the cup to its brim and kept pouring. The professor watched the cup overflowing in astonishment until he could no longer restrain himself. 'It is overfull,' he said. 'No more will go in!' 'Like this cup,' the Zen master said, '*you* are full of your own opinions and speculations. How can I show you Zen unless you first empty your cup?'

Indeed, how can we ever hope to grow and learn and flourish, when our minds are overfull with the unyielding, despairing, false certainty of atheism and fanatical 'progress'? Whenever we are certain, we are full, and when we are full, we are stupid. Uncertainty, an emptiness in our cup, a sense of wonder, is crucial for life, sanity and survival.

What Zarathustra also Said

In his book *Thus Spoke Zarathustra*, Nietzsche applied the *coup de grace* to God the supernatural personality; to God the fierce, judgmental overlord. Nietzsche emptied our cup of some of the nonsense of irrational superstition and, for this, we are indebted to him. But he did not stop there. He had something more in mind, something better, and in the same book he tells us the three things we need to get it.

He tells us that we must have the strength of the camel in bearing the burden of doubt across the wasteland of modern emptiness, that we must not dump our burden at the foot of some new false certainty. So, too, he tells us we need the courage and power of the lion in roaring a sacred 'No!' to the eternal golden dragon of social 'wisdom', with 'Thou shalt!' written on each of its scales (Thou shalt produce, consume and have fun, for example!). He demands doubt and courage from us.

The third thing Nietzsche demands is that we should become the 'self-propelling wheel', the creator of new values, of new belief, that we should whisper—with all the hope and innocence and life-affirmation of a little child—a 'Yes!' to some new truth, some new, truer idea of life. Yes, God is dead, but not mystery, not hope, not the ability to affirm and love this life. Can it be that atheists have really forgotten that Nietzsche also said with all his heart:

'...by my love and hope I entreat you: do not reject the hero in your soul! Keep holy your highest hope!'[9]

In many ways, atheism has been an understandable reaction to the escapism and excess of much (often cynically manipulative) religious nonsense. It has also, and more importantly, however, become a vital tool in the armoury of those who would have us keep ourselves on our knees. And, now, the killers of the old God worship the new God, just as Nietzsche warned they would.

Power Religion

Not only, then, is atheism a religion (a provisional answer to life like any other) but it is one ideally suited for the promotion of unrestrained consumerism. As the alternative to believing in a Cosmic Father Figure, atheism has loyally served to limit the debate between two suitable alternatives, leaving the genuine and far less suitable interpretation of religion out of the picture (an interpretation to which we shall return in the next chapter).

Atheistic consumerism is simply the latest version of a perennial religion which may be called power religion. Power religion, unlike true religious endeavour (for which Fromm used the term 'humanistic religion'), has nothing at all do with the search for fundamental, adequate answers to human life, but is purely a means of justifying, enforcing and facilitating the exercise of power.

Power religion does not consist in a particular set of beliefs, but in a set of functions supporting power. Because these functions remain essentially constant, we discover close similarities between versions of power religion widely separated by historical time, geography and superficial appearance. The differences between these beliefs represent a sort of superficial clothing over an essentially identical framework of underlying function. This unchanging framework operates to ensure that the mass of people:

—be over-awed and pacified by esoteric knowledge incomprehensible to, and therefore unchallengeable by, mere mortals who are not 'in the know'.

—be incapable of forming a coherent picture of the world on the basis of which they might offer criticism of power.

—be intimidated into obedience and loyalty by reference to life-threatening, 'demonic' enemies.

—be seduced into conformity by the promise of utopian future happiness.

—defer to and idolise their leaders.

Two versions of power religion which, while outwardly different, both satisfy the above requirements, are:
—traditional, theistic, church-based religion and
—modern, atheistic, corporate-based religion.

Experts: High Priests of Incoherence
From the sun Gods of Egypt to the modern Vatican, old-style theistic religion has long promoted the belief that an élite few have secret access to mysterious, esoteric knowledge revealed by a supreme cosmic intelligence. The utility of this type of belief is clear—it ensures that all merely mortal citizens do not dare challenge ultimate authority as embodied in the earthly ruler. What, after all, could be more absurd

than that the average person—with no special knowledge, temple, or access to the very creator of the universe Himself—should dare suggest that the revealed word of God could somehow be mistaken? How could such a person dare suggest that the earth revolves around the sun, in contradiction to the book of Joshua?

The obvious advantage of revelation as the basis of law, truth and political legitimacy, is that it is not open to discussion or rational argument. Indeed, once the basic ideational framework has been established—that there is a supreme being actively intervening in human affairs—to challenge revealed truth is to challenge the word of God, which, by definition, is to threaten the ultimately 'evil' revolution. The only way to realistically challenge these revealed truths is to argue either that there is no supreme being, or that there may be a supreme being but He is not revealing the truth as claimed (and that therefore the king and his priests and everyone else must be lying or deluded, and therefore have no legitimacy).

Both these views are so incompatible with the truisms of theistic society that they would be expected to be met by ridicule—or by torture and death. History does not disappoint in this expectation. Views not merely inconvenient but also dangerous to the ruling powers have almost no chance of being discussed within the mainstream channels of communication, education and discourse that are controlled by power.

Frequently the need for drastic measures is avoided by limiting the parameters of discussion and thought between two alternatives—'Did God mean this?', or 'Did God mean that?'—so preventing individuals from moving beyond to the real questions: 'Did God speak at all?' 'Is there a God able to speak?' 'What might the real goals and interests of power be beyond the rhetoric?' and this, in turn, prevents any radical questioning of the legitimacy and rationality of power. More generally, it serves to maintain the passivity, delusion and stupefaction of the general population—it has long been understood that stupidity is the oxygen of power.

Even from this cursory discussion, we can recognize that the 'death of God' pronounced by Nietzsche has certainly not meant the death of power religion. For this self-same function can be seen to be very much alive in modern atheistic, consumer society.

Because state and corporate power depend on a similar set of unchallenged, unquestionable distortions and delusions, incoherence remains vital for their survival. After all, to present a coherent explanation as to why the Third World is starving, why the environment is falling apart, why there was a Cold War, why Panama was invaded, why there was a Gulf war, why forty per cent of British children live below the poverty line, and so on, would immediately involve revealing the truth that society is built on a set of necessary illusions. Consequently, the news we see and read, like education at school, must consist of a stream of disconnected, disembodied facts, with no context, no coherent explanation of meaning or significance, no background and no logical framework by means of which they could be understood. Because the only logical framework that fits—that the Western world is motivated by corporate profit at very nearly any human and environmental cost—is disallowed, a confused hotchpotch of ill-fitting, irrational frameworks must be invented and bolted together. Any number of surveys have revealed the extent to which the majority of people have no coherent grasp of what is happening in the world. (This does not at all indicate, as many claim, that the mass of people are stupid; only that they have been, in effect, brainwashed by the actions of the filter system discussed in chapter one.)

This failure to comprehend ranges from imagining that ozone depletion is caused by leaded petrol to the notion that Third World poverty is a tragic act of God, or the result of overpopulation, or 'African nature' and 'Asian corruption', for which the West bears no responsibility. Few people today understand why there is violence in the Middle East (why the Palestinians are so dissatisfied), how it can be that starving Africans are armed to the teeth with military hardware, why South America seems to breed dictatorships as a matter of course, why countries as naturally wealthy as Brazil and Venezuela are crippled by poverty, and why there was an arms race. People know of these problems, but they do not understand them in any meaningful way. As in earlier times, people must be made to worship the revealed 'truth', unquestioningly:

> 'In the modern secular age, this means worship of the state religion, which in the Western democracies incorporates the doctrine of submission to the masters of the system of public subsidy, private profit, called free enterprise. The people must be kept in ignorance, reduced to jingoist incantations... and 'emotionally potent oversimplifications' that keep the ignorant and stupid masses disciplined and content.' Noam Chomsky, *Necessary Illusions*[10]

The modern secular priesthood promoting this level of required stupefaction are those we call 'experts'. Their function, as with the priests of old, is to suggest that only an élite few are in a position to fully understand the esoteric secrets of domestic and world affairs. How, then, could ordinary modern men and women dare to suggest that the infinitely complex modern world of technological and economic society could be improved, or changed—or is, perhaps, redundant? How absurd that we—who know not the first thing about the intricacies and secrets of piloting a ship of state—should have the idea of commenting on its direction (actually, our direction). We must leave that sort of thing to the 'expert' priests of finance, foreign affairs, diplomacy, behavioural science, and so on.

No doubt this is how our forebears felt and reacted before the high priests of the geocentric universe. In our case, it is not necessarily that these 'experts' consciously try to befuddle and bemuse us; rather, the various filters see to it that the facts fit the ideology. Because the Nicaraguan Sandinista regime was more concerned with implementing social welfare and land reforms to help Nicaraguan peasants than with serving US corporate interests, and because this could not be allowed to become 'the threat of a good example' (Oxfam) to other Third World victims in thrall to Western corporate needs, and because this truth could not be allowed to pass through the corporately-run filter system, a whole web of fabrications and distortions simply had to surround the 'monstrous', 'totalitarian' Nicaraguan regime bent on global revolution (how else could we explain our hostility to a regime bent on ameliorating the condition of the poor?). There had to be some explanation, something to fill the vacuum of understanding. Thus, the Sandinistas had to come to be seen to have a much worse human rights record than El Salvador and Guatemala (supportive of US corporate interests), and to be threatening the US with non-existent Mig jets.

Because this account of reality is a result of the distorting influence of the propaganda filter system, it is a version of reality that cannot be coherent, that cannot make sense. For the same reason, when we listen to news commentators, we inevitably find their accounts bewildering, superficial, disembodied and incoherent. Because we do not understand anything, we do not feel in a position to resist (or even complain). Clearly, we cannot become outraged, let alone act, unless we have a grasp of why we should be outraged, or act. Anyone challenging the 'expert' runs into essentially the same set of unquestionable truths by which the likes of Copernicus were faced. Today's eternal truths are only superficially different—the government is dedicated to maximising the well-being of all by a passionate commitment to democracy, equality and fraternity, achievable only by the harsh medicine of pursuing maximum corporate growth as the only reasonable answer to life, with all else deemed sinful, pagan blasphemy, or, in modern parlance—'mystic psychobabble'. The terms of abuse change, but the function does not.

'Wherever I Lay My Hat…': Devils on the Move

James Joyce wrote of how old-style religion employed soul-hungry demons to terrify potential sinners, especially the young. Here, his character Stephen Dedalus recalls a talk given by one of his teachers:

'… Last of all consider the frightful torment to those damned souls, tempters and tempted alike, of the company of the devils. These devils will afflict the damned in two ways, by their presence and by their reproaches. We can have no idea of how horrible these devils are. Saint Catherine of Siena once saw a devil and she has written that, rather than look again for one single instant on such a frightful monster, she would prefer to walk until the end of her life along a track of red coals…'[11]

The function of belief in a physical hell populated by devils is plain enough—failure to be adequately virtuous (actually, obedient) in the eyes of God (actually, in the eyes of church-based power), will result in ever-lasting torment at the hands of devils. This, of course, is no more than an imaginative way of frightening people into conformity and passivity. Indeed one of the worst sins, by this doctrine, is to suggest that the whole notion of vengeful Gods and fiery devils is more worthy of a Bugs Bunny cartoon than serious discussion (for, then, the soul must surely be utterly beyond redemption).

Fortunately, of course, since the advent of modern science and so on, we have discarded all such nonsense talk of soul-munching devils… or, rather, we have not! Consider, for example, the aim of practical politics according to H.L. Mencken:

'The whole aim of practical politics is to keep the populace alarmed by menacing it with an endless series of hobgoblins, all of them imaginary.'[12]

Thus Hitler's dire warnings of Czechoslovakia as a 'dagger pointed at the heart of Germany'.

Thus Lyndon Johnson's warning in 1948 of the need for overwhelming US military superiority if it was to avoid becoming 'a bound and throttled giant; impotent and easy prey to any yellow dwarf with a pocket knife.'[13]

Thus Ronald Reagan's tragi-comic declaration in May 1985 of a 'national emergency' to deal with the 'unusual and extraordinary threat to the national security and foreign policy of the United States' posed by 'the policies and actions of the Government of Nicaragua.'[14] Far from eliciting roars of laughter, the last statement was received with great solemnity by the US population (which had, after all, previously fled for its life from Orson Welles' only marginally less credible Martian threat).

Thus we discover that the dread demons once said to be living in some giant, underground cave, were, until recently, to be found residing happily in the 'evil empire' of the former Soviet Union. Subsequently they have been forcibly evicted both to and from Panama, the hills of Nicaragua and, more recently, to the streets of Baghdad. Latest (as yet unconfirmed) sightings report a convoy of demonic mobile homes moving in the general direction of Haiti, North Korea and Cuba. There is, indeed, it seems, no rest for the wicked.

No matter where they happen to set up camp, however, these modern devils, be they 'baby-eating' Germans, 'merciless[ly] savage' Indians (as the Declaration of Independence had it), or 'Rabid Dogs' of the Middle East, all perform the same function of old—that of frightening the populace into passivity and submission. As we discussed when examining Chomsky's and Herman's fifth filter of 'anti-communism' in the first chapter, the fact is that if we can be persuaded that our lives, our very souls (as 'free democrats') are in danger, we are unlikely to offer much resistance to our leaders' heroic calls for action in their defence. Long and bloody experience indicates that we will be only too eager to offer our grateful support to our brave leaders (and their expanding arms industries, with profits willingly donated by quaking taxpayers) as they invade political minnows like Panama, Grenada, Haiti, or slaughter 250,000 effectively defenceless Iraqis, even cheering at the video footage. Psychologists tell us that it is precisely when a population feels helpless and afraid in the face of an 'overwhelming threat', that it will be most inclined to abdicate responsibility and power to an idolised figurehead.

'Most groups, whether they are primitive tribes, nations, or religions, are concerned with their own survival and upholding the power of their leaders, and they exploit the inherent moral sense of their members to arouse them against outsiders with whom there is conflict. But they use the incestuous ties which keep a person in moral bondage to his own group to stifle his moral sense and his judgement, so that he will not criticize his own group for violations of moral principles which if committed by others would drive him into violent opposition.' Erich Fromm, *Psychoanalysis And Religion*[15]

This, as we have indicated, has long been old hat to the totalitarians of our world. Devils can be found more or less to order—among villainous immigrants 'flooding' the country, among 'dirty' Gypsies, even among single mothers and their ten year-old children who, as required, become unaccountably possessed of a demonic destructiveness that will soon bring society to its knees.

Free at Last: Again!

Modern corporately-sponsored, atheistic power religion performs exactly the same function as earlier church-based versions. In this chapter, we have seen how atheism encourages people to unquestioningly accept the goals of fun, consumption and status as the only answers to life. Indeed, we saw that any questioning has come to be presented as a dangerous threat to our happiness and sanity—to go 'too deep' is to risk plunging into madness and despair. On reflection, this really is startlingly similar to the threat made by old-style religion that any doubt, any loss of faith, would result in the ground collapsing beneath our feet and our souls being sucked into the dark, despairing pit of hell. Similarly, we have seen how both types of religion encourage a necessary incoherence, a necessary humbling and stupefaction of the individual in his or her search for understanding and truth. Both are tools designed (both consciously and unconsciously) to reduce us to meek conformity and passivity. So, too, we have seen that the devils remain to once again scare us into obedience and idolatry of our only source of hope and salvation—our honourable and courageous leaders.

If it is true, as Thoreau said, that we laugh at the old generations while devotedly following the new, then the same is certainly true of power religion. For power religion is a chameleon—beneath the different colours and styles, the function remains the same. It is disturbing, then, to consider that, when we look back and wonder how on earth our forebears could have believed 'all that nonsense?' they too undoubtedly looked back just as we do and, like us, rested assured that they, too, were free from the lies of all that old-time superstition—at last!

Chapter 4

KILLING THE DREAM
OF RIGHT CONDUCT

Because the filter system acts to maintain a framework of beliefs that are essential to corporate capitalism but utterly superficial, inadequate and absurd as an answer to human life, the search for more adequate answers is limited, and effectively stifled as far as the majority of the population is concerned. It is not even that most of us no longer perceive the possibility of different answers; we no longer even perceive the existence of a *question*; the lives into which we are born are simply 'how life is'.

Doubt, like the search for fundamental truth generally, has come to be seen as sentimental, deluded, self-indulgent, and impractical. This, of course, is not always true of particular individuals, but it is almost always true of the mass media and all other economic, political, social and educational institutions that support business: all have a job to do, and that job almost always supports the corporate goals (euphemisms include being 'realistic', 'pragmatic', 'practical').

It is not, for example, that our schools are somehow neutral, that they have nothing to say on the issue of fundamental truth. Despite the efforts of well-meaning individual teachers, the framework of government curricula ensures that schools end up training young people to function efficiently as part of the economic system in a way that is competitive with our industrial rivals (certainly this is the prime criterion by which the success of our education system is judged by government and much of the mass media). This business-friendly syllabus for education is cited quite openly, with barely a murmur of dissent to suggest that it might compromise individual freedom, let alone amount to a massive programme of brainwashing the young. After all, who in the 'respectable' mainstream doubts that maximum economic growth is the rational and primary goal of modern society? (any such doubts would be assailed by appeals to 'jobs', 'the recovery', 'standards of living', although not the forbidden p-word: profits). But then who, in respectable society, doubted that the book of Joshua documented the ultimate truth? Who challenged subservience to the Fuhrer as the supreme ideal? Who questioned the defence of 'the people's revolution' as the ultimate good? No one, of course, because these were self-evident, incontestable certainties— like all necessary lies that support power. Today our assumption that we live in a free democracy goes unquestioned for the same reason, as does our understanding of what we mean by freedom and democracy. Here we can formulate a general law of social life: where we find an unchallenged social goal, we are in the presence of a great lie supported by power. From this we can see that the unquestioning acceptance of economic growth as the natural goal of human endeavour is all the evidence we need to confirm its complete fallaciousness. If there were any possibility at all that it might be a rational goal for the greater proportion of humanity, there would be some dissent, some argument, for these are universally absent only where irrationality and exploitation reign. It is worth repeating that we should not delude ourselves by thinking that all previous absurdities were held with any less conviction than our own (Hitler really was the saviour of the nation, sin really did lead to a fiery hell, the Spanish Inquisition really did act to save souls). They, also, were 'special cases'; they also were the first to find something genuinely, self-evidently true beyond all earlier superstitious nonsense, beyond all deviant calls for discussion and doubt (proof, merely, of possession by a devil or a neurosis). This, then, is how we know the absolute lie—it must call itself the absolute, unquestionable truth because any questioning, any rational consideration, threaten it with its own absurdity, and vested interests of institutionalized power simply will not permit this to happen in any meaningful way.

Returning to the matter of education, there is therefore no place for genuine doubt, questioning, learning, or freedom of thought in our exam-oriented education system. For our exams are designed to test, not our ability to think, but our suitability for the corporate programme, as automatons able to produce what we have been told to produce on time, under pressure, every time—no matter how meaningless, confusing, repetitive, boring and absurd the task.

In similar vein, the mass media are not indifferent to issues of doubt, questioning and truth; their primary role is to create a buying environment which maximizes advertising sales. This requires the careful avoidance of stimulating deeper thought that interferes with the buying mood (what, after all, could be worse than the potential consumer deep in thought about some critical issue raised by a programme, thus barely noticing the advertisers peddling their soft drinks, snacks and other essentials of modern life? Programmes will inevitably tend—by a process of 'natural selection', rather than active censorship—to be reduced to the lowest common denominator of advertising product vacuity). Above all, the creation of a buying environment requires the avoidance of any notion or implication that gratuitous consumption for status and luxury might not be the natural and sensible goals of life. This immediately rules out most profound human thought which, as a consequence, has almost ceased to exist for modern humankind—except as the fossilized bones of 'superstition'.

In the previous chapter, we saw that atheism is, in fact, merely old-style power-religion (complete with devils) brought up to date and preached by far the most powerful 'church' the world has ever seen. The price we pay for our submission to this church of trivial lies, however, is not itself trivial—it is (in a very literal sense) unimaginably high. In this section we will begin to identify some elements of that price. For the required misinterpretation of all deeper questioning as a choice between belief in a cartoon God, or atheistic consumerism— is there more to life than fun?—has facilitated a very necessary misunderstanding of what is meant by right and wrong conduct as described by the masters of religious thought the world over. Because a rational interpretation of truth, and especially fundamental religious and moral truth, is diametrically opposed to the modern system of illusion, we must be consigned to lives of complete moral chaos, caught between the rock of a cosmic cartoon and the hard place of moral nihilism.

Enlightened Ethics: Why Not?

All of us have an idea of what we imagine to be right and good as opposed to wrong and evil. Perhaps we define these concepts in terms of being kind as opposed to cruel, loving as opposed to hateful, generous as opposed to selfish. We all use words like virtuous and moral, and we all talk in terms of our vices, our evil impulses to be resisted. Regardless of how we happen to define our particular versions of good and bad, we in the West are haunted by a set of simple but fundamental questions—Why be a good person? Why not be a bad person? Why, in fact, is vice to be resisted and virtue pursued? If being bad gets us what we want, then—why not?

These are crucial questions, yet, even a moment's reflection reveals the vague manner in which most of us answer them, if we answer them at all. Most often, we resort to tired clichés, we talk of the importance of having a 'clean conscience', of being able 'to sleep at night', of being able to 'look ourselves in the mirror'. This is all very well, but the counter-argument is close at hand: if we genuinely do not care about the consequences of our actions, if we are genuinely without conscience, why should we not gaze in the mirror to our heart's content? If we are able to abandon our conscience, then what is the benefit of being good? We might go further and argue that conscience is simply a feeling of guilt resulting from the brain-washed notion that we should feel ashamed at disobeying rules stuffed into our heads as children. And, if we decide that this is true, what power does conscience have over us then?

These are the elementary ethical questions by which we moderns are confronted. We must surely ask ourselves: can we believe in the importance of virtue without resorting to the nebulous concept of a conscience, or to the even more nebulous concept of a Cosmic Father Figure keeping score on a cloud?

In this section, I would like to examine the real meaning behind the notion that sin is destructive and bad, and virtue is productive and good; why it is that we should seek to avoid the one and pursue the other; why this does not at all involve our becoming slippery with the 'slimy benignity' so loathed by Thoreau; and why we are not able to understand these simple truths in modern society. My argument will be that we can choose to be virtuous for one of two funda-mentally different reasons. The first is both superstitious and irrational but required by the modern propaganda system. The second is based on rational psychological grounds but is incompatible with—and therefore denied meaningful access to—the propaganda system. On closer examination, we find that the first reason is a misinterpreta-tion and corruption of the second.

The Short Arms of Cosmic and Earthly Law

According to the first argument, punishment for being sinful (greedy, cruel, violent, dishonest), and reward for being virtuous (humble, kind, loving, peaceful), are dependent on the existence of external supernatural and/or human powers.

Thus according to the orthodox religious view, a rich landowner cruelly exploiting the peasants around him may think he has 'got away with' his crimes but ultimately he will be punished by God—perhaps later in this life, perhaps after this life in hell. The landowner may appear to have escaped with his greed and cruelty but eventu-ally the long arm of the all-knowing, all-just, cosmic law-giver will reach out and punish him, and he will pay a terrible price.

Similarly, the alternative (but in fact closely related) view is that there is of course no God of this sort at all because everyone knows that God has long since been declared dead. Rather, in the brutal real world, the cruel landowner able to get away with his crimes in the short term will also get away with them in the long-term, unless the peasantry, or some other very earthly human agency, succeeds in enforcing equality and justice, perhaps meting out an appropriate punishment (this, essentially, defines the moral standpoint of much atheistic socialism—the evil-doer benefits from his brutality and greed unless he is made to pay).

Despite their differences, the two arguments are united in suggesting that sin is to be avoided and virtue practised in order to avoid punishment and to receive reward from an *external agency*, in the absence of which (we can only assume) we might well be forgiven for gorging ourselves on the wicked delights of 'forbidden fruit'. In this event—in the absence of a heavenly or human deterrent—we must assume that sinners would 'get away with' being sinful, that they would benefit from their sin.

Both of these arguments are compatible with the requirements of the propaganda filter system and are therefore commonly understood and discussed. Today, of course, the atheistic view most often prevails, existing uneasily and often cynically alongside notions that 'we should be good people anyway', that we should live by 'moral imperatives' regardless of whether we can 'get away with' wrong-doing (the 'moral imperatives' guiding foreign policy, like the ethics of 'corporate responsibility' guiding business, perform the same function—that of camouflaging the inhumanity of the dominant profit imperative). The point is that both versions are suitable to the long-standing goals of state and corporate power—an authoritarian God has always been employed to legitimize authoritarian power and is therefore perennially invoked by presidents, prime ministers, kings and queens—'We pray for the blessing of The Almighty on this task', 'Today, in the sight of God', 'God bless America', etc. Likewise the atheist concept of a Godless universe, with the state imposing (and conserving) some semblance of order and decency in opposition to the forever simmering anarchy implied by this version of reality and human nature. This provides the ideal rationale for state control to limit our freedom (to go on a Hobbesian rampage), whilst also removing any serious concern for ethical issues (there's nothing to discuss, the universe is meaningless and amoral), so providing the ideal vacuum to be filled by gratuitous consumerism—pleasure and status now, or nothing. Consumerism needs us to say: Why not? It requires a whimsical, ethically indifferent attitude to life. The last thing consumerism wants is for us to be seated before our televisions detained by the question of whether we should or should not be consuming more for some reason; the question should be—who cares, how can I *get* more, and get it now?

Clearly both arguments leave virtue in a perilous position. For when we consider the real world, we see that an all-powerful God apparently does *not* intervene to restore balance by striking down the evil doer. Instead, in the real world, we find that a cruel or greedy person stealing money from the sick and poor generally does not run into either bolts of lightning or bad luck. On the contrary, tyrannical dictatorships regularly demonstrate an ability to become self-supporting: through a process of escalating fear and intimidation; an entire population can become dedicated to informing on the smallest signs of resistance to tyranny, for fear of being associated with (and liquidated as part of) that opposition themselves. This brutal system of kill-or-be-killed can survive for many decades, and certainly as long as the natural lives of people like Stalin, Suharto, Deng Xiaoping, Pol Pot, and Saddam Hussein. Given this evidence from the real world, it is difficult to take seriously the idea that evil-doing is punished by an external, all-powerful father-figure.

Similarly, the notion that motivation for virtuous behaviour can be found in today's social welfare and utility is equally unconvincing. In the real world, we know that notions of social justice have a long tradition of being simply mischievous devices for precisely facilitating the exploitation of the weak and poor by the powerful and strong. As Plato said in *The Republic*:

'All societies we know of are governed by the selfish interests of the ruling class or classes.'

This is not, in fact, universally true, but it will certainly do for our own society. Indeed, if we are living virtuous lives on the basis that so doing benefits our society, this may well amount to allowing the powerful to pick both the wallet from our back pocket, and the heart from the Third World (a glance at US government records since 1946, for example, demonstrates that US military aid has often increased in direct proportion to increases in human rights abuses).

Given the self-evident imbalance between the punishment of the innocent and the 'prospering' of the bad in the real world, people quite rightly see little credible evidence for either a cosmic or an earthly system of justice. But if we believed that evil-doing was to be avoided for fear of punishment, or in the hope of protection by cosmic or human law-enforcement, and now decide that those agencies are either non-existent or at best hopelessly corrupt, where does that leave us?

It seems to leave us in a world where we might as well attempt to get away with whatever we can because, well—why not? After all, everyone seeks happiness and if what we call sin can deliver that happiness without punishment, if there is no cosmic overlord, no long arm of the Lord and only a vestigial, cynical, earthly concern for social justice then surely all self-restraint is mere sentimentality based on redundant notions of sin and virtue, punished and rewarded by 'God', now dressed up as society's moral imperatives to be used and abused by power as required.

Clearly, when the idea of cosmic intervention is exploded by the likes of Nietzsche, a moral vacuum will inevitably be created, and only inadequately filled by a human system of reward and punishment on the basis of social utility. In short, when we get it into our heads that sin is to be avoided to escape punishment by an external justice system, be it cosmic or human, and when both types of deterrent are found to be illusory, we have a recipe for moral nihilism.

Many have seen here the cause of the extreme violence of the twentieth century: evil has been unleashed and goodness abandoned simply because these words have lost all genuine meaning; they seem to have lost both their cosmic assent and their social credibility. Consequently if today we can get away with satisfying our greed, ego, or hate at someone else's expense, we might as well go ahead—no one is going to stop us. God doesn't exist and society will probably even support us if our actions benefit big business (as recent events in Timor, Iraq, and the stratospheric ozone layer confirm). Thus we might as well act as monstrously as we like, if we can get away with it, if it gets us what we want.

This, I would suggest, is the situation in which the majority of people find themselves today (beneath the perennial rhetoric of devotion to various causes, beliefs, and so on). While the notion of a personal God has become more or less incredible, most of us nevertheless have a strong idea of what it means to be virtuous and sinful. We feel that it is important to be a good person, but without really knowing why. As a consequence these notions are extremely vulnerable; they are not deeply rooted in our belief system and few are gullible enough to believe they are deeply rooted in the state. A person will therefore be virtuous up to a point, often constrained by fear of negative social consequences. But if that person feels he or she can 'get away with' something without punishment, then he or she will perceive few compelling reasons for not doing it. Indeed, should a person perceive no external deterrent, he or she may well enter into vice with great enthusiasm, because the only reason for not doing so has always been seen to lie in external punishment, and the realization that there will be no punishment releases the weak ethical brake which strains to contain the drive towards 'forbidden fruit'.

Zen and the Art of Living: A Rational Basis for Morality

However, I would like to argue that both of the above are hopeless (albeit necessary) misinterpretations of the true basis of morality. I will suggest that, even in the absence of a cosmic or human system of justice, human beings will not 'get away with' what we call sin, and will benefit from the practice of what we call virtue. To understand this argument, we need to take a radically different look at the essential meaning of words like religion, virtue and sin; for beyond the choice between a cosmic overlord and moral nihilism, humanistic religion has something very serious to say.

As discussed earlier, the word religion derives from the Latin *religare*, meaning to re-bind or re-connect. This emphasis on re-connection lies at the heart of all the great systems of religious thought and refers to the requirement that we human beings re-connect ourselves with the universe around us, following our evolutionary jump beyond the tram-lines of instinct to self-awareness.

Although the question of how to live does not arise for animals, the problem for human beings is very real, as we have transcended the limitations of our instinctual programming. If this fact is still not clear in an immediately personal way, we need only refer to some representative questions: Am I a basically nice person or a bad person? Am I too hard-hearted or too trusting? Am I too self-indulgent or too giving? (If the latter, is my giving itself a form of self-indulgence?) Am I too arrogant, or is my arrogance a cover for my lack of confidence? Do I like or love the person I am with? What is love anyway? Does it even exist? Should I indulge or resist my lust, hate, greed?, and so on.

The truth is that we are only *potentially* Homo Sapiens. We are set apart from the animals precisely by the fact that we are born without any clear guide as to how to deal adequately with the problems of our human condition. The great marvel and misery of humanity is this capacity for bewilderment. This is not, of course, to deny that human beings have instincts; it is to affirm the fact that each of us is required to find our own non-instinctual answers to the problems of life, freedom and happiness (instinct is silent in the face of all the above questions). The sum total of answers we give to the problem of our relationship with the universe, we call religion.

By implication, then, the human condition demands that we are born not once, but twice. Our second birth—uniquely human—is to be born gradually and progressively into understanding and personal relationship with the world.

From this point of departure we can appreciate the essential message of religion—that we are fully born as human beings only to the extent to which we are successful in overcoming our ignorance in understanding the true reality of our nature and needs and in fulfilling and adapting that nature and those needs to the realities of the world. Clearly, this is of ultimate importance—a human being can be happy and fulfilled only to the extent to which he or she is successful in living a real life in the real world. At first sight, this statement may strike us as absurd: how, after all, could we live an unreal life in an unreal world? Yet surely the great tragedy of human life is that, in the face of this task, we are supremely capable of living lives lost in illusion—illusions which are often promoted by social forces. Obvious examples might include the anorexic who thinks she is fat when she is skin-and-bones; the SS guard who sincerely believes that to massacre 'inferior people' is a moral act; the government official who believes Western foreign policy really is founded on the twin concerns of freedom and human rights; the sadistic parent who believes his or her control is based on a profound love for the child, and so on.

This already implies a very different meaning for words like sin and virtue. The word 'sin' was originally a term used in archery meaning 'to miss the mark', while virtue means skilful, powerful, or excellent. Quite simply, then, that which is declared sinful by humanistic religion, is that which 'misses the mark' with regards to reconnecting the first-born human in his or her attempt to be fully 'born' in a realistic relationship with the world as it actually is. Similarly, virtue is that which promotes success in our striving for reality and understanding. (Note that there is nothing here about being a 'good' person, and certainly nothing about being punished by some external, cosmic law-keeper).

We may be forgiven for asking what this search for truth has to do with traditional notions of morality, with which we associate qualities like kindness, humility and compassion? By way of an answer, it might be useful to examine two humanistic religions which have preserved the central, underlying themes of all religion in a way that has remained relatively free from deliberate and accidental distortion.

Sin as Mistake

For Buddhism, the goal of religion is Enlightenment, which is, indeed, defined as the connection of the individual in understanding and experience with the ground of reality. This goal is deemed to be of ultimate importance, not because it pleases some cosmic overlord (the Buddha, as we have discussed, is not a God; he is an archetype, a human map tracing both the possibilities of, and means of achieving, liberation through truth), or because it makes us good citizens, but for the simple reason that when we fail to understand and live in harmony with the workings of ourselves and the universe as they really are, we must (self-evidently) live in conflict with the way we and the rest of the universe actually work—it is the chaotic effect of this failure on ourselves and the world more generally that we call sin.

The same point is made in Taoism, where the goal of life is not to become powerful, important, successful, or good, but to live in right relationship with the Tao—that is, with the way you and I and the universe are constituted and operate. Taoists talk in terms of being 'in accordance with the Tao', of flowing like a leaf on a stream. This has sometimes been misinterpreted as a call for passivity but is really a recommendation that we live as completely in accordance with the workings of the universe as a leaf moves in accordance with the ripples of a stream. This fits exactly with the definition of religion cited above: re-connection with reality. For both religions, the great obstacle to human freedom and happiness is illusion, ignorance, mistaken thinking and, in the social context, the promotion of these by thought control.

Indeed, according to Buddhism the great obstacle to Enlightenment—to understanding the reality of self and world—is the symbolic Threefold Fire of Desire, Hate and Delusion (all being both the cause and result of false understanding). These are the roots of the Buddhist version of what we call sin, but it is important to recognize that sin is here not perceived to be evil or wicked in (for example) the evangelical Christian way, but is seen in a way much closer to the original meaning of sin as 'missing the mark', that is—as a *mistake*. Sin serves to obscure the truth so that we think and live in mistaken ways. For this reason there is no hatred or desire for revenge in Buddhism.

The sinful person is not wicked, he or she is simply mistaken, has failed to solve the problem of life adequately and thus both causes and suffers chaos. For Buddhists, the notion that a sinner should 'not be allowed to get away with it' (as our newspapers perennially fume) is a nonsense because human 'wickedness' is precisely the result of a self-punishing, mistaken answer to life which places the greedy, hateful, or proud individual in conflict with both his or her own real needs and the merciless demands of the real world. After all, do we punish the child for burning its finger in the flame? The mistake is its own punishment.

Thus we find the tale of an early example of Enlightened humanity—the sage Muni, who innocently incurred the wrath of the local king. Even after the king had flashed his sword and severed both the wise man's hands, his arms, feet, ears and nose, the legend assures us that Muni felt no anger towards his assailant. On the contrary:

> 'What gave him anguish was to see the king so far estranged from Dharma [truth, reality, virtue].
>
> Those who are great in true insight, whose minds are governed by pity,
>
> Heed not the ill that befalls them, but that which troubles their fellows.'[1]

Clearly the king is a sinner if anyone is, but the point is that he is as much a victim of the delusion of his sin as his ostensible victim. Indeed, it is precisely because he is a victim of his sin, his mistake, that he is so maddened—*homo ignoramus* unable to become *homo sapiens* is a wounded, dangerous animal. A thoughtful individual understands this and feels only compassion for those who are made both destructive—and self-destructive—by delusion. Added punishment would only fuel the flame of hate and promote even greater error and suffering. For, according to Buddhism, the uniquely human phenomenon of malignant destructiveness always results from the deluded individual being lost in wrong thinking and putting him or herself in agonizing conflict with the world as it actually is. Mistaken thinking blocks the capacity of the individual to live and to express his or her real needs; it is this damming up of life that explodes in frustration, hate and destructiveness. The answer, therefore (except for those suffering from the same sickness of Delusion), is not hate, or violence, but compassion and wisdom by which oxygen is denied to the fires of Desire, Hate and Delusion. To understand is deemed a healing light to the darkness of hate which is the result of failing to understand; we can only cure misunderstanding with understanding, not with more misunderstanding. Personal experience surely confirms that 'to understand all' really is 'to forgive all'. To respond with hate, on the other hand, is to try to extinguish fire with petrol, to bring light by increasing the darkness, to cure the wound by deepening it, whatever the short-term satisfaction and sense of 'doing something'.

According to this philosophy, the great issue is our perceived (as opposed to real) separateness from the world. After all, our self-awareness and comparative freedom from instinct, our sense of ourselves as alone, fragile and fleeting in an unimaginably vast world and cosmos, inevitably mean that we suffer uncertainty, self-doubt, guilt, loneliness and feelings of worthlessness (as Rumi said, 'Anyone who is calm and sensible is insane'; so too anyone who is completely confident and certain).

The great mistake, according to Buddhism, is that we often try to escape the pain of perceived separateness by, for example, trying to gloss over the real problem, believing that when we manage to obtain some strongly desired goal, we will at last be happy and satisfied—even though the real, burning, human issues remain unresolved (the Buddhist sin of Desire).

Alternatively, we might try to escape the problems that are brought by our sense of separateness by projecting our sense of worthlessness and shame onto someone else, a tendency manifested as the phenomenon of creating scapegoats—to be found far and wide, from bullying in the classroom to genocide in the concentration camp (the Buddhist sin of Hate).

Similarly, by becoming lost in delusions (of grandeur, for example), by trying to delude ourselves that we are enduring, important and invulnerable, we become ever more separate and isolated from the reality of ourselves and the world, and find that the more 'successful' we become in living our deluded lives, the more irrelevant our achievement seems (the Buddhist sin of Delusion).

These are all seen as attempts to avoid confronting and resolving the real, painful issue of life—the pain of perceived separateness and the delusions it inspires—and all are doomed to failure. By losing ourselves in the sin of Desire, Buddhists say we become like men and women with giant bellies and tiny mouths and necks—the more we indulge our attempt to satisfy our desire, the less we are able to find true satisfaction because, in our dedication to hedonism, we have completely neglected to address, or even identify, the real problem.

'When you consider what suffering these sense-pleasures entail, by way of their acquisition, and so on, you will be prepared to cut them off at the root, for they are false friends. Sense-pleasures are impermanent, deceptive, trivial, ruinous, and largely in the power of others; avoid them as if they were poisonous vipers! The search for them involves suffering and they are enjoyed in constant disquiet; their loss leads to much grief, and their gain can never result in lasting satisfaction.' [2]

Taoists predict a similar result:

'He who is empty within welcomes idle pleasures as diversions. He lacks inner stability and so needs to be amused. He will always find opportunity for indulgence. He attracts external pleasures by the emptiness of his nature. As they overwhelm him, he loses himself more and more.' [3]

Similarly the projection of our hate clearly cannot resolve our sense of separateness and guilt, but serves only to create more separateness from, and antagonism with, the world—so that we are endlessly at war with our own shadow of guilt and self-hatred projected onto the screen of the world around us.

In a later chapter, we will see how Tolstoy came close to being destroyed by the haunting question posed by his own life lost in Delusion:

'Thinking about the fame my own writing brought me, I would say to myself, "Well fine, so you will be more famous than Gogol, Pushkin, Shakespeare, Moliere, more famous than all the writers in the world, and so what?"

And I had absolutely no answer.' [4]

Because his overgrown ego had isolated him from real life, much of Tolstoy's inner life had atrophied and died. This, say the Buddhists, is the fate of all who refuse to face, and attempt to escape from, their sense of worthlessness by becoming 'important'. It is also the fate of those who attempt not to make the self 'important', but to dissolve the self in an external symbol of importance: a greater fatherland, party, state, or other ideology. The conformist seeks to avoid his sense of separateness and guilt by finding approval and a sense of belonging in some truly 'worthy' cause. As with Tolstoy, this does not resolve the problem of separateness and worthlessness but simply projects it elsewhere, serving only to continue the strangulation of the real human being beneath the weight of a fallaciously 'important' life.

These mistaken solutions to the problem of human separateness and the need for re-connection are familiar to Westerners as Dante's division of hell:

Upper Hell—site of the sins of gluttony, lust and hoarding,

Hell—site of the sins of violence to others and the self, and

Lower Hell—site of the sins of fraud, hypocrisy and deception.

In other words Desire, Hate and Delusion.

The question 'Why be a virtuous person if I can get what I want by being a sinful person?' is absurd to Buddhism, because being virtuous is precisely about finding out what *is* truly best. It is like asking 'Why be a sane, alive, happy person when I can get what I want by being a deluded, deadened, suffering person?' It is a logical absurdity. The central point is that, according to Buddhism, virtue does not at all require a sacrifice, just the destruction of seductive illusions; the reason we should not indulge our greed, hatred and egotism, is because these things are bad for us no matter how much we might believe (or might have been persuaded to believe) otherwise. The secret lies in being sufficiently open-minded to doubt our cherished, mistaken 'certainties'.

The primary motivation for abandoning greed, hatred and delusion is not to reduce the suffering of others. Buddhism does not seek sacrifice and justice for the sake of the exploited, it seeks liberation of both oppressor and oppressed through the abandonment of absurd beliefs. Buddhism appeals not primarily to conscience or obligation, but to our real self-interest; it seeks also to improve the lot of the powerful, wealthy and successful, the supposed 'winners' in an unequal society, and certainly its most deluded section. It does not seek to affirm the value of greed and egotism by angrily demanding that the wealth and symbols of delusion be shared more equitably, it asks that we abandon concern for such things for the sake of true wealth, true power and success, which are to be found only in a life free of such delusions. This is why there is no sense of confrontation in Buddhism—a radically different approach to that of Marxist and much socialist thought, which is highly confrontational, demanding that the fruits of the 'good life' be appropriated and more equally distributed, by armed struggle if necessary. For Buddhism this is dangerously mistaken, for here we are talking of poisonous fruits; calling for their redistribution only serves to hide the truth of their illusory, inadequate and destructive nature.

In short, Buddhism argues that when there is greed, hatred and delusion, leading to injustice, exploitation and repression, all suffer; when the causes rooted in deluded thinking are understood, all gain. Clearly Buddhism is imbued with a spirit of compassion and full-blooded psychological adventurousness. It has nothing at all to do with retreating from life, as has long been claimed in the West; rather it involves a determined and life-affirming retreat from *fantasy* life to life as it actually is.

The central point is that because the responses to life that we call sinful avoid facing the central problems of human existence that result from our self-awareness and consequent sense of separateness—isolation, insignificance, guilt, and so on—they are all seriously mistaken, and can only lead to chaos and suffering for the sinner as well as those around him or her. The more successful individuals become in avoiding these problems through Desire, Hate and Delusion, the more completely will they become lost in lives of chaos and destruction. For all these errors attempt to build a healthy life on the basis of smothering the great human wound. But the wound remains and festers. Far from living as harmoniously in the world as the leaf moves with the ripples of a stream, the sinner is dedicated to an appalling, lifelong war against self and against life, building defences against the infinite force of the workings of the universe, both in the world and in ourselves, so that destruction and misery are guaranteed. One such war is the greed-inspired drive for unending economic growth, currently being waged (and inevitably lost) against the finite carrying capacity of the environmental support systems of human life—a classic sin in the sense of a doomed attempt to make reality fit the deluded requirements of the human mind.

Thus sin is to be avoided not because we will be punished in some mysterious after-life, nor because it offends some dyspeptic cosmic father figure, not even because the state police may catch up with us, and not even to save suffering humanity, but because failing to deal with the central problem of human separateness and delusion can only lead to suffering and chaos in our lives. We are bound to pay in terms of confusion, isolation, desperation, rage and deadness as our real needs are not addressed. We are bound to be subject to an almost infinite number of psychological and physical diseases.

'The iron itself createth the rust,
Which slowly is bound to consume it.
The evil-doer by his own deeds
Is led to a life full of suffering.'[5]

According to Buddhism, the alternative to the chaos of sin is to become attentive to the truth of what we imagine makes us happy, so that we can perceive the real cost of wealth, luxury and selfishness. This most certainly does not mean that we should damn sin as being 'monstrously wicked'. For the young, nothing could be more virtuous than that they should experience the Threefold Fire—that they should experience the effects of hating other people, of trying to convince themselves that they really are more valuable and important than others (perhaps by becoming successful and tasting the applause of life), of dedicating themselves to desire and the satisfaction of all appetites—and find how utterly inadequate these attempts are as answers to life. The only danger arises when we refuse to listen to our inner dissatisfaction and keep trying to make the impossible possible.

In our society, for example, sexual consumerism is presented as a desirable goal in life—sex with as many desirable partners as possible. Nothing could be more instructive than a degree of success in this aim, for we would surely find that sex is to love, what masturbation is to sex—a poor surrogate. But, just as masturbation does not somehow corrupt people so that they reject sex, sex does not corrupt people so that they reject love, and sin does not corrupt people so that they reject better answers—if (and, in our society, this is a big if) we have a realistic opportunity for discovering better answers beyond the perennial lies of power religion.

The great problem today is that many people seek satisfaction in absurd ways; they fail, but are then goaded back into trying and failing again and again by the propaganda system, both by its perpetual promotion of absurd lifestyles and by its massive censoring of all more adequate alternatives (including even the notion that it makes any kind of sense at all to talk in terms of alternatives). As Erich Fromm said so well:

'To see himself without illusions would not be so difficult for the individual, were he not constantly exposed to being brain-washed and deprived of the faculty of critical thinking. He is made to think and feel things that *he* would not feel or think, were it not for uninterrupted suggestions and elaborate methods of conditioning.

Unless he can see the real meaning behind the double-talk, the reality behind the illusions, he is unable to be aware of himself as he is, and is aware only of himself as he is supposed to be.'[6]

And when we try to live as we are *supposed to be*, as society needs us to be, we are trying to force the world to fit our delusion and this always spells disaster:

'In refusing to turn back, in defiantly seeking to attain one's objective by force, one incurs misfortune both from within and without, because one's attitude is wrong.' *I Ching*[7]

Sex, for example, is a part of human life and neither wicked nor sinful (there would be no one to condemn sex as wicked and sinful if we had not evolved the capacity for finding it delightful; animals, no doubt, have many other activities they could be getting on with, such as eating and not being eaten!). Only when sex is seen as some sort of goal in life, as some sort of answer in itself, does it become a mistake.

That sin is not to be regarded as wicked has been given great emphasis by Buddhist sages both ancient and modern. Consider the urgent message contained in the following account of the spiritual development of the Buddha himself:

'He [the future Buddha's father] selected for him [the future Buddha] from a family of long-standing unblemished reputation a maiden, Yashodhara by name, chaste and outstanding for her beauty, modesty, and good breeding, a true Goddess of Fortune in the shape of a woman. And the prince, wondrous in his flashing beauty, took his delight with the bride chosen for him by his father... [For] It must be remembered that all the Bodhisattvas, those beings of quite incomparable spirit, must first of all know the taste of the pleasures which the senses can give. Only then, after a son has been born to them, do they depart to the forest.' [8]

What could be clearer? Desire is one of the three great sins, but not in itself, not because it is infectious and wicked, only because it is inadequate. And to become aware of this, we may first need to indulge in it. But when we see sex (or luxury, status, hate, and the other sins) as some kind of final answer to life, we have both devoted ourselves to an inadequate answer and abandoned the search for more serious answers and, therefore, must both experience and cause great suffering.

Why the Above Interpretation is Absurd

We suggested earlier that the argument for and against the existence of an authoritarian God as the basis (or absence of a basis) for morality, is well suited to the propaganda system and so is freely debated. Similarly, we suggested that the atheistic emphasis on immediate gratification as the only reasonable goal has served well corporate ends, with their requirements of mass production, mass consumerism, and the related rape of the Third World and destruction of the natural environment.

The above interpretation of the ethical message of humanistic religion is badly suited to the propaganda system. In fact as soon as we shift the discussion of religion away from belief or non-belief in a cosmic overlord, we begin to move into areas of understanding to which the interests of our corporately-run society are inherently hostile. For our society requires that we believe in the supreme value of status and consumption (in Buddhist terms—Delusion and Desire) as answers to life because only by these beliefs can we be persuaded to endlessly produce and consume highly processed commodities in the required, profit-maximising way. Similarly, as we have already discussed, our arms industries and corporate beneficiaries of 'good investment climates' in the Third World have a vested interest in demonising obstacles to profit; hence the vigorous promotion of hatred for various life-threatening 'devils'—Russians, Iraqis, Libyans, Nicaraguans, North Koreans, et al—in order to terrify and enrage us into supporting brutal interventions.

In short, our society has powerful reasons for wanting to promote pride, greed, hate, selfishness, chaotic living, conflict, ruthlessness, illusion and ignorance. It will forever seek to breathe life into the Threefold Fire of Desire, Hate and Delusion. It requires that we live by answers that do not remotely deal with the problem of the human condition. This is the price of living in a society devoted not to life, but to non-life—namely profit.

The above discussion suggests that it has long been understood by the masters of human understanding that, no matter how initially seductive and seemingly adequate, the solutions to life described as sinful are desperately mistaken and inadequate. Yet this understanding remains almost completely alien to the West, where religion is seen as a matter of believing in a cartoon cosmic overlord, or rejected altogether. The sinful are chastised because they hurt others; the notion of guilt (and the force of the law) are employed to deter them; so reinforcing their conviction that they really are benefiting from their behaviour, albeit at someone else's expense.

Truth and a Good Buying Environment

In the first chapter, we saw how the filter system ensured that a buying environment was maintained in support of corporate advertisers and business interests generally. We saw how this served to promote and reject facts, issues, programmes, literature and news according to the extent to which they were in accordance with this requirement. And to what extent is the above interpretation suitable for the creation of a buying environment? I would suggest that it is not only unsuitable but is the absolute antithesis of such a goal, as it presents a diametrically opposed view of life and how human happiness may be attained. Given this, how could deeper religious questioning today come to be seen as anything but a matter of believing in a cosmic overlord, or of believing in nothing but fun as the only antidote to a meaningless life? Once more, what is being suggested here is not some diabolic conspiracy that acts to censor these views, but a process of filtering by which our culture has inevitably tended to become swamped by ideas, information and entertainment supportive of the goals of society's controlling corporate power groups, namely mass production and mass consumption.

Because the ideas outlined above are not only not in tune with corporate consumerism, but blow a loud whistle on it, they are bound to be misinterpreted, passed over, attacked, and above all ignored, for the same reason that we have been kept in almost complete ignorance of the fact that, since 1975, Britain and the United States have been responsible for arming the genocidal Indonesian regime which is, at the time of writing, still murdering the people of East Timor. For to become aware would necessitate the most powerful institutions in society turning vigorously against the very goals they have been evolved to achieve—a logical absurdity. They will not and indeed cannot do this, if only because even if several individuals (no matter how powerful) were to attempt to do so, they would very quickly be removed from the institutions they serve. (One common delusion is the idea that something cannot be true because we would have 'heard about' such an important idea before in the mass media. In fact quite the reverse is true. Anyone concerned with the truth must look to the margins, to tiny magazines like *Z, Lies Of OurTimes* and *Resurgence*, as well as marginalized authors like Chomsky, Herman, Fromm, Clark, and so on. These exist on the margins for the same reason that they are able to tell the truth—they do not depend on corporate advertising and support.)

In our society, the approved distortions of religion and morality are not open to discussion—serious exploration of the alternatives is far too incompatible with the framing goals. Thus we can see how, in a way reminiscent of the Polish state, religious truth has long been the victim of powerful abusers. Just as Poland was 'liberated' from Hitler into the tender care of Stalin, so religious truth has been 'liberated' by Nietzsche from the lies of church-based power into the lies of corporate-based power.

In the last two chapters, we have shown that the corporate propaganda system has a powerful interest in seeing to it that we 'miss the mark', that we fail to answer, and even perceive, the real issues of human life—it will seek to ensure that we are unable even to imagine that there is anything to think about.

On occasions, the true implications of this level of thought control in our own lives may begin to dawn on us. We may begin to experience very clearly a sense of just how logically impossible it is for the vested interests of society to present us with a real picture of the world, at which point it may come to seem almost a fact of life. We can hardly blame society for lying to us—for what else could it do, given the internal logic of its goals and construction? Giant corporations and other business-supportive institutions have, in a very real sense, no choice—they must attempt to grow as rapidly as possible in order to pay the interest on loans, satisfy their shareholders, and so on.

It does not matter whether or not society can be *blamed* for adhering to its own logic; the question is whether that logic is the logic of humanity and life. No doubt it is natural and internally logical for a psychopath to rampage through the streets, and no doubt he or she cannot be blamed for being the way he or she is. But the question remains: Is the modern, catastrophic state of affairs really as far as the fight for human freedom is able to go? Is this system actually reconcilable with human sanity, well-being and even survival? What are the alternatives? Are they achievable? If not, why not? How can we be so sure? Who are we to say that the situation is hopeless?

In the next three chapters, we will look at some of the very real human and environmental costs of 'missing the mark', of failing to live life according to our own reality and the reality of the world. We will first examine the modern malaise resulting from our conformity to the required illusions of consumerism, a sickness which has been variously described as 'alienation', 'anomie', 'ennui', 'the deadening of life', 'the automization of man'. Subsequently, we will examine a real-life case which, we will find, closely mirrors our fictional model.

Chapter 5

THE DESOLATED DAY-TRIPPER

'Walled in boredom, hard work, or "culture", the subject loses the power of significant affirmative action and becomes a victim to be saved. His flowering world becomes a wasteland of dry stones and his life feels meaningless—even though, like King Minos, he may through titanic effort succeed in building an empire of renown. Whatever house he builds, it will be a house of death; a labyrinth of cyclopean walls to hide from his Minotaur. All he can do is create new problems for himself and await the gradual approach of his disintegration.' Joseph Campbell, *The Hero With A Thousand Faces*[1]

In the first four chapters we have argued that current affairs, literature, psychology, religious and ethical understanding are all subject to distortion through biased omission and misinterpretation, and the dismissal of some ideas as being simply 'irresponsible', 'extreme', 'un-American', 'un-Swedish' (a less familiar but equally ridiculous concept) regardless of their rationality. Even if we agree with this analysis, the real question for many people with jobs, careers, families and futures, undoubtedly still remains: So what? Why should we spend time and effort seeking to understand the ways in which our view of the world is distorted to suit a particular set of political and economic goals?

For some, one motivation is already clear enough: to the extent to which we and those around us are able to become aware of what is being done in our name in places like East Timor, Nicaragua, El Salvador, Iraq, throughout the Third World generally and in the natural environment, we may be able to generate pressure to constrain those responsible and so limit the extent of their crimes, as has been the case in the past. The Pentagon Papers, for example, reveal that the option of significantly escalating the Vietnam war in 1968 was rejected at least partly because of high level fears regarding the domestic consequences. The Joint Chiefs of Staff recognized the need for sufficient forces to be available 'for civil disorder control' if more troops were sent to Vietnam in response to the disaster of the 1968 Vietnamese Tet Offensive. Pentagon officials feared that escalation might lead to massive civil disobedience, with the risk of 'provoking a domestic crisis of unprecedented proportions'.[2] These are facts that we would do well to bear in mind when considering, for example, the fate of the East Timorese today.

If we are among those who believe that compassion and the rights of all human beings to life and liberty dwarf mere accidents of geography and pigmentation, if we have a sense of the fundamental (and remarkable) unity of human thought and experience beneath our comparatively superficial differences (which, all too often, have been exploited or concocted by power religious zealots in need of scapegoats to divide domestic populations against each other and Great Satans to join the same populations against foreign targets of exploitation), then this is indeed a powerful motive for seeking to understand the mechanisms by which people are deceived and destroyed.

One result of such an understanding may be the realisation that it is not that we need to learn tolerance and respect for black, white, yellow and pink people, but that the whole issue of skin colour is a cultural obsession (and controlling device) of an order of foolishness close to madness. The suggestion (or more often, presupposition) that judgements can somehow be made about human beings on the basis of differences of this degree of superficiality is to enter (again) into a cartoon version of reality where 'good guys' wear white hats, tea leaves document the future and bumps on the head explain our personality (or, more realistically, some of our beliefs). It is all too easy to imagine that in a society where a few did not gain from the promotion of inequality, division and hatred among the many, the notion would be considered unworthy even of discussion. Similarly, the level of effort élites generally devote to concealing their destruction of foreign peoples and to generating hatred towards different nationalities and colours (with propaganda campaigns containing all manner of fabricated lies), suggests that such a society is a real possibility and that the innate compassion, understanding and peaceableness of the average individual are tendencies not easily overcome.

Another motivation for understanding the ways in which we are deceived is that of our long-term self-interest—if you and I continue to believe what we are told, if we continue to trust in the 'experts' and to doubt our own ability to understand and change the world, sacrificing our self-respect at the altar of absurd sentiments like 'I'm no expert, but...' then there seems every chance that those same 'experts' will succeed in dancing us down the cul de sac of short-term profit maximisation to final catastrophe (as they have previously led us to lesser catastrophes—huge wars, lethal arms races, the devastation of the Third World, and so on). With all eyes fixed firmly on the short-term—on the next quarter, the next financial year, at best the next five year plan—there is no reason to expect the corporate system to see (or want to see) the brick wall of environmental collapse before the point of collision. On the contrary, there are enormous institutionalized forces which make a collective raising of heads to look ahead virtually impossible. By gaining an understanding of how we are deceived, of how we are kept blinkered, we may be able to change the social forces that are themselves preventing a change in the direction of sanity (if we reject the possibility of achieving this awesome task then, by so doing, we certainly guarantee that there is no hope—the choice lies between hopelessness and a slim chance of success).

Arguably most dissident groups demand change primarily on the basis of these motivations—concern for others and enlightened long-term self-interest.

Here, however, we are stressing a third and, perhaps, more urgently personal motive for understanding and extricating ourselves from the deceptions of thought control. This third motivation lies in the implications of the propaganda system for our own sanity, for our own psychological well-being and happiness.

Earlier, we examined the extent to which the science of understanding psychological ill health has been degraded to suit the requirements of dominant economic and political forces. At one point, however, Freud, the founding father of modern psychotherapy, did manage to pose the following question (with which, in essence, this entire book is concerned):

> 'May we not be justified in reaching the diagnosis that, under the influence of cultural urges, some civilizations or some epochs of civilization—possibly the whole of mankind—have become 'neurotic'?'[3]

Clearly the question is of critical importance in any serious consideration of mental ill health: is it possible that whole societies could be so constituted that the root of individual mental illness might be located in the social conditions of society, such that, for many people, the achievement of mental health would be possible only as the result of the radical restructuring of society itself? In a moment of self-revelation, Freud answered that it was indeed a possibility but:

'I have not the courage to rise up before my fellow-men as a prophet.'[4]

Understandable enough. Had Freud chosen to pursue this line of questioning, his reputation would not now be firmly ensconced in the Western hall of intellectual respectability but would long since have been bundled out the back door, in the understanding that here was a tragic case of someone who (like Chomsky) began brilliantly but later went off the rails (trundling off, in fact, to the margins of 'respectable' discourse to join the other 'wild men on the wings'.

To grasp the importance of Freud's question for our understanding of ill health and our motivation for escaping the delusions of the modern propaganda system, it may be helpful to return again to the widespread psychological malaise said to be afflicting modern individuals: that of alienation.

The Soluble Self

The word alienation was originally used to denote an insane person (the French *aliene* and Spanish *alienado*, meaning psychotic). Later, Hegel and Marx used alienation to refer to the condition in which an individual's acts come to seem unrelated and disconnected from him- or herself, as a result of their being determined by economic and political forces.

In modern Western society, where people are assigned a defined range of functions as cogs in the corporate machine, many individuals come to experience themselves (as revealed, for example, through psychotherapy) not as powerful, creative, living beings acting from a productive centre, but as inert, powerless, externally-directed *things* manipulated by the outside world. The reason why this should be so was explained by A.R. Heron:

'The human being who has resigned himself to a life devoid of thinking, ambition, pride, and personal achievement, has resigned himself to the death of attributes which are distinctive elements of human life. Filling a space in the factory or office with his physical body, making motions designed by the minds of others, applying physical strength, or releasing the power of steam or electricity, are not in themselves contributions of the essential abilities of human beings.'[5]

Alienated individuals can come to lose the sense of being in control of life, and so feel estranged from what they do, from themselves, and from other people. Where a human being completely loses the sense of self, he or she will indeed have become insane.

The gradual loss of an independent self and the associated loss of any sense of connection to a real world 'out there', is experienced as extreme boredom and anxiety; life is pervaded by a sense of dissatisfaction, depression, a vague sense that existence is meaningless and grey. However, where realisation of the catastrophe of the loss of self begins to come to awareness this vague dis-ease may be replaced by something far more acute. As Erich Fromm wrote, after many years of encountering in his role as a therapist the phenomenon of the modern alienated individual:

> 'The anxiety engendered by confronting him with the abyss of nothingness [of the loss of self] is more terrifying than even the tortures of hell. In the vision of hell, *I* am punished and tortured— in the vision of nothingness I am driven to the border of madness— because I cannot say 'I' any more. If the modern age has been rightly called the age of anxiety, it is primarily because of this anxiety engendered by the lack of self.'[6]

Chronic boredom and anxiety are two of the commonest (indeed almost ubiquitous) forms of mental ill-health in the modern world. A key as to why this should be so is suggested (again by Fromm) in a way which resonates strongly with much of our discussion so far on the modern system of thought control:

> '...man can fulfil himself only if he remains in touch with the *fundamental facts of his existence*, if he can experience the exaltation of love and solidarity, as well as the tragic facts of his aloneness and of the fragmentary character of his existence. If he is completely enmeshed in the routine and in the artefacts of life, if he cannot see anything but the man-made, common-sense appearance of the world, he loses his touch with and the grasp of himself and the world.' (my emphasis)[7]

In this book we have of course been suggesting that modern men and women are largely *unable* to remain in touch with the fundamental facts of their existence because these are filtered out and replaced by necessary illusions better accommodated to the requirements of the corporate- and state-run propaganda system. In other words, we have been suggesting that modern alienation is a direct and predictable result of the operation of the propaganda system.

In order to gain a clearer understanding of the implications of the propaganda system for individual ill-being let us, by way of an experiment, take an imaginary example of the modern individual at a point of extreme alienation, and attempt to interpret and explain his descent into boredom, anxiety and emptiness by reference to that propaganda system, to that same 'influence of cultural urges' that Freud reluctantly postulated might be able to generate mental illness *en masse*.

The intention will not be to suggest that all people today suffer symptoms of alienation to the same extent—an extreme case is presented to more sharply define the underlying problem, in the understanding that nothing is more difficult to see clearly than the nose on one's face! (or, indeed, the loss of self in one's heart)—rather, the intention will be to suggest that we are all subject to the same destructive social, economic, and political 'cultural urges' with the same interest in promoting a set of profitable deceptions and half-truths; and that this has important implications for us all. For as Jung said (albeit largely unheard):

> 'A collective problem, if not recognized as such, always appears as a personal problem, and in individual cases may give the impression that something is out of order in the realm of the personal psyche. The personal sphere is indeed disturbed, but such disturbances need not be primary; they may well be secondary, the consequences of an insupportable change in the social atmosphere. The cause of disturbance is, therefore, not to be sought in the personal surroundings, but rather in the collective situation. Psychotherapy has hitherto taken this matter far too little into account.'[8]

'Can't Find The Wound From Where I'm Bleeding'[9]

Our modern alienated individual—let us call him the desolated day-tripper, to contrast the depth of his crisis with the banality of his socially-sanctioned response—is on the verge of panic. Inside, he feels he is standing on the edge of a psychological abyss; the rising of his fear is like the rising of an ill-wind pushing him towards that abyss. He senses that his fear may eventually escalate to some altogether unknown extreme and that, if and when that happens, he will somehow be annihilated, will be destroyed, that his life will somehow come to an end (in fact, as we have discussed, it is his sense of self that may come to an end). Thus, while it is fear that seems to be propelling him towards some abyss, the abyss itself seems to take the form of a strange new version of total fear, of which he has no experience. Thus, the fear he feels as he stands on the edge is actually a response to fear. In other words, he is afraid of being afraid and is in a vicious circle, all his psychological resources being rapidly consumed in an effort to hold back the growing tide of panic.

Not all his resources, perhaps, because while all this is happening, he is sitting in a car with his wife beside him and his two children playing happily in the back. Outside, the sun is shining and it is a beautiful day; in fact, it is the perfect day for a day-trip.

He feels required to act normally and so, despite the ever more terrifying scene being played out inside him, despite the rising panic, he is required to smile, to joke with the kids, to comment on the lovely weather and talk about what they will do on their day-trip. He appears to be happy and light-hearted, and this all the more sharply defines the fear he feels inside. It leads him to feel an appalling claustrophobia, being trapped in his hidden real world that must not be revealed. Indeed, the dramatic emotional dissonance between how he feels and how he feels he must act leads him to believe he is going insane, and this only increases the sum total of his fear because the end point of fear seems to be total madness.

One of the extraordinary aspects of the nightmare experience that his day-trip has become is the extent to which the pleasant little day-trip itself has become a source of horror and threat. For one question that seems to hang over everything and that seems somehow intimately related to his fear, is 'Why?' Every time he asks this question the fear surges inside him. The point is that he does not know why he is going on a day-trip. This is utterly bewildering, but he just does not know why. He does not know why he and his family have got into their car and are driving down to the seaside. He does not know what they are going to do when they get there. Are they going to have an ice-cream? Are they going to look at the sea? Are they going to sit on the beach? But *why?* He just does not understand and he does not understand why he does not understand—all he knows is that when he asks 'Why?' he feels afraid. He knows he is in deep trouble and senses that it can only end badly, in some catastrophe. And he feels helpless because he cannot find the wound from where he is bleeding.

The Natural History of the Desolated Day-Tripper

The natural history of the desolated day-tripper begins in boredom. Of course his real life did not begin in boredom; it began in exuberant, vital, 'trails of glory'. It began with an intelligence and sharp-wittedness which, when compared by him to that of the average (desolated) adult, left Freud woefully depressed. It began with a flourish of infectious happiness and sparkle-eyed curiosity.

But almost immediately his vitality, his curiosity and love of play became 'bad'. He was told off for showing his love of life, and as this intensified (rather than resolved) his innate human sense of guilt and shame (we all know we could be more adequate), he was made to feel guilty for showing his love of life and even for *having* a love of life.

He had no idea of what his terrible shame might consist. He did not understand that his teachers and family shamed him into conformity because they felt it crucial for his future well-being that he learn to 'smile' in a disciplined, obedient way at the system.

'A skilled teacher sets up many situations in such a way that a *negative attitude can be construed only as treason.* The function of questions like, 'Which one of you nice, polite boys would like to take (the observer's) coat and hang it up?' is to blind the children into absurdity—to compel them to acknowledge that absurdity is existence, to acknowledge that it is better to exist absurd than not to exist at all.' R.D. Laing, *The Politics of Experience*[10] (my emphasis)

The alternative, his teachers and family supposed, was that his head would be a world full of pretty, coloured butterflies, rather than the strictly controlled war-room required for survival in the corporate offensives of school and work. They were undoubtedly thinking only of his best. But then, as Vauvenargues said:

'The common excuse of those who bring misfortune on others is that they desire their good.'[11]

Those who love him want only the best for him. Unfortunately, what they believe is best for him is what they have been made to believe is best for him; which, in fact, is what is best for someone else.

For these reasons, he became ashamed of his love of life and sought to hide and control it. Progressively consumed by self-doubt, his spontaneity became replaced by a search for the source of his shame.

Thus did the desolated day-tripper lose his love of life, his wild, exuberant curiosity and playfulness. In its place, he learned to doubt himself, to distrust and dislike himself. And if the people outside him had caused him to doubt himself, then it only made sense that he should look to them for acceptance and approval. His desire for approval replaced his desire to express himself. His love of life had been punctured, processed, penned inside a system of conformity by which he might be safely controlled. And the price he paid was in terms of what we call boredom for—make no mistake—this was not a joyful submission. He did not willingly go into that dark night of conformity and loss of love of life; he found it all desperately boring. Occasionally, during adolescence, he fought back in wild explosions of life—signs of resistance, soon to be submerged beneath conformity. So what is the nature of this boredom by which our developing day-tripper is being progressively desolated?

Boredom may be contrasted with interest which, from the Latin *inter-esse*, means to be 'in amongst' something. But what might it mean to be 'in amongst' something? We feel interested when we are 'in amongst' the world. By 'we', I do not necessarily mean our physical selves, so much as our deepest needs, drives, aspirations, desires. One such need is the need to be loved and accepted—a need springing (as we have discussed) from the deepest sense of human separateness from the world, from the loneliness of self-awareness. On occasions, when we are able to express and satisfy this need for acceptance, we feel deeply involved with the world. It is as if a central part of ourselves has been released from solitary confinement into intimate relationship with the world. In this situation, for example when we are in love, we feel intensely the happiness of interest, of being 'in amongst' the world.

But for our desolated day-tripper it is a very different story. He has been taught to be ashamed of spontaneously showing his love of life. He has been made to feel ashamed of allowing his deepest, ultimate concerns, desires and needs, to be 'in amongst' life. He has been shamed into taking his deepest concerns *out* of life and hiding them away and feeling guilty about them. Thus does life become boring.

In earlier chapters, we discussed how the propaganda system of conformity requires that we be confused and terrified by a distorted picture of the world; a picture that supports the necessary illusions on which our corporately-run system depends. We saw how attempts to coherently examine the truth, to break through the veil of lies, are powerfully suppressed by ridicule, expert obfuscation, or just plain silence. Thus the circle is complete. Not only is our desolated day-tripper shamed into withdrawing his deepest needs and concerns from 'in amongst' the world, but the world in which those concerns might otherwise be 'in amongst', has itself been destroyed. It has been replaced by a pseudo-version of reality suitable to state and corporate requirements.

Even the occasional stubborn individual who has not been

sufficiently shamed into completely withdrawing his or her ultimate concerns from the world, will find no real world to connect them with anyway. Our deepest, most urgent need to understand life tentatively reaches out to find truth and finds a maze of incoherence, distortion, lies and damned lies, false friends and answers that are deliberate deceptions. And what happens in this situation? Our deepest concern for understanding—like a psychic plant reaching for sunlight—strives, falters, fails and falls back, or is lost in some useless intellectual cul-de-sac. Our attempt at understanding collapses before the lies, especially the lies that insist that:

—all truth is relative
—all views are equally valid
—there are no answers anyway
—no one has ever found any answers
—we must not go 'too deep'
—we should not take life so seriously
—we should not think so much
—we should not take responsibility for the world's troubles
—we should make the most of our lives in the short time we are alive by enjoying ourselves
—we should relax and have some fun, because
—what we need is to go out and find ourselves a nice girlfriend or boyfriend and leave all that 'thinking stuff' to hundred year-old professors (experts).

All this, despite the clear fact that the search for truth, reality and understanding beyond delusion is our only hope.

It is no surprise that our attempt at understanding retreats with barely a whimper and joins the other defeated attempts to be 'in amongst' a coherent world. Not only is the attempt defeated but the dream itself is killed, the fragile dream-mist of early morning youth is burned off by the ferocious sun of 'economic requirements', leaving only a cold, hard and very, very crazy industrial wasteland in which we must somehow attempt to live.

As our desolated day-tripper grows older, the extent to which his deepest concerns are able to be 'in amongst' the real world is more or less limited (if he is lucky) to romantic love. Indeed, because this is one of his few sources of connection (assuming he is not too ashamed to show his feelings), he will load everything—all his need for reality and relatedness with the world—in this one relationship, which will rarely stand the strain. Otherwise, he will be dedicated to utterly inadequate corporately-suitable surrogate answers—being 'the best', buying the 'dream' car, climbing the ladder.

But his obsession with romantic love cannot help him either, for this too is a victim of conformity. What does he know about love? He knows nothing. He is not born with an understanding of how to relate to the opposite sex. Love is the greatest mystery to him. In fact, his biggest tragedy as a young man seems to be precisely that he *does not* understand love. Everything he knows about love he has learnt, copied, made up for himself. But what he copies, he copies from a system where sex is sold as a type of consumerism, or status, where the girls around him are cajoled and taunted into obsession with, and hatred for, their physical appearance, where they are tortured (for the sake of profit) into judging themselves physically inadequate, and hence insufficiently loveable. Because appearance sells, love must become a matter of appearance. The world of romance must become the fantasy world of 'love at first sight'. Deeper thought, questioning, understanding, relationship have been suppressed—any suggestion that there might be an alternative question beyond the answers we are given, any suggestion that there is even a question to be solved at all, has been suppressed. And when there can be no understanding, there can only be surfaces, pretty surfaces, to be dressed up, expensively and profitably, to be 'consumed' by other pretty surfaces; and this is 'love' for the desolated day-tripper—'Love at first sight', love without understanding, coherence, or communication, love as best-looking girl, love as maximum-points-conquest-consumption, love as a good enough package to marry.

Because he has been persuaded to feel ashamed of himself, to be dependent on external judgements and authorities, because he has been taught to abandon his capacity for creative, independent thought and coherent understanding, his ability to stand with strength, understanding and independence in love has been crippled and he will tend to fall—not in love—but into dependence on some other person, some 'magic helper' able to solve all the problems he has been made to feel incapable of solving himself. He seeks strength, solutions, coherence and affirmation in the only place he has ever been told to look for them—outside himself.

As we have discussed, coherence is not possible within the mainstream, because society is built on a series of destructive lies. There can be no understanding of the issues of life, no understanding of the problems of life or their answers, and so there can be no understanding of the possibilities of love, of the understanding of relationship between man and woman. True relationship between man and woman can be a part of the answer to life, but the desolated day-tripper is not in a position to know what life is really all about. So he stands in the pub, and the disco and the party and dreams of the 'ultimate screw' that will give him the ultimate 'high'.

But these dreams are not his dreams, they are the dreams he is required to dream by a system that cannot allow understanding but must use sex as a tool for consumption. When he is unsuccessful in his efforts he is alone; but when he is successful, he is even more alone. And each time he is on the verge of waking from the dream—and abandoning it—the dream-masters return to cajole him to keep searching—to keep buying and looking. Though it has all failed time and time again, it is simply because he has not met the right girl—he does not know that the right girl cannot possibly be found so long as he and she are crippled by the lies of conformity and remain incapable of coming together as strong, independent, thinking individuals. The dream of truth has been killed, and his search for love is not a survivor. It is one of the nails in its coffin, one of the bars on its prison.

Obsessive romantic aspirations apart, his world is a dull, grey world of conformity. At school, he is bombarded with disembodied facts which do not even begin to consider the ultimate questions which might make them meaningful and interesting. Paulo Freire has described this as the 'banking' concept of education in which the role of students is limited to receiving, filing and storing the information deposited in them. The aim is to turn students 'into "containers", into receptacles to be filled by the teacher. The more completely he fills the receptacles, the better a teacher he is. The more meekly the receptacles permit themselves to be filled, the better students they are.' [12]

The logic of this education is not, of course, the logic of understanding, of human well-being, but of conformity to the requirements of corporate consumerism:

> 'The more students work at storing the deposits entrusted to them, the less they develop the critical consciousness which would result from their intervention in the world as transformers of that world. The more they accept the passive role imposed on them, the more they tend simply to adapt to the world as it is and to the [necessarily] fragmented view of reality deposited in them.' [13]

The final worth of this system for preserving the *status quo* is clear:

'The capacity of banking education to minimize or annul the students' creative power and to stimulate their credulity serves the interests of the oppressors, who care neither to have the world revealed nor to see it transformed. The oppressors use their 'humanitarianism' to preserve a profitable situation.'[14]

The desolated day-tripper does not know it, but school is actually teaching him the seven lessons outlined by John Taylor Gatto (a teacher for twenty-six years, and winner of the American Teacher of the Year Award three years running).

The first lesson he is taught, Gatto reminds us, is confusion; a multitude of unrelated, disconnected facts are hurled at him. Meaning is not sought and so, by implication, is shown not to exist—confusion, he is told, is his destiny. Yes, there is mass starvation in fabulously wealthy countries like Brazil and Venezuela; yes, Panama was invaded to arrest one man at the cost of 3,000 civilian lives; yes, the Gulf War was fought against a dictatorship armed with US, British and French weapons—he knows the facts but he does not know why, he cannot know why, he must not know why.

The second lesson is class position: he is told his place in the hierarchy, he is 'streamed'. He is taught to envy the 'bright' and despise the 'slow' and to believe the concrete reality of both. Take your pick—failure (shame, rejection, relative poverty) or success (conformity).

The third lesson is indifference: he is taught not to care too much. When the bell goes, his enthusiasm is left to flounder before the greater logic of the school timetable—he is there to learn but, more importantly, he is there to stick to disciplined schedules. He must turn 'on' and 'off' like a switch as required. Obedience, not enthusiasm, is primary.

The fourth lesson is emotional dependency: by stars and ticks and frowns, prizes, honours and disgraces, the desolated day-tripper is taught to surrender his will to the chain of command. The judgement of right and wrong, value and worth is abdicated to external authority. God forbid that anyone should be able to evaluate themselves as successful beyond conformity.

The fifth lesson is intellectual dependency: good people wait for the teacher to tell them what to do. Only the 'expert', the authority, can decide what it is good for him to know. Successful children are those who believe what they are told with a minimum of resistance. Only the High Priests of conformity must be considered free to think for themselves (in fact, as the propaganda system requires).

The sixth lesson is provisional self-esteem: confident people make bad conformists. Self-respect, therefore, is taught to be dependent on 'expert' opinion. The desolated day-tripper is constantly evaluated and judged. Dissatisfaction is crucial for his continued conformity. Self-evaluation—'Know thyself'—the heart of every major philosophical system, is rejected out of hand. People must be *told* what they are worth.

The seventh lesson is that he can't hide: he is always watched. There is no private time, no private space in which his non-conformity might flourish (a device employed with particular intensity and conspicuous success in Japan, where children are schooled six days a week).

He is told who did what, when, where, how, but he is not told why learning about algebra, plant reproduction, the periodic table and the French Revolution are in any way important to him as a living being. All he is told is that learning this stuff will help him pass his exams, which will help him get to university, which will help him get a 'good' job, that is to conform as part of the economic system. This, of course, is presented as being an entirely adequate answer to life; he need not detain himself with seeking or considering alternative answers (unless he is suffering from some form of anti-establishment neurosis).

But despite this great weight of brainwashing, he is not really convinced that this is the best path, he does not really believe it answers his deepest needs. He takes it on trust, because there seem to be no other alternatives, for none may be seriously proposed. Even discussions of vegetarianism and environmental issues in the classroom are liable to be denounced by our mass media as left-wing or Fascist propaganda, or politically correct preaching (threatening to swamp the occasional, diffident appeals made by fizzy drink, hamburger and cigarette manufacturers and the like, which is not brainwashing but simply giving kids 'what they want'—that is, what they are required to want).

Our future day-tripper acts 'responsibly'; after all he does not know what the future holds and so he plays safe to give himself more options later, not knowing that by then he will have been brainwashed so powerfully, for so long, that he will almost certainly be unable to extricate himself. After all, he will then say to himself that he has certainly not done all those exams just to throw them away: what sort of investment would that be? By then, half-way up the career-ladder, to leap off will seem a sort of suicide, a sort of madness. Who chooses to earn less? Who chooses to 'fail'?

Because the answer he has effectively been forced to choose does not answer his deepest needs, but answers the deepest needs of the economic system into which he has been born, our desolated day-tripper continues to suffer endless boredom. The career work he is required to do is that of a cog in a giant machine. Above all, it does not involve his deepest need as a living being—his need to be self-directed rather than 'employed'. Instead it requires that he hide all aspects of his personality which do not fit the necessary template. He wears a dark (grey or black) suit to indicate his conformity, his submission to the norm. The characteristic quality of black is, after all, that it absorbs all the colours of the spectrum. In the business context, this property, together with the impersonal, uniform-like style of the suit, symbolizes the primacy of the goal of professional profit-orientation (black) and the absorption and subordination of all secondary, compromising human goals and values (red, orange, yellow, green, blue, indigo, violet). True, the brightness and colour of his tie does loudly insist on his maverick individuality, but only in the way that government PR departments insist on their 'yearning for freedom and human rights' and corporations declare their commitment to 'green consumerism' and 'corporate responsibility'. Beyond this, there is no colour, no individuality, no distracting spare fat or idiosyncratically human baggage. The dark suit announces that he is there to serve the absolute goal of profit, and all his individual likes, dislikes, interests, goals, values, have been subordinated to this aim. The dark suit represents the smothering of his ultimate concerns, and their replacement by those of the company automaton. This is why he sometimes has difficulty breathing, why his tie sometimes seems a little too tight, why he hates doing up that last, top button on his shirt.

The need to withdraw his ultimate concerns from the world becomes far more intense at work than it was at school. He must smile, speak, shake hands, think and discuss in exactly the right way; or at least he knows he will be a success only to the extent to which he succeeds in mastering these black arts of conformity (and why else is he there, if not to succeed?). Our day-tripper unconsciously knows that he will be successful only to the extent to which he succeeds in cutting the cloth of himself to fit the requirements of the system; that he will be successful only to the extent to which he becomes outer-directed as opposed to inner-directed; that is, to the extent to which he succeeds in becoming an essentially dead *thing* as opposed to a living *being*.

Because his ultimate needs conflict with this goal, they are a real danger. The more he is aware of them, the more he attempts to fulfil them, the more he will find himself in conflict with the world around him. So he tries his best to become unaware of his ultimate needs, because he does not want to become a shameful failure, does not want to become even more disgraceful and shameful than he already believes himself to be. For then (he knows) they will say—'I always said he was a bit strange'—and it is precisely this 'strangeness', this inadequacy, that he has dedicated his life to concealing and overcoming through 'success'.

Thus we have one successfully desolated day-tripper.

Desolate: Meaning 'Alone'

We have examined the ingredients that, to our day-tripper, seem intimately connected in some way. He does not understand what he is doing on this cheery day-trip. This lack of understanding seems intimately connected to his fear, his feeling of panic, his feeling that he must get away, that he must escape. But from what? How can he escape when he is afraid of his own fear, when the fear is inside of him? How can he escape from himself? The key lies in the meaning of the word desolation.

Desolate means 'solitary, barren, neglected, ruinous'. We read that desolation often means 'to overwhelm with grief'. We read that desolate derives from the Latin 'desolare', meaning 'leave alone', which in turn derives from, 'solus', meaning 'alone'.

Because the desolated day-tripper—for all his success, for all his well-adjusted conformity, for all his wealth and status—is *completely alone*. But he is not simply alone in the usual sense of being apart from other people. He is alone from the entire world, from the entire universe of which he is actually a part. For he has been utterly crushed and imprisoned inside his own conformity. Yet his authentic self, the self that burst wailing, laughing and questioning into this world, lives so long as he is alive and ceaselessly demands release.

The claustrophobia he feels is the claustrophobia of his authentic self entombed by conformity and confusion. His panic is the terror of that claustrophobia, the terror of being trapped, of needing to escape, of needing to live a coherent life but of being caught, of being unable to live whilst life runs through his hands. The question—'Why?' Why go on a day-trip?—is a pertinent one. Why, after all, is he in this car? Why go to the seaside? Why sit in the sun? Why talk about the weather? Why discuss how beautiful the little sailing boats look? Why think, say, or do anything when you are dead? What is there for a cardboard cut-out, a machine, to do at the beach or anywhere else? For he is so cut off from life, his concern for the real world is now so vestigial, his understanding so superficial, that everything seems utterly unrelated, utterly meaningless, just as it all once seemed utterly boring.

The claustrophobia, despair and panic of our desolated day-tripper is the despair of all living things in a world that sacrifices life for profit and truth for necessary illusions. His personal agony is a psychological problem, but it is also a philosophical problem, a religious problem and perhaps above all a political and economic problem, for political and economic forces are able to control his understanding of all other aspects of life; and it is this ability, not guns and barbed-wire, that is the most effective form of control.

There can be no solution in our desolated day-tripper fixing his relationship with his wife, so long as he must bury himself alive the following day in the conformity of the economic machine. How can he be intimately related to his wife, or anyone else, when he lives in a social system at war with his desire to be intimately related to truth? There can be no solution in re-living his childhood trauma, in de-activating some of his terrible shame, when that shame is re-activated every time he speaks or acts 'unprofessionally' in a meeting, thus failing to show a correct sense of decorum. There can be no solution in stress-counselling, in jogging, in time management, in extra training, in taking a couple of months off, just as there can be no solution in green consumerism, sustainable growth, economic recovery, wage rises, and corporate responsibility. The framing conditions always fix it so that the news, information, ideas, and we the people, inevitably drop into the correct positions to build the pyramid. As long as the framing conditions go unchallenged, people will always counter any ideas for, or attempts at, change by asking: 'But how, then, are we going to maintain the pyramid we have all agreed on?' 'How are we going to maintain employment in car manufacturing if taxes on pollution cripple the industry?'

But once we reject the framing conditions, the pyramid has lost all validity. If the framing conditions, the goals of corporate capitalism, are inappropriate for our human life, the building of the pyramid which was dependent on those conditions retains no credibility whatsoever. The agreement is over, and now you and I may say that we want to build different shapes. We want new framing conditions, and those marbles are just going to have to shift round. If you don't agree with us, if the whole world does not agree with us, that is okay, because we are going to try to escape as far as possible from the chains of society's delusions and the values (Desire, Hate and Delusion) that persuade us to conform to them. We will seek to create new framing conditions and try to get our marbles (which we had previously lost!) to form a new shape of our own. This is difficult, as the giant pyramid constantly tries to manipulate us into a good place in itself; but we believe it is possible, and it is at least life, it is at least hope (who knows what is possible in this world?). And, in a way, it is beautiful and it is certainly faithful to the desire to live. One thing is clear: unless we reject the framing conditions currently operative in individual and social life, there can be no solutions—for either individual or society—to the essential questions that life puts before us.

The only solution is the ultimate revolution—the revolution of framing conditions whereby the dead is subordinated to the living; where life rides economics and politics rather than being ridden by them; where the test of economics is what allows life to fulfil itself, to live—not what allows politics and economics to exploit life for profit.

We have listed only a few of the truly ingenious devices (perfected and repeated over millennia) for controlling the thought and behaviour of human beings. It would be surprising indeed if human beings, who are so inventive, had not developed extremely efficient mechanisms for controlling other human beings. We must expect that level of expertise to have evolved, and we must seek to understand and so disarm it.

Our hope is truth. We must seek the truth about ourselves, and especially about our most cherished beliefs; for as we have seen, our most cherished beliefs may be our worst enemy, our solutions may be our problem, our hope our despair, our virtue our vice, our friends our false friends. This applies as much to everything written here as it does to everything else. We must seek to understand, trusting in truth and life, sceptical of all certainty.

In the next chapter, we will examine a real-life case study of the inevitably destructive results of the modern corporately-required (and entirely deluded) version of happiness, reality and truth.

Chapter 6

BEYOND 'SUCCESS'—TOLSTOY'S
CONFESSION

The Self-Defined

Though we may rarely be consciously aware of it, the most important task facing us is always that of creating our own lives. We have jumped the tram-lines of instinctual programming and no longer have any pre-set biological rails to follow—we are fated to choose our lives, to create our own personal and social culture. The human being is the animal that must define happiness for him- or herself.

It might be thought that our task would be made easier by the pre-existing cultural frameworks into which we are born but, as this book seeks to show, it is more often made supremely difficult. For as we have seen, we never begin from scratch. On the contrary, society vigorously promotes a particular way of life, a required version of happiness. We call a society free to the extent to which it permits an individual to choose his or her own path. In reality, however, the difference between the power of dictatorship to force individuals to conform through violence and of 'free' democracy to persuade individuals to conform through propaganda is far less clear cut than we might like to imagine.

Most of us are simply not able to assert the authority of our own selves against the massive conforming power of our 'free' society and question its aims. We are unable to question their validity, to such an extent that we often do not even doubt them when they have catastrophically failed us. This, fortunately, was not the case for Leo Tolstoy.

In his remarkably candid book *A Confession*, Tolstoy—one of the most successful writers of his or any other time—graphically describes the truth of the human price paid for the modern version of success and happiness. For, at the very height of his success, he experienced an almost complete psychological, spiritual and physical collapse.

Tolstoy's collapse revolved around an overwhelming sense of the meaninglessness of life, which had come to seem utterly absurd and pointless, to the extent that he could not summon the will to perform even the simplest tasks. For years, while haunted by a desperate desire to escape the desolation of his life through suicide, Tolstoy worked courageously to discover the cause of and solution to his crisis. The one thing of which he was sure, however, was that the root of his disaster somehow lay precisely in that which he had deemed his success.

In the previous chapter we analysed the crippling price of modern conformity; here we will examine the crippling price of modern 'success'. We will see that the common goal of modern men and women is built on a terrible illusion that can only lead to despair. Tolstoy's illness, and the solution he found to save himself, are of tremendous relevance today. For his illness is our illness; his spiritual malaise is the great alienation and desolation of modern man everywhere. His solution is our answer—our hope.

When Life Is A Lie: Tolstoy's **Confession**

Tolstoy—who came to call his greatest success, *Anna Karenina*, 'an abomination that no longer exists for me'[1]—is frank about his early motivation for writing. In describing his own slavish conformity to the ideal of success during the ten-year period in which his great name as a writer was made, he confesses:

> 'During this time I began to write out of vanity, self-interest and pride.' [2]

He goes on to describe how he became involved with a group of similarly motivated writers.

> 'Horribly strange, but I now understand it all. Our genuine, sincere concern was over how to gain as much money and fame as possible. And the only thing we knew how to do in order to achieve this aim was to write books and journals.'[3]

For many years, Tolstoy's greed for the fruits of fame overwhelmed his underlying awareness of the falseness of his life.

> 'But strange to say, even though the utter falsehood of this creed was something I came quickly to understand and to reject, I did not discard the rank these people bestowed on me: that of artist, poet and teacher.'[4]

Tolstoy denied his awareness of the lie that he and those around him were living, preferring instead the aggrandisement of his ego, and the status conferred upon him within an environment so utterly divorced from reality that he describes it as 'a madhouse'. Thus we have a picture of a man who, like so many men and women today, had dedicated his life to the pursuit of wealth, status and fame. The result, Tolstoy declares, was the acquisition of 'an unhealthily developed pride'.

As we know, Tolstoy was extremely successful in achieving his egotistical aims—today he is still considered one of the great novelists. Yet even as his fame rocketed skywards, he came to realize that, whilst he had devoted his life to the acquisition of fame and wealth through writing, he actually had nothing at all of any substance to say. The utterly false nature of his existence was already beginning to haunt him.

'I, an artist and poet, wrote without knowing myself what it was I was teaching. And I was paid money for doing this. I was provided with excellent food, lodgings, women, company, and I was famous.'[5]

With fame and wealth as motivations, Tolstoy's life became empty of authenticity. During this time, the conflict between his desire to be honest and genuine—to live a real life—and the lie of his actual life, quickly drained his resources, so that he began to encounter the symptoms of exhaustion that later led to his almost complete disintegration. As the Japanese proverb says: 'The gods only laugh when men pray to them for wealth.'

'For a year I involved myself with arbitration work, with the schools and the journal, and soon exhausted myself. This was largely due to my confusion; the struggle as arbitrator became so burdensome, my school activities so complex and my journalistic prevarications so repulsive to me, since they always consisted of the same thing: the desire to teach everyone while concealing the fact that I did not know what I was teaching.'[6]

The self-destructive consequences of living a lie are familiar to many today who are required to appear dedicated to work and goals which are utterly disconnected from their ultimate concerns as human beings. As Erich Fromm wrote about modern, desolated man:

'...he senses his gifts or talents, his ability to love, to think, to laugh, to cry, to wonder and to create, he senses that his life is the one chance he is given, and that if he loses this chance he has lost everything. He lives in a world with more comfort and ease than his ancestors ever knew—yet he senses that, chasing after more comfort, his life runs through his fingers like sand. He cannot help feeling guilty for the waste, for the lost chance... Thus, alienated man feels guilty for being himself, and for not being himself, for being alive and for being an automaton, for being a person and for being a thing.[7]

The resourceful Tolstoy managed to stave off disaster (which was actually to be his salvation) for fifteen long years.

'Despite the fact that during those fifteen years I considered the writer's task unimportant, I continued to write. I had already tasted the temptations of authorship, the temptations of enormous financial gain and applause for my trivial work, and I devoted myself to it as a means of improving my material position and of stifling any questions in my soul regarding the meaning of life, or of life in general.'[8]

With appalling determination, Tolstoy—like so many people of our own day—refused to fully recognize, or act to alter, the illusion that his life had become. It would take total exhaustion, devastating collapse—the complete rebellion of mind and body—to wake him from his lie.

When Life Comes to a Standstill

'And so I lived until five years ago when something very strange started happening to me.' Tolstoy writes regarding the onset of his collapse.

'At first I began experiencing moments of bewilderment; my life would come to a standstill, as if I did not know how to live or what to do, and I felt lost and fell into despair. But they passed and I continued to live as before. Then these moments of bewilderment started to recur more frequently, always taking the same form. On these occasions, when life came to a standstill, the same questions always arose: "Why? What comes next?" '[9]

We know that in numerous mythological tales the struggling hero, the lost soul, is visited by strange powerful forces, symbolising the forces of the unconscious. Often these are personified as monstrous Demons arriving from the underworld to confront the lost hero. Though terrible to behold, these visitors are never merely malign— their essential purpose is always to lead the hero away from danger and onto the right path. (Of course it is precisely *because* the deluded individual believes he or she is on the right path that these forces seem so appalling.) The temptation not to face but to run from these awesome guides is ever-present and utterly mistaken.

'I who pursue thee am no enemy. Thou knowest not whom thou fleest, and for that reason dost thou flee. Run with less speed, I pray, and hold thy flight.' Ovid, *Metamorphoses*[10]

Yet if the individual is unable to face, or to act on, these psychological rumblings, then surely they will become genuinely dangerous.

'Because I have called, and ye refused... I also will laugh at your calamity; I will mock when your fear cometh; when your fear cometh as desolation, and your destruction cometh as a whirlwind; when distress and anguish cometh upon you... For the turning away of the simple shall slay them, and the prosperity of fools shall destroy them.' (Proverbs)[11]

Tolstoy's Demon was a manifestation of his unconscious desire for authenticity. It showed him the pointlessness of his egotistical obsession with fame.

'At first minor signs of indisposition appear, which the sick person ignores; then these symptoms appear more and more frequently, merging into one uninterrupted period of suffering. The suffering increases and before the sick man realizes what is happening he discovers that the thing he had taken for an indisposition is in fact the thing that is more important to him than anything in the world: it is death.'[12]

The questions of meaning, of the emptiness of the life he was living, which he had denied for so long, finally became unavoidable, and at last he was forced to face them.

'...Thinking about the fame my own writing brought me, I would say to myself, "Well fine, so you will be more famous than Gogol, Pushkin, Shakespeare, Moliere, more famous than all the writers in the world, and so what?" And I had absolutely no answer.'[13]

Tolstoy had begun to admit the reality screaming at him from inside, thus taking the first step towards the dissolution of the fantasy of his ego. Yet, his dedication to pride and status was such that the struggle would be a long and bitter one.

Into the Abyss

'My life came to a standstill.' Tolstoy says. 'I could breathe, eat, drink and sleep because I could not help breathing, eating, drinking and sleeping... The thought of suicide now came to me as naturally as thoughts of improving my life had previously come to me. This idea was so attractive to me that I had to use cunning against myself in order to avoid carrying it out too hastily... And it was at this time that I, a fortunate man, removed a rope from my room where I undressed every night alone, lest I should hang myself from the beam between the cupboards; and I gave up taking a rifle with me on hunting trips so as not to be tempted to end my life in such an all too easy fashion.'[14]

It must be remembered that this extraordinary collapse of a talented and intelligent man into illness and loathing of life happened at the height of his 'success'.

'All this was happening to me a time when I was surrounded on all sides by what is considered complete happiness: I was not yet fifty, I had a kind, loving and beloved wife, lovely children, and a large estate that was growing and expanding with no effort on my part. I was respected by relatives and friends far more than ever before. I was praised by strangers and could consider myself a celebrity without deceiving myself... And in these circumstances I found myself at the point where I could no longer go on living and, since I feared death, I had to deceive myself in order to refrain from suicide.'[15]

Extraordinary? Not at all, to cultures less deluded than our own. It is interesting to compare the above quotation with the ancient mythical declaration of King Muchukunda after his Enlightenment, having beheld Krishna—symbolising the breakthrough to an experience of the truth of life. Suddenly, Muchukunda saw his earlier life for what it was.

'My Lord God! When I lived and wrought as a man... I sought and suffered, nowhere knowing cease or rest. Distress I mistook for joy. Mirages appearing over the desert I mistook for refreshing waters. Delights I grasped, and what I obtained was misery. Kingly power and earthly possession, riches and might, friends and sons, wife and followers, everything that lures the senses: I wanted them all, because I believed that these would bring me beatitude. But the moment anything was mine it changed its nature, and became as a burning fire.'[16]

Or compare the tale of King Midas, to whom Bacchus offered anything his heart desired. As we know, Midas chose not wisdom, nor truth, but that everything he touched be turned to gold. Leaving the God, the 'blessed' King touched the twig of an oak tree and it turned to gold; on taking up a stone, it too became gold, while the apple he picked became a gleaming nugget. In delight, Midas ordered a great feast of celebration. But, when he sat down to eat—alas!— the roast turned to gold at his touch, while the wine became liquid gold at the touch of his lips. And when his beloved daughter came to console him, she too became a pretty golden statue at the moment of embrace (a powerful symbolic depiction of the condition of alienation and desolation described in the previous chapter: in our devotion to an illusory answer to life rooted in greed, our deepest needs become completely isolated from life so that everything, even our loved ones, come to seem completely unrelated, uninteresting and dead to us).

Let us be clear that Tolstoy's illness did not come about *despite* his success. On the contrary, it was his success—his commitment to pride and egotistical advancement—that came crashing down around him when he realized that it was an illusion, that his importance was also illusory, and that the price he had paid was in truth and real life. Tolstoy indeed tells us that his spiritual catastrophe presented itself to him as a kind of malignant joke—he had spent his one precious life searching for importance, status and fame, only to find that all life is change and all that we gain is ultimately lost.

'Today or tomorrow sickness and death will come (and they had already arrived) to those dear to me, and to myself, and nothing will remain other than the stench and the worms. Sooner or later my deeds, whatever they may have been, will be forgotten and will no longer exist. What is all the fuss about then? How can a person carry on living and fail to perceive this?'[17]

With this terrible realization, Tolstoy had at last fully re-opened the debate which had previously been closed as a result of his single-minded pursuit of fame. If we are to understand the significance of his crisis and the answer he found to his own despairing question, we must examine the means by which he escaped that despair. He himself was clear on the matter.

'The thing that saved me was that I managed to tear myself away from my exclusive existence and see the true life of the simple working people, and realize that this alone is genuine life. I realized that if I wanted to understand life and its meaning I had to live a genuine life and not that of a parasite.'[18]

'In order to live… one must renounce all the comforts of life, work, be humble, suffer and be merciful.'[19]

'I discovered in my soul a feeling that helped me to endure… It was a sense of self-abasement and humility. I humbled myself…'[20]

Tolstoy had been the victim of his own ego, his own sense of self-importance and superiority. He saw himself as the victim of a spiritual and religious crisis, and in this he was correct. But for a long time he sought a solution in the question of meaning: What is the point of life?

However, as we have discussed, to arrive at this question was itself not the answer, but a *symptom* of his illness. Only when he realized that the answer to his problem lay in understanding that the question itself was meaningless, could there be a possibility of recovery. To understand this more clearly, we need to understand the nature of human beings, our egos, and the universe in which we live.

Returning to the Real World

In chapter three we saw how we so often seek a fallacious certainty on which we can depend—in some mother, father, lover, leader, state, Cosmic Father Figure, or even in some supposedly certain philosophical rejection, anything that can promise security in an inherently insecure universe. But we also do this by attempting to make something solid and certain and important out of *ourselves*. We idolize ourselves.

Thus we seek to become special and important, as a response to the transitory nature of our lives. Our ego seeks security, a sense of permanence; the greater our ego (that is, the more we believe in the reality of our importance), the more ardently we demand a meaning to life, a final result from life. Tolstoy's own monstrously inflated sense of self-importance meant that he was haunted by the question almost beyond endurance.

Our ego seeks to be special and important in a thousand subtle ways. We may prove our worth by being better in business, sport, love, art, or any number of competitive activities. We may seek it by believing that we are part of a superior, more valuable nation or race. So, too, we may seek it through being good or righteous—through being nicer, kinder, better, than other people. Most insidiously of all, we may even seek to be special by being the righteous one who seeks not to be special—ego being our secret motivation.

We, like Tolstoy, seek success, status, power, wealth, goodness, all to prove that we are valuable. Unfortunately, the attempt to be special, as Tolstoy came to realize, involves nothing less than the denial of the most fundamental realities of human existence. For as the Zen master mischievously commanded his pupils: 'Point to the important and worthless in the world.'

It is interesting to try! The rather self-evident truth is that valuations such as important and worthless, good and bad, do not lie in the real world—they lie in the human mind. A person may declare a certain experience to have been bad; yet later the lessons he or she gained from that experience may lead the same person to decide that the same experience was, after all, good. A little Chinese story illustrates the point:

One day, a poor, old peasant's farm was hit by violent storms. As a result, his fences were broken and his one and only horse escaped and ran away. On hearing this, the old man's friends in his village shook their heads at his misfortune. 'What bad luck!' they said.

The old man shrugged, saying, 'Maybe'.

The next day, the farmer's horse returned, bringing with it four beautiful wild horses which the old man easily caught by simply re-erecting the fallen fence. When they heard the news, his friends were delighted—'What great good luck it turned out to be after all!' they laughed.

'Maybe', the old man replied.

Then, a day later, while taming one of the new horses, the old man's son was thrown to the ground and broke his leg. The villagers couldn't believe that the old man's luck had turned sour again— 'What a terrible thing to happen!' they said.

'Maybe', the old man replied.

The next day, government troops arrived in the village and set about conscripting all the young men to fight a distant, bloody war. With his leg badly broken, the old man's son was the only young man to be left behind. Once again, the villagers were delighted 'What a good thing it all was in the end!', they said.

'Maybe', the old man said.

Although we inevitably ascribe values to people and things in our world, there are no intrinsic values in the universe: as far as we can tell, from a cosmic perspective nothing is more or less important than anything else. Is a leaf more important than a wave, than a mountain, than a man, than a star? To what end? When the sun finally expands into a Red Giant engulfing and destroying the Earth (or the universe as a whole comes to an end) what, then, from our lives, will be more or less important? Will Tolstoy be more or less important than you or I? That nothing in the world is permanently good, bad, important or worthless, becomes even clearer when we consider the fundamental nature of material objects. All things, including of course people, are in a process of continuous change—nothing stands still, nothing stays the same even for a moment. The universe is an ever-changing interconnected network of energy in which nothing can be important, if only because no thing actually exists as a permanent, enduring entity. As Santayana said:

'What man strives to preserve, in preserving himself, is something which he has never been at any particular moment.'[21]

The worms and decay that Tolstoy's ego feared so much do not begin their work in the grave—they are here and now, in every moment. All is change—here, now, continuously. All phenomena are continuously destroyed and created anew and there is no pause in between, when they become fixed, unchanging, important things.

As Zen Buddhists would say, our attempts at assigning worth and value to things are as sensible as attempting to stick labels on fountains of water. We find that the fountain is not a solid object; it is a process of continuous change which, from a certain distance, may give the illusion of being an object. If we could look closely enough we would see that we, too, are men- and women-shaped 'fountains' of energy pouring into the world, and would see the absurdity of attempting to attach labels like valuable or worthless to that which is continuously changing.

In desperation, we (like Tolstoy) may even look for a meaning to the universe as a whole, asking: 'What is the point of the universe?' which asks the nonsensical question 'To what does everything lead?'. Yet because the word *universe* denotes everything that exists, there is nothing to which it could possibly lead. This is all there is; life is not leading anywhere special or important. If this sounds like a declaration of despair, perhaps it is as well to say that when we are living a sane, real, life in the universe as it is—that is enough!

We know that beyond our fantasies, galaxies spiral, planets revolve, universes expand and contract, life comes and goes, we breathe in and out, the planets circle, the seasons cycle, as do our lives; we know that everything has a rhythm, and that rhythm is circular, not linear; everything is impermanent. Tolstoy's crisis came with the realisation that his enormous wealth and fame notwithstanding, his own life was not permanent, and was not contributing to some cosmic purpose. This was a crisis because this undeniable reality collided with the fact that his whole life—his whole sense of security—had been built around his attempt, by acquiring fame and status, to escape from the central fact of the transience and meaninglessness of life. His crisis was the price he paid for the extraordinary 'success' on which his whole sense of self rested. Tolstoy came to realize that the life he was living was meaningless and futile, and also that the irresolvable quest for importance and superiority was a sort of sickness of the mind. Yet although his own life was empty and wretched, he came to recognize that this did not apply to human existence as a whole.

'I realized that my question as to what my life is, and the answer that it is an evil, was quite correct. The only mistake was that I had extended an answer that related only to myself to life as a whole. I had asked myself what my life was and had received the answer that it is evil and meaningless. And this was quite true, for my life of indulgent pursuits was meaningless and evil, but that answer applied only to my life and not to human life in general.'[22]

The turning point for Tolstoy came when he finally succeeded in letting go of the fantasies of his ego by abandoning self-importance. In the end, he realized that although life does not contribute to a further end, it is neither valuable nor worthless, for these are two poles of illusion—life is something other (the mysterious other that Buddha, Jesus, Mohammed, Lao-tse and the other masters of understanding found).

It is a nice irony that one of the giants of worldly success and reputation found his answer in the common life of the peasantry—in humility, realism, in the day-to-day labours of ordinary life.

Tolstoy had the courage to look deep into the heart of the abyss of meaninglessness. What then was the result of this cataclysmic change in world view?

'Just as the life force within me was extinguished gradually and imperceptibly, and I came upon the impossibility of life, the cessation of life and the need for suicide, so too did this life force return to me, gradually and imperceptibly.'[23]

With the abandonment of both the ego and its nonsensical questions regarding the meaning of life and the universe as a whole, Tolstoy had completed his psychological journey back to where he had always been. Instead of sinking into despair, the recognition that nothing in the universe is more or less important, meaningful, or worthless, removed a giant weight from his shoulders. It allowed him to become reconnected to the real world—life once more began to flow through his veins.

What is known as spiritual growth is often seen as a journey *to* some new plane of experience. Actually it is a return *from* nowhere— from fantasy—to the world as it actually is, through a sort of shrinkage of delusions. Tolstoy realised that he had spent the better part of his adult life living just such a fantasy. The result of this had been nothing less than his exile from reality—from an authentic experience of what it is to be alive. Above all, it had separated him from any possibility of relating to the universe as it is. He became one of the many alienated, tormented souls, who dedicate their lives to denying the value-free, ever-changing world as it is. His efforts to make the impossible possible drained him of all strength, and disconnected him from the source of life. Only when he returned to the real world without importance, only when he finally faced what, to his ego, was the dark Demon of 'So what!', did he begin to feel his body once again grow warm with life and reality.

Tolstoy's story is so interesting because he was so 'successful', and is considered to be a giant of modern culture. He journeyed to the very heart of where so many of us aim to be and saw the fearful truth that awaits us there. The magnitude of his lie, the magnitude of his success and the magnitude of the failure of his success, make his story of great importance for us.

The Reasonable Demand of Life

One thing is sure: *life loves to live*. Where people lose their love of life, we can be certain that they are lost in fantasy, often in the necessary illusions of society. Tormented by the tricks of ego-desire, chained by their own words into deeming the world permanent and important, they are as terrified of becoming worthless as they are desperate to become valuable, and so are cut off from the simple world of the present in which they belong. But life will not rest in its violent struggle with our illusions until it gains reality—it is the 'thunder and lightning' of this battle that we call neurosis.

When the desire to live is blocked, it becomes transformed into a desire to destroy life (in Tolstoy's case the desire to destroy himself;

in Hitler's case, the unconscious desire to destroy the entire world). The social goals of status and success that we are persuaded to pursue lead to a destructive society naturally given to hatred and violence. Beyond egotistical pride, we can transcend notions of our importance and worthlessness, of our superiority and inferiority, and gain a sense of acceptance, of humility—of things simply being as they are. Then we find that what we lacked all along was not a meaning to life, but a genuine experience of it. We find that when we live in the real world beyond our ego fantasies, simply living is enough. As living beings, all we really need is to drink of the reality of life, and drink as deeply as possible; but this is what we are unable to do whilst disconnected and lost in the fantasy-world of our ego and its absurd questions. Tolstoy saw this truth in the strangely contented life of the humble, away from the boudoirs of the rich and proud. The following is recommended reading for all who aspire to, or enviously despise, high society and its wealth:

> 'I saw that those people who laboured hard throughout their entire lives were *less dissatisfied* with life than the rich. In contrast to the people of our class, who resist and curse the privations and sufferings of their lot, these people accept sickness and grief without question or protest, and with a calm and firm conviction that this is how it must be, that it cannot be otherwise and that it is all for the good.' (my emphasis)[24]

The critical difference between the two is not money, but realism; between those relatively free from delusion and so able to live in the real world, and those lost in an absurd, fantasy universe of their own making.

The Need to Know

Just as there is a difference between hearing and listening, there is a world of difference between intellectual understanding and affective *knowing*. When we read of the fantasies of the ego and the malaise that results from them, they may seem entirely unrelated to the realities of our own lives. Yet on reflection we can see that the complete standstill at which Tolstoy arrived has its counterpart in our own lives.

When Tolstoy talks of the extinction of the 'life force' within him, he is surely talking of our own boredom, the great ennui of the twentieth century—the great sense of greyness, dullness and emptiness of modern life that so haunted our desolated day-tripper. When we face our own 'So what!' in middle-age—or earlier—we are confronting the same Demon of truth faced by Tolstoy. So I ask you: do we not recognize his ennui, his malaise, in our own lives? Have we not all experienced first-hand the greyness and boredom in our own lives? Do we not know, do we not genuinely feel, that the quest for the fool's gold of status and importance turns everything we touch to lifeless metal? When we choose the modern version of success, do we not become King Midas?

The Demon Cities of the Underworld: Where the Jewels Glow!

When all the great spiritual leaders have taught humility, that the rich man cannot enter the kingdom of heaven, that enlightenment comes with the death of ego—they have all been referring us to the same truth: that we can only be happy and sane when we are living in the world as it is, and not the world of fantasy.

And this is indeed possible. But first we must confront and accept our own Demons from the underworld—the aspects of our life and reality generally that we would rather not accept. We must look deep into the source of our modern neurosis—our alienation, depression, boredom, emptiness—and see their cause not in this or that job, relationship, or weakness, but in the central fact of our lives being dedicated, as was Tolstoy's own, to the pursuit of status, progress and conformity—that is, to the required illusions of society rather than the authentic needs of life.

If we can succeed in doing this, we will see that our sickness, like Tolstoy's own, is actually a benevolent guide calling us away from deadening conformity to life; as in so many fairy tales, the fearsome and ugly becomes beautiful if only we can face it and accept it. As Joseph Campbell has told us, the princess's golden ball—representing the sun, the source of life and happiness—must be collected from the darkest of dark places by the darkest of creatures.

'The disgusting and rejected frog or dragon of the fairy tale brings up the sun ball in its mouth; for the frog, the serpent, the rejected one, is the representative of that unconscious deep ('so deep that the bottom cannot be seem') wherein are hoarded all of the rejected, unrecognized, unknown, or undeveloped factors, laws and elements of existence. Those are the pearls of the fabled submarine palaces of the nixies, tritons and water guardians; the jewels that give light to the demon cities of the underworld... The herald or announcer of the adventure, therefore, is often dark, loathly, or terrifying, judged evil by the world; yet if one could follow, the way would be opened through the walls of day into the dark where the jewels glow.'[25]

We must dive deep into the abyss to collect these Demon jewels, for they are nothing less than the rejected jewels of the sun—which is, after all, nothing less than the source of life!

Let us then not shy away from the fact that we cannot become important; let us feel instead the full passionate delight of living life for itself in the only moment that exists and therefore matters—*now*. Let us accept ourselves as we are, without categorising ourselves, or other people, as important and worthless, good and bad. Let us see that the unique human destructiveness we call evil is the result of the damming up of the human psyche by suppressing the 'worthless and bad', and promoting the 'important and good'.

Let us rescue our Demon jewels and air our less socially acceptable (though equally natural and vital) sides. When we are angry, let us be angry, so that we do not store old dynamite in our cellars. If we feel passionate, let us show passion, so that our natural delight in love and life does not rot and sicken us. If we feel greedy, let us stuff ourselves, so that we may learn of the self-destructive nature of selfishness and so that we do not feign generosity while keeping a balance sheet for every smile and gift we give. Let us turn our Demons into guides and trust in life, so that we can live deeply and completely and fully in the time that we are alive. Let us reject the lies of respectable conformity.

In the preceding four chapters we have suggested that the propaganda system of thought control demands that you and I live by absurd religious, ethical and philosophical notions; and that the truth is not compatible with the exploitative and irrational goals of corporate consumerism and so is filtered out, not by conscious collusion, but by natural operation of market forces. Thus the widespread occurrence of mental and physical ill-health among people in the West today can be seen not as a strange accident, nor as an indication of the inevitably tragic nature of life, but as an inevitable result of the distorting influence of the propaganda system, for which human well-being (as the poor of the Third World know all too well) is completely expendable.

If human beings are expendable, what price the rest of life on this planet? The answer is clear—after less than 150 years of industrial war against nature, the life-support systems of human life are beginning to crumble. The wound inside—your desolation and my desolation— is reflected in the wound outside—in the warming seas and in the thinning stratospheric ozone layer—and it is bleeding.

Chapter 7

THE WOUND OUTSIDE

Pyrrhus Recalled

The devastation of the psychological lives of Westerners is not, of course, the only form of desolation afflicting our world—a gloomy litany can be reeled off *ad infinitum*. Today over a billion human beings are living in conditions of absolute poverty as defined by the United Nations. The UN Human Development Program (UNDP) has reported that the gap between the rich and poor nations doubled between 1960 and 1989. While 'favourable investment climates' generate massive wealth for transnational corporations and the top few percent of élites, the majority of people in the Third World live in an almost literal hell. Despite their country's fabulous natural wealth, 40% of the Brazilian population goes hungry and seven million children work as slaves or prostitutes. In Guatemala, 87% of the nine million population live below the poverty line (a quarter of a million children having been orphaned by political violence). In Mexico, 60% of households are unable to meet basic needs. In Venezuela, 33% of the population cannot meet basic nutritional requirements. In El Salvador, 90% live in poverty. In Thailand, one million (ever younger) girls are recruited every year by a combination of poverty and force into the sex tourism industry, with whole villages being wiped out by AIDS.

The list goes on. The University of Mexico reports that 200,000 children are being sold to the United States each year "for supplying illegal traffic in vital organs, for sexual exploitation, or for experimental tests". UNICEF reports that half a million children die every year as a direct result of Third World debt repayment, and eleven million die from easily treatable diseases, described as a 'silent genocide' by World Health Organisation Director-General Nakajima. Nor has the underclass of the North escaped—40% of children in New York City and 36% of all British children now live below the poverty line. According to *The Boston Globe*, In the United States, hunger grew by 50% during the last half of the 1980s, affecting 30 million people. And according to the *Wall Street Journal*, the number of full-time British employees with weekly pay below the Council of Europe's 'decency threshold' had risen from 28.3% in 1979 to 37% in 1994. The arrival of capitalism in the former Eastern bloc countries has had predictably dire consequences, with health, welfare and education collapsing as the usual Third World system of rich élites ruling impoverished majorities ('flexible labour') is established with Western aid. In Russia, 87% of the population live below the poverty line, with a sharp deterioration of food consumption since 1989, while forgotten diseases like tuberculosis and diphtheria are rapidly spreading. UNICEF estimates that the yearly deaths in Russia between 1989 and 1993 increased by over a million. Over the same period, death rates increased by 17% in Romania and by 12% in Bulgaria, Albania and Ukraine. Life expectancy for men had diminished by two years in Russia. In Poland, the number of suicides had risen by 33%, and in Romania by 25%. In the relatively well-off Czech republic, the percentage of the population living in poverty rose from 5.7% in 1989 to 18.2% in 1992. In February 1993, an EC poll found that most Russians, Belarussians and Ukranians opposed the move to a free market system and felt that 'life was better under the old communist system'. In the same year, 53% of the Hungarian population agreed, saying life was better before the collapse of the old system (remarkable sentiments, given the nature of the old system).

This human misery is mirrored in the environment. Northern Europe experienced 20% ozone depletion in January 1992 and 40% depletion in January 1993. On the basis of an extrapolation of data collected over the last 30 years by the British Antarctic Survey team, Jonathon Shanklin recently predicted (in September 1994) that stratospheric ozone levels in the Antarctic spring could drop to zero by 2005. Researchers at the British Antarctic Survey (BAS) reported (September 1994) 'the greening of Antarctica', with one flowering grass 25 times more common than it was 30 years ago; BAS scientist Ron Lewis Smith reported that 'This is part of the global warming situation'—Antarctic summer temperatures having been present for 50% longer than in the 1970s. In September 1993, Norwegian scientists reported that data collected since 1983 revealed that the polar ice cap is melting 10% faster than it can be replaced.

By 2020, there will be only fragments of the Earth's rainforest left untouched anywhere in the world. Indeed, animal and plant species are disappearing faster than ever before, with the food chains of the North Sea on the verge of collapse as a result of over-fishing. Birdlife International reported in August 1994 that 40% of all bird species are in decline, with 10% threatened with extinction—a hundred species may disappear within five years. On the basis of this decline, the same report suggests that as many as ten million plant and animal species could be under threat globally. In 1993, the British Forestry Commission revealed that almost all trees were afflicted by a mystery disease (58% seriously), which caused their leaves to turn to autumn colours from July onwards. The 1994 figure for seriously afflicted trees dropped to 16.9% but only as a result of changes in assessment; calculating by the old method, the figure was 54%. The disease may well be due to increased levels of poisonous, low-level ozone pollution generated by car exhaust gases reacting with sunlight; this form of pollution exceeded World Health Organisation limits over much of Britain between May and September 1994.

The sperm count among European men has declined by fully 50% over the last 30 years (quite possibly as a result of water-borne pollutants able, even in tiny quantities, to imitate the effects in unborn babies of the female hormone oestrogen, so altering the sex of what would otherwise have been male sperm-producing cells in adulthood). Today, one in seven British children suffer from asthma. In some areas, such as London, the figure is as high as one in five, with the incidence of asthma having doubled in every health region of the UK between 1979 and 1991, reaching a peak of 186% in the West Midlands. At the same time car and lorry traffic grew 44% in the decade to 1992, with pollution emissions rising by 50%.

The point is that these are not isolated phenomena. Of course, on the few occasions when these ever-worsening statistics are discussed by state or corporate spokespeople, a wide array of imaginative arguments are employed to indicate the short-term, isolated, superficial, or unknown nature of these problems; this is a continuation of the more general attempt to separate and isolate related aspects of the world to prevent our comprehending the whole picture. Thus unleaded petrol is a 'step forward', a 'solution' to the problem of lead-inhalation but not to the rising epidemic of respiratory diseases and not to global warming; and is therefore a solution in a superficial way, representing a step forward only in facilitating short-term profit by giving the impression that something is being done—to knowingly choose to remove just one of several detonators from the same ticking environmental bomb is not a solution—it is a deception. Similarly, the mass premature colour-change of leaves was blamed on the British drought, which had in fact ended three years earlier, with water-tables long since back to normal levels.

Another common device is for government bodies to demand that 'more research needs to be done' because the reasons are 'by no means fully understood' and involve 'a complex interplay of factors' (meaning that the issue is far too complex for the public to understand which should therefore leave it to the 'experts'—in obfuscation and inaction, that is). This tactic has been used for everything from the carcinogenic effects of power-lines to the effects of car pollution on the incidence of asthma, fears over pesticides, and so on—and is transparently a delaying tactic and an attempt to pacify people by feigning concern and vigorous action. In effect it amounts to sweeping the problem under the short-term balance sheet—the only real concern.

Such cynical devices aside, it is clear that global warming, ozone depletion, species destruction, general pollution and all other major environmental problems, have the self-same cause—they are all symptoms of the same massive trauma resulting from industrial intervention interfering with the natural life-support systems of global life.

The significance of this is clear enough. To all intents and purposes, the ozone layer is our skin, the rivers and seas our arteries and veins, the forests our lungs, the food chains our blood cells; if we destroy a sufficiently high percentage of the web of life on the earth, we must eventually destroy the global life-support systems on which our own survival depends. This is so self-evident that no further explanation should be required. Yet it remains the declared intention of the three main political parties in the UK and every element of the corporately dominated system to pursue with all vigour the great task of maximising economic growth *ad infinitum*. This intention has nothing whatsoever to do with the realities of the situation, with the possibility of maintaining infinite growth on an already hobbled, finite earth; it has to do with the internal logic of the corporate machine, which recognizes few concerns beyond next quarter's sales targets, and the need of our political and economic system to deliver endless growth to stave off collapse.

The Pathology of Profit

Business, as exercised by modern companies, is a matter of generating maximum profits at minimum cost in minimum time. This is their absolute goal. I use the word 'absolute' advisedly: maximum profit generation, for the modern company, is the final, unconditional reason for being. By implication this means that all other goals are secondary, and justifiable only in terms of their contribution to the absolute goal of profit. Thus all recruitment, training, accommodation, administration, advertising, production, storage, profit-sharing—

all aspects of company activity—are justifiable only to the extent to which they contribute to the absolute goal. Any activity compromising or conflicting with that goal is not, in corporate terms, justifiable. As we have discussed, this logic applies as much to human behaviour as it does to everything else. All human behaviour at work is justifiable only to the extent to which it serves the absolute goal: generating revenue, minimising costs, cutting time, in order to generate more profit.

The point is that there is no room for compromise in the essentially fanatical system of profit-orientation. Indeed, given the (economically logical) indifference with which corporations maintain 'a good investment climate' at the expense of human life in the Third World, it is more accurate to describe the corporate system as essentially psychopathic. The corporate system genuinely does not have the capacity for compassion and remorse in the face of the suffering of its victims. Like the psychopathic individual, its 'logic' cannot comprehend the immorality of its actions—concern for human suffering simply has no place on the balance sheet, beyond PR costs and benefits. The political extension of this truth was neatly encapsulated by US Secretary of State Dean Acheson in 1950, arguing that 'should starvation break out in mainland China the United States should give a little food aid—not enough to alleviate the starvation, but enough for a psychological warfare advantage.'[1]

Compromise, in corporate terms, is failure. Success is defined *only* in terms of profitability. It is not defined in terms of profitability *and* the happiness and contentment of the staff, or profitability and the preservation of the environment. As Sydney Smith said:

'You never expected justice from a company, did you? They have neither a soul to lose, nor a body to kick.'[2]

Indeed so—for the modern company, anything is justifiable if it contributes to profit. This includes actions which destroy both human and environmental well-being but whose cost and negative public relations impact are less than the revenue generated. As David Jack, former head of research at Glaxo pharmaceuticals said of the company's Chairman, Paul Girolamo:

"I can tell you quite frankly he doesn't have any great regard for scientists, or for science as a way of living. His whole purpose is to make money. I don't think there is much folly in his mind about doing good."[3]

This may sound extraordinary and exceptional, but it is not: it is an inevitable product of our unrestrained, cut-throat system of economic evolution: the survival of the most profit-oriented. Good guys—people who place human well-being above profit—do not win in this game. Consequently, this evolutionary system tends to throw up the sort of individuals found at the top of our corporate trees. It is they and the logic of the system by which they are produced that are responsible for so much of the chaos in our world.

Undoubtedly the prime example is the devastating role corporate activity has played in the history, fortunes and catastrophes of the Third World. As we would expect, this fact is almost never discussed in a serious way. One exception appeared in 1972 in *The Annals of the American Academy of Political and Social Sciences*. The author, Dennis Ray, investigated two hundred major works of what he termed 'respectable' literature on international affairs and foreign relations. He discovered that 95% of these books made no mention whatsoever of the relationship between corporations and government foreign policy and that less than 5% gave the subject 'passing mention'.

One reason for this oversight on the part of 'respectable' academics is that the impoverishment and death through starvation of millions in the Third World is a direct result of collusion between Western governments and corporations in maximising exploitation. Woodrow Wilson expressed the guiding philosophy behind this co-operative venture succinctly enough:

'Since trade ignores national boundaries and the manufacturer insists on having the world as a market, the flag of his nation must follow him, and the doors of the nations which are closed against him must be battered down.... Colonies must be obtained or planted, in order that no useful corner of the world may be overlooked or left unused.'[4]

Consequently, as Susan George has written:

'Food has become: a source of profits, a tool of economic and political control; a means of insuring effective domination over the world at large and especially over the "wretched of the earth"... Multinational agribusiness wants to grow cheap and sell dear (meaning mainly to Western markets that can afford to pay) and totally ignore the needs of poor people who cannot become 'consumers'.'[5]

Feeding the millions of non-consumers would compromise the profit drive. The great lie of initiatives like Band Aid and Live Aid is that they serve to bury the truth of institutionalized Western exploitation beneath the idea that, not only are we not responsible for mass starvation, but are passionately committed to doing all we can to alleviate the problem. As David Pepper has said:

'Western false consciousness about the Third World is amply illustrated by Band Aid and other mass-media charity events. The cloying self-congratulatory tone of the 'generous' stars melds with the frenzied pointlessness of the supporters' sponsored activities to produce a rich cocktail of hypocrisy. Purged of some of their guilt, the participants then return, none the wiser, to lifestyles and politics (masquerading as non-politics) that create the very situation which their 'charity' had sought to alleviate.'[6]

The truth beyond Western philanthropy being that:

'Every time weaker nations have attempted to reallocate their resources and undertake land reform [to feed starving populations], powerful interests emanating from the rich world and its multilateral bodies have thwarted their efforts.'[7]

By means of economic strangulation, proxy armies, or outright invasion, as the peasants of Chile, Nicaragua, Vietnam, El Salvador, Cuba and Haiti among many others know only too well. The reason for the opposition to local, self-preserving initiatives is simply that the goal of the Western powers:

'...is not, and never was, to feed today's undernourished or starving millions, but to perpetuate poverty and dependence for altogether "valid" political and economic reasons'.[8]

Indeed, Susan George continues:

'Today the State more often than not protects not the right to food but *those who violate* the right to food. This is the case in countries in the First or Third Worlds which are governed on behalf of banks, corporations or the landholding classes; where the rights of property always supersede the right to eat.'[9]

The filter system ensures that these truths remain generally unknown, buried beneath the perennial diversions of overpopulation, innate Third World stupidity (the classic device of blaming the victim, to which we will return) and tragic Acts of God. Despite the fallacious nature of such arguments, Susan George argues that they persist for the simple reason that they help to maintain 'as thick a smokescreen as possible around the problem of world hunger'. This is vital to obscure the fact that the starvation and torture of the Third World are the results of deliberate policy designed for '"valid" economic and political reasons', namely to ensure the enrichment of a Western élite through the profitable activities of giant corporations, all this being facilitated by the same smiling, eminently respectable politicians talking of their 'yearning for democracy and human rights'. To quote Susan George one more time:

> 'At this point you are entitled to ask whether every case of hunger truly implies a wilful violation of the right to food. It's true that acts of God like drought and flood or population pressures can aggravate hunger. But climatic extremes and environmental destruction can often be traced to human action or inaction. Pushing this statement to its limits, I will even say that there *are* no ecological problems, only the social and political problems that invariably underlie and cause ecological damage....Wherever and whenever hunger occurs, I'm convinced that human agencies and agents are at work; that hunger is basically a reflection of inequity at the local, national and international levels. This is why, ethically speaking, the correct response to hunger, and the cardinal virtue we need to respond to it, is justice, not charity.'[10]

Similarly, if anyone wonders how it can be that Western corporations have sold $300 billion worth of arms over the past thirty years, fuelling the 150 global conflicts at the cost of 22 million lives; how it can be that companies like ICI can export ozone-destroyers to the legislation-free and PR-safe Third World; how it can be that the US-led consortium of fossil-fuel interests can continue to insist on a 'wait and see' approach to global warming, when all climate models agree that global warming will happen between 10 and 100 times faster than living systems have ever experienced while man has walked the Earth—they need only look to the absolute and unconditional goals of modern business.

Thus we can see that corporate capitalism is fundamentally at odds with life. It is not even against our lives and for its own long-term survival; the logic of profit maximisation in a free-market economy dictates that longer-term planning is subordinated to the needs of the day, the next quarter, the next financial year; and rarely beyond.

Over and over again in this discussion we have surely been struck by the complete disregard the corporate system has for life generally—

be it the poor of the Third World, the sanity of the first world, for the living creatures generally who get in the way. Concern for life just does not belong in the profit/loss equation. In our discussion of the desolated day-tripper, we saw that he was overwhelmed by a sense of deadness rooted in conformity. This is the real truth of the corporate industrial system—it is against life, it is a system for using living beings to create things, to create capital. To do this, it must turn human beings into producing and consuming devices that serve the needs of capital rather than the needs of human life. The environment provides the raw material for the machine, to be processed and transformed into profit, regardless of the needs of global environmental integrity.

Because this system is against life, a shadow of death is spreading over the planet—over the minds and lungs of European children, as over the people of East Timor, as over the poor of Africa, as over the peasants and rainforests of South America. It is the shadow of life sacrificed for non-life. Remarkably, this process is only able to continue because you and I continue to believe that it is really on the side of life, that it is really for our best, for the progress of man and all life. Once again, we may remind ourselves that, just as the fiend is said to speak in the name of God, so the corporate killing machine speaks in the name of life.

Two Voices of Resistance

I think the reader will agree that it is one thing to perceive the falsity of the goals of the modern propaganda system; quite another to believe it really is important to reject them; and quite another again to believe it is possible and sane for us, as individuals, to do so. Moments after reading a critique of modern life—no matter how rational, no matter how relevant—we may well find ourselves laughing at some media distraction, and moments later again, we may find ourselves wondering what on earth all that 'thought control stuff' we had been reading was about.

This is how we are kept in line—not by force, not by violence, but by a humorous, worldly joke, by the intent look on the face of the reporter telling us that Noriega, Ortega and Saddam Hussein are threats to Western civilisation, by the friends and parents clapping us on the back and hailing us as heroes when we pass our exams, when we get our job, when we buy our new car, when we get our promotion. All around us celebration, concern, condemnation and conviction are presented with certainty, often with complete sincerity, all based not on deep consideration of the facts, not on independent thought, not on an understanding of truth, but on what is *required*, what is *supposed* to be true. The question needs to be asked—is all resistance hopeless?

The Real Foundation of Skyscrapers

Anyone wishing to gain a perspective on the magnitude of modern corporate power need only visit the Parisian industrial complex of La Defense. Here we can walk a fantastic corridor between two towering rows of skyscrapers. For all who recognize the fundamental conflict between life and corporate capitalism, this is a daunting experience. How could it be possible that we, as individuals, might hope to resist power on this scale—power which appears to be rooted in foundations of immovable solidity? It is important that we focus on the apparent impossibility of change because it is in this area of fundamental belief that thought control is at its most effective; it is in these moments—when we feel we have understood that there is a problem—that we are most likely to fail. The truth is that very often our awareness of the existence of a problem does not at all indicate that we have escaped the propaganda system.

Consider, for example, how we may argue with someone that there is a deep, underlying, systemic problem with the way we are living. The other person may duck and dive, ridicule and mock until, eventually, perhaps persuaded by sheer weight of evidence, he or she concedes there is indeed a problem. Very often we find that the discussion continues along the following lines: 'I agree there is a problem, but there's nothing you or I can do about it. We are just individuals. Even if what you say is true, people aren't going to listen, they aren't going to change. We might as well forget about it and get on with our own lives while we can. We can't change anything.'

Here it may seem as though we have succeeded in breaking through the rationalisations of the status quo. In reality we have simply advanced to the next line of defence against change—the atheistic 'So what!' discussed earlier. This involves a complete dislocation of what might have been a rational argument to a new, much more fundamental argument—that nothing can be done about anything anyway. As discussed earlier, this 'So what!' is often a device for avoiding the pain of an idea by resorting to some spurious certainty. No evidence is provided for this certainty, on the unspoken, worldly-wise assumption that it is common sense. But in fact no evidence is presented because the idea that human beings are unable to shape their destiny is nonsense. History is the record of human beings doing just that, for better and for worse.

The idea that nothing can be done anyway is a means of resistance to abandoning the entrenched version of 'normality'. Although it gives the appearance of being a compromise, a partial climb-down, it is an attempt to construct a sort of psychological force-field around irrational views of society, so that they are protected from fact and reason.

The power of this tactic is clear—it appears to offer a compromise, a reasonable, middle way between the two poles of the argument, between the person who believes there is a problem requiring a solution, and the person who claims there is no problem at all. The second person appears to have agreed that there is a problem, but asserts that nothing can be done about it; which appears to be a compromise. But clearly a problem is not a problem if nothing can be done about it; it is a fact of life to be accepted. So in reality the second person is keeping to his or her original position that there is no problem and therefore there is nothing to be done about the situation. Meanwhile the first person, arguing that there is a problem, and sensing a compromise, may agree that the second person may be right that nothing in fact can be done. Thus the argument has been resolved in favour of the *status quo*, with the added benefit that the person in favour of change now believes that his or her effective renunciation of the idea that there is a problem, is a reasonable compromise.

Even if we manage to win the argument that change is possible, the other person will often respond by saying, 'Well, maybe you're right, we'll have to see', and will then abandon the conversation. In the last analysis, the system by which they have been convinced does not require defence—only silence. As we have seen, silence is a common resort of the powerful. Beneath the silence, these people have probably not been changed by our arguments; they remain convinced that the repetitious voices around them must be telling the truth, because they all say the same thing. To quote Aldous Huxley again:

> 'The students nodded, emphatically agreeing with a statement which upwards of sixty-two thousand repetitions in the dark had made them accept, not merely as true, but as axiomatic, self-evident, utterly indisputable.' *Brave New World* [11]

Even indisputable fact and rational argument, even looming catastrophe, have no power to change their minds. This is what makes human beings so interesting—our ability to not recognize what we do not want to recognize because it would be just too troublesome, awkward, or painful.

It is impossible to overemphasise how much political change must depend on psychological change. In the past, we have been prisoners of tyrants and dictators and consequently have needed to win our freedom in very concrete, physical terms. As black slaves, we needed to literally break our chains and win the right to live as human beings. As peasants, we needed to win freedom from physical coercion— from the whip and the stocks. As Soviet dissidents, we needed to free ourselves from the Gulag and the executioner's gun. These were physical controls requiring physical solutions.

Now we in the West (though not in the South) are more or less free from this type of coercion, but nonetheless we are not free. We remain in psychological chains. We now need to free ourselves not from a slave ship, a prison, or a concentration camp, but from our own minds, from our brains that have been washed whiter-than-white by the adverts, by the TV soaps, by the sports and quiz programmes, which are freely allowed and freely chosen but only because other, more adequate but less business-friendly interests and pursuits are filtered out. Although we are not under the same sort of physical restraint as a concentration camp victim or a slave, we seem to be paying a similar price. Each year in the United States *thousands* of anorexic and bulimic young girls *are dying* of hunger under the heel of the $32 billion global dieting industry and the allied fashion industry (see chapter nine, and Naomi Woolf's book *The Beauty Myth*). We are not being forcibly incarcerated in asylums, but those who cannot adjust to the insane 'normality' of modern life, *are* being shipped-off to sanatoria to be made normal again.

The thought police have become you and I policing ourselves. Victim and gaoler have become one. The revolution now is not simply a matter of taking to the streets, but must be a psychological one, a matter of freeing ourselves from ourselves.

Yet resistance is not hopeless, because the smallest truth is ultimately more powerful than the largest lie. We may have been slumbering whilst the lies have been trumpeted at us for decades, yet when we hear truth even faintly whispering to us, we may become immediately alert and alive. Today, that truth is growing to be more than just a whisper, and is beginning to be heard.

Returning to the skyscrapers of La Defense: each and every one of them is built not on bedrock foundations, as appears to be the case, but on nothing more concrete than a set of fallacious beliefs, a set of illusions and lies. In a very real way, you and I keep them standing by a sort of psychic magic—by believing the illusions on which they depend. As we have discussed, these illusions include the idea that endless economic progress is possible or desirable, that consumption is the answer to the problem of human happiness, that freedom and happiness are the priorities of our profit-oriented society, that happiness and automaton-like conformity are reconcilable, that a meaningful life is defined by being somehow important in terms of consumption, by the idea that infinite luxury, passivity and comfort constitute 'the good life', and so on. But take a look: they are still standing, those skyscrapers. What, then, maintains them?

Their support can be imagined in terms of a voice. The skyscrapers of La Defense are maintained by the incessant shouting of the giant, global voice of state and corporate propaganda, which shouts so loudly that many of us are unable to collect our thoughts or independence of mind sufficiently to question what is being said. This is the process of brainwashing by relentless brain-scrubbing, to which Aldous Huxley was referring. We are driven on by the voice, and though the answers it proposes do not remotely begin to satisfy us, every time we try to doubt, we find the voice calling us back to the dream from which we had been on the point of waking—and, suddenly, all doubt, all uncertainty, seem somehow strange, absurd, unreal (despite the fact that our entire life in this universe is characterized by tremendous uncertainty).

However, because the voice of corporate propaganda is based on a set of lies and distortions, it can make us listen by sheer volume of noise, but it does not have the penetrating clarity and conviction of truth. In the same way that totalitarianism can chain our bodies but not our minds, so corporate propaganda can chain our egos but not our need for life; it can satisfy our superficial desires but never our need to live freely, it can make us greedy but not happy. Ultimately, both totalitarianism and corporate thought-control must run into the same insurmountable problem—the demands and requirements of real life, of both human beings and the environment. For the more successful either system becomes—the more it succeeds in crushing life to suit its own ends—the nearer it comes to its own failure. To the jovial sages of the East, this was all a matter of common sense. We need only look to the winter and summer solstice, or indulge our love of food and drink to excess, to understand the principle that the one, at its extreme, must eventually become its opposite. Over the last 150 years or so, this voice of corporate propaganda has been rapidly increasing in pitch and volume. Inevitably, two contrary voices of infinitely greater power have begun to grow. The factories of the industrial revolution have whistled; their Demon has heard, and is coming. It is the same Demon that assailed and humbled Tolstoy—the Demon of denied life.

The twin voices of this Demon could hardly present a greater contrast in scale and type, yet they speak the same language and cannot be resisted for very long. The first is the desolated cry of wounded life inside our unconscious minds and bodies; the second is the devastation outside in the environment. For the wound inside us is the same wound we behold before us in the world.

In our tale of the desolated day-tripper and in our examination of Tolstoy's crisis, we found that though the needs of life may be repressed in an individual, often as a result of the conflicting demands of society, they do not simply disappear and die; rather they go 'underground', fester and ferment and become psychologically explosive. In other words, any individual or social victory over life can only ever be pyrrhic and temporary in nature—for life must eventually reassert itself.

It seems to me that the task now—the only task that matters—is to attend to the two voices of resistance, to the wounds inside and out, and to act on their message in the understanding that it is not that we already have so many personal problems that we cannot also deal with the world out there, but that our personal problems are a reflection of problems out there and that only by attending to the root causes of both—the necessary lies of state and corporate thought control—can we hope to resolve either.

Chapter 8

JOINING THE TWO WOUNDS
Personalizing the Global,
Globalizing the Personal

'For those, however, in whom the authorized signs no longer work
... there follows inevitably a sense both of dissociation from the
local social nexus and of quest, within and without, for life, which
the brain will take to be for 'meaning'. Coerced to the social pattern,
the individual can only harden to some figure of living death; and
if any considerable number of the members of civilization are in
this predicament, a point of no return will have been passed.'—
Joseph Campbell, *Creative Mythology*[1]

In the summer of 1991, after two decades of climbing the educational and occupational ladder—from school, to college, to university, to salesman, to manager, to group manager—I abandoned my
business career. Until as late as the spring of 1991, it had never seriously occurred to me that I might actually do this. Of course I do
not mean that I had not thought of it—like many people, I had dreamt
of just walking out one day, of perhaps making my way to the airport
and leaving it all behind. But these were just fantasies and, more
importantly, I felt sure that was what they would remain. After all, it
had taken an enormous effort to get where I was and to earn what
I was earning. I was beginning to achieve my goals, and the future,
supported by an ever more qualified and experienced past, was
looking reasonably successful and comfortable. It seemed as if I was
just beginning to get under way in business, albeit, as Thoreau assured
us, 'on my way to the devil'.[2]

The idea that I should simply throw away this huge investment of
time and energy really did not seem to me to be a serious option.
And who could blame me? I was surrounded by friends, family, an
entire culture, that insisted that life was more worthwhile, more
impressive, and more likely to be happy, the more successful and
wealthy I became (for just one example of the type of unrecognized
propaganda by which these values are promoted, see the film *Pretty
Woman*). I felt deeply that my ability to consume more or less as I

pleased was a capacity to be treasured. Whilst I could certainly not buy the bigger consumer items at will, I could buy many lesser ones more or less as I pleased. To give up such a source of pleasure and freedom did not seem something to seriously consider. And of course in the early days of the current recession, the attention of the nation was focused on precisely how to earn and consume more, not less. Leaving did not seem an issue—my parameters of possibility extended to changing jobs, industry and perhaps country—but never to leaving business itself, never to 'jumping off the ladder'. And all this despite the fact that I was not at all happy in what I was doing.

I had always found the work of a corporate salesman and manager desperately boring. I always found an impossible contradiction in having to work at maximum effort under maximum stress to execute tasks of minimal intrinsic interest. Like most people, I was required to perform extremely repetitive, trivial tasks which were important only as a means of generating revenue. And as Adam Smith said:

> 'The man whose life is spent in performing a few simple operations, of which the effects too are, perhaps, always the same, or very nearly the same, has no occasion to exert his understanding... and generally becomes as stupid and ignorant as it is possible for a human creature to be...'[3]

Moreover, I was required to drastically constrain my own individuality within parameters set by the need to interact with customers and staff in a way that maximized profit.

It seemed to me that overshadowing every relationship within business was the whole reason for our employment: profit. Everyone understood—too well to even consider the fact—that there was no legitimate place for values conflicting with this goal. As a consequence, a deep commitment to caring for people and the environment, the demonstration of sincerity, honesty, kindness and love had no place within the corporate culture, as these things had to be subordinated to the profit drive. (What we call—and, indeed, what feels to us like—embarrassing 'sentimentality' and naïvety at work, is actually anything which openly compromises the profit motive. We find honesty, sincerity, caring, and the candid declaration of human sentiments more generally embarrassing because in the business context they are indeed absurd and foolish. No one can seek to hold to these ideals in the business environment without living in a state of permanent and extremely stressful conflict. We take the expression of these sentiments as a sign that people have lost sight of the whole reason they are there, that they are 'cracking up'. Needless to say, in a sane economic system, these sentiments would not be considered sentimental at all; they would be considered realistic and healthy, indeed the whole basis of whatever we happened to be doing.)

The point is that sincerity, for example, is by definition not subordinated to the business goal; it is motivated by human, and not purely economic, values. As such, it threatens to compromize the business goal and so is incompatible, inappropriate, a sign of inefficiency, weakness and failure. Sincerity cannot be manipulative, but conversely the corporate need for manipulation cannot function efficiently if there is a genuine commitment to sincerity.

One of the reasons we are so profoundly lonely, bored and stressed at work is that the manipulative logic of business is simply incompatible with our behaving as human beings in relation to each other. We are allowed to act only in ways that do not compromise the profit culture; nothing else makes sense in the business context.

'The concrete relationship of one individual to another has lost its direct and human character and has assumed a spirit of manipulation and instrumentality... The word 'employer' contains the whole story: the owner of capital 'employs' another human being as he employs a machine. They both use each other for the pursuit of their economic interests; their relationship is one in which both are means to an end, both are instrumental to each other. It is not a relationship of two human beings who have any interest in the other outside of this mutual usefulness.' Erich Fromm, *The Fear of Freedom*[4]

I can only liken my experience of corporate employment to eating some grey, tasteless porridge as fast as possible. In order to safeguard prospects of promotion and enthusiastic references to future employers, I had to look extremely enthusiastic about the eating of my porridge. This strange recipe of pressure mixed with boredom, together with the necessity of hiding my true feelings about both, made the whole business highly painful, tiring and stressful to me (beneath my well-honed corporate perma-grin!).

All the time that I was working flat out to cope with this work, I was haunted by the meaninglessness of the effort I was making—whether we sold more or less of this or that; whether this proposal, report, business plan, or whatever, was perfect or not, mattered not at all except as a means of generating revenue to achieve our sales targets. The work itself (like the people doing it) was simply an incidental means to an end. When the money had been collected and the profits calculated, the work was forgotten in the rush to the next campaign. And in this war of attrition there was no end, no time to pause; the pressure never slackened, and you were only ever as good as your last performance. The next quarter's sales targets were always waiting around the corner, and they were always a little higher than you could comfortably manage.

I felt like a hamster running inside a revolving wheel. I had no time to look up in order to take stock, because to lose concentration, to lose my footing, would have resulted in my being swept out of the wheel, with the loss of everything I had worked for. And the weeks and months seemed to rush by without offering any essentially new or interesting experience. The requirement of maximum concentration and effort seemed to make any fundamental doubt extremely dangerous and threatening, like deliberately choosing to fight an opponent with one arm behind your back—the fight is bruising enough even when fully committed, but if that commitment begins to waver, life becomes very difficult indeed. (As we discussed earlier, this is surely why business people become so fanatical, so profoundly alienated and unwilling—or unable—to doubt their conformity.)

At this time, I had an extraordinary recurring dream—I dreamt I was either inside a crashing airliner, or outside watching it crash. If I was inside, I saw the plane slowly descending towards the ground, trees sweeping past the window; my feeling, quite markedly, was one of excitement, of eager anticipation, and not one of fear. I awoke feeling excited by this dream. It seemed an extremely positive one; I had an idea it symbolized what I really wanted—to crash the ludicrous, ascending career-plane that I was piloting.

For several years while this was going on, the doubting side of my personality had been concerned with considering and questioning the 'normal' life I was leading. I had long been interested in environmental issues and felt increasingly aware of the contradiction between what was said to be 'normal' and the abnormal results of that 'normality' in the world around us. I had read a range of ideas from Hobbes, to Rousseau, to Popper, to Nietzsche and so on. But it was my concern for the environment that brought me in touch with ideas I would never normally have encountered. I read of the Taoist notion of progress as adapting the self to the way of Tao, the way of nature, which contrasted so completely with our own notion of subjugating nature to our own requirements. I read of the oriental conception of the insubstantial nature of the world—of the world as illusion and of how this seemed to accord with the view of modern physics describing the world as a network of relations. If everything was so fundamentally interconnected, and not after all made up of separate 'bits', then surely the supposed gain of one part of nature (humanity) at the cost of another (the environment) must eventually mean that the winners also lose. It seemed that today's crises of pollution, ozone depletion, global warming, species depletion, deforestation and so on, were inevitable, according to the logic of sages both ancient and modern.

But the important point I want to make here (and the reason the reader has been subjected to an account of my personal experience) is that this was not nearly enough to change my life. It was all very well to doubt progress, to be fascinated by ancient philosophies, but I also had my life to live. I wanted freedom, comfort, love, life. Quite simply, there seemed no real connection between these two sides of my life. On the one hand I had my interest in ideas and understanding; on the other, I had my 'real' life. For long periods of time I abandoned my interest in ideas. When those ideas became resurgent, I would begin to feel again the great tension of the deep-rooted conflict between the two sides of my life. It is interesting to me that, shortly before the conflict was finally resolved by my abandoning my career, I more or less completely abandoned my ideas, my books, my writing of ideas and stories, even selling or throwing away many books on philosophy and psychology. I decided that they were just holding me back, making me impractical, miserable—what I needed was to be practical and take action to get a better job, move elsewhere and sort my life out in 'the real world'. The ideas disappeared, and I remember that shortly after accepting a new job outside London, I had genuine difficulty in remembering what they had been about (a good example of what psychologists call resistance, the inability to remember or perceive what we do not want to remember or perceive), in the same way that you cannot quite remember the subject of a dream when swamped by the awaking of consciousness. But then everything changed and giant, irresistible ideas began to revolutionize my life— I stumbled across mythology.

What a terrible word this is—mythology. It sounds moth-eaten, with something of the dusty bookshelves of dark college libraries about it. It seems to belong to the realm of academic ideas, of no relevance to the real world. What good could a lot of ancient superstitions, fairy-tales and 'lies', do for the ladder-climbing, money-piling, managerial man-missile of the real world? My concern with the environment and philosophy and the rest had been irrelevant enough, but myth—what could be more useless! Thus it is one of the more important facts of my life that I nevertheless picked up, bought and read a book on mythology, namely Joseph Campbell's *The Hero With A Thousand Faces*. The inspiration had been a brief glimpse of Campbell being interviewed on television by Bill Moyers in the series 'The Power of Myth'; I had been surprised to find my ears prick up at what he said. Here was someone who seemed to understand what I was interested in better than I did myself. Why then did mythology have such an impact?

'The Wound That I Beheld Bleeding, Is Bleeding, Now, Within Me'

The key psychological function of myth appears to be one that is currently not being performed by modern psychiatry—it personalizes the global and globalizes the personal in order to enhance the health of both. It suggests that personal suffering is often an indication of a social, cultural, or global problem; and that social, cultural, or global suffering is often an indication of problems at a personal level—'as above, so below'. In other words, when society 'misses the mark', individuals lose their marbles and the world loses its ozone layer.

The great obstacle that had prevented me from responding to the many global, systemic crises that beset us—that made me feel that problems 'out there' were irrelevant to my individual life—was the notion that I already had far too many problems to deal with, that I had nothing left for the world, that I dare not fight for my career with one doubting arm behind my back. Thus not only did I seek to ignore, but actually to avoid all such concern. I remember viewing my interest in environmental, philosophical and political concerns with great suspicion and even hostility, as being a threat to my happiness, to my capacity 'to have fun'. What I needed was to lighten up, to stop taking things so seriously and start concentrating on getting what I wanted. (I can even remember chastising myself for being forever irritated by adverts and their attempts to manipulate me. What is wrong with me, I thought, that I can't stand on a tube platform without grumbling away at the adverts on the opposite wall? Ignore them, I told myself, it's not important!) But let us remember the sublime exhortation of Ovid's God:

> 'I who pursue thee am no enemy. Thou knowest not whom thou fleest, and for that reason dost thou flee. Run with less speed, I pray, and hold thy flight.' *Metamorphoses*[5]

This is the critical message of all mythology and, more recently, of radical psychology and politics: the fearsome social and global environmental crises from which we mentally flee are not unbearable additions to our already extreme weight of personal problems; they are the key, the answer to those problems. It is only when we recognize that the cause of our personal suffering and unhappiness is rooted not simply in our individual lives, relationships, sexual repressions, childhood traumas, but in a collective missing of the mark that is wreaking havoc right around the world, that we are able to begin to identify solutions to our personal suffering. Only when we realize that our desolation, our sense of meaninglessness, our boredom, our anorexia, our inability to meet someone we genuinely love and care for, our inability to be interested and interesting, our inability to make sense of the world, our anxiety, our depression, our paranoia and fear, are rooted in precisely the same series of economically necessary false answers to life that are also responsible for ozone depletion, global warming, Third World starvation, rainforest devastation, species extinction, South American human rights atrocities, inner city chaos, educational chaos, and so on and so on— only then can we begin to find answers. Only then can we start to genuinely question the corporate life-raft that we thought was keeping us afloat and see that it was actually a sea monster preventing us from striking out for dry land, while beginning to drag us down into the depths.

The forbidden truth is that we are living by a set of lies which are necessary for short-term profit, at the expense of human physical and psychological life and global environmental integrity. We are living in a system where power ensures that the requirements of profit take priority over the requirements of living things—including the need to know that this is the case. Consequently our freedom extends as far as, and no further than, the satisfaction of these requirements, with all else being declared neurosis, paranoia, communism, extremism, the work of the devil, or Neptunian nonsense.

I can only find answers, you can only find answers, the world can only find answers, when you and I as individuals escape the pacified herd, escape the system of control around us and in our heads and recognize the two voices shouting louder even than the massed might of propaganda—the voices inside our desolated hearts and outside in the desolated environment. When I realized this, I happily crashed my career-plane and came down with barely a bump!

'Hooray for Peter Pumpkinhead!' The Task of the Hero [6]

The main purpose of many mythological tales is to bring these personal and trans-personal concerns together, reconciling them as elements of one healing concern. In these stories, the hero is shown to be living an essentially wretched life in a world that has become a wasteland without health, hope or happiness. Everything has a deadness, a dullness to it. Yet, the hero instinctively feels that he or she cannot remedy the situation simply by battling away against his or her own personal concerns (in trying, for example, to find the source of the problem in personal physical or psychological failings, as so many modern teenagers are effectively forced to do by the censorship of adequate alternatives), but must find an altogether deeper solution. Often, this solution lies in waking up to the truth that the life the hero is leading is unsatisfactory because it is not in fact his or her real life at all, but is rather the life programmed and maintained by the social version of what is 'good and sensible'.

'The Waste Land, let us say then, is any world in which… force and not love, indoctrination, not education, authority, not experience, prevail in the ordering of lives, and where the myths and rites enforced and received are consequently unrelated to the actual inward realizations, needs, and potentialities of those upon whom they are impressed.' Joseph Campbell, Creative Mythology [7]

The hero comes to realize that he does not feel depressed and empty because of personal weakness, he is not unhappy at work, or in relationships, because he is not trying hard enough, because he is too fat, or ugly, or stupid, but because he has been tricked into living the life prescribed by society (perhaps, as in Tolstoy's case, by encouraging absurd ego-inflation) at the expense of his own. Upon perceiving this truth (either consciously or unconsciously), the hero answers this 'call to adventure' and leaves the social boundaries to disappear into the heart of the forest (of radical doubt) to search for his or her own true life. (The word 'hero' should not be imagined to refer to a superior, perfect person, in the sense in which the word is generally used, but to the person who is determined to radically challenge the assumptions and certainties of conformity. The hero is not a superior person. On the contrary, the hero is any person prepared to throw off the baggage of social delusion, including the notion that some people *are* superior to others.)

In the Grail Legend, for example, the grail represents life and truth, a genuine experience of life. Consequently, the heroic knights begin their search by avoiding all conformity, symbolized by the avoidance of all worn paths:

'And now each one went the way upon which he had decided, and they set out into the forest at one point and another, there where they saw it to be thickest... all in those places where they found no way or path.'[8]

The truth to be found in this forest is always essentially the same— the individual, social, global environmental wasteland has the exact same cause: the crushing of real life beneath the lies of irrational social requirements (usually the manipulative requirements of a system that has come to support a powerful, wealthy few). The individual wasteland is the result of living according to the needs of conformity rather than according to the human need for genuine freedom, expression, growth, relationship and life.

In social terms, the cultural wasteland is the result of society expressing not its truth and life as a society, but its obedience to the demands of power. The life of human culture dies beneath the weight of national pride, feudal tyranny, or economic obsession (the death of our own culture can currently be experienced as a descent into infantile triviality).

In environmental terms, the wasteland results from the same sacrifice of real life to the social (in fact élite) goal that is deemed somehow more important than life. Once again, life is subordinated to the notion that the pride of a king, the triumph of a war-lord, the maximisation of economic power, is somehow the supremely important goal of existence, to which the well-being of life should be subordinated.

It is only by becoming self-directed, as opposed to externally controlled, that we can become fully human and alive. Having gained this realisation, the hero returns to society with an essentially simple message—*DOUBT!* The only lead that the hero offers is that we must all search for our own answers. In this sense the hero is the leader who does not want to be followed, who does not want to be taken seriously but urges us to follow ourselves, to take *ourselves* seriously. Thus the Buddha urged:

'Be ye lamps unto yourselves
Be your own reliance
Hold to the truth within yourselves as to the only lamp.'[9]

Similarly, the Tao Te Ching suggested:

'If anyone desires to take and remake the empire under his own reforming plans, he will never be successful. The empire is a spiritual thing that cannot be remade after one's own ideas....Therefore, the perfect Sage does not seek to take and remake the empire. He does not seek to enforce his own ideas upon it, but is content to give up extravagant comforts and indulgent egoism himself and thus to set the nation an example of returning to simplicity.'[10]

Or, in more recent times, as Chomsky explained when asked how he would advise the young to follow him:

'I don't want any followers. My message, especially to students, is that they shouldn't be following anyone.'[11]

These all express the same, age-old understanding of the true qualities of a genuinely democratic leader—a mentor, catalyst and example, rather than a commanding father-figure. This, of course, is an altogether alien idea in our society with its PR specialists and 'spin doctors' bent on manufacturing leadership cults in order that we might defer to the superior wisdom, courage and intellect of those who steer the 'bewildered herd' (with the idea of the 'Lord our shepherd' as a version of this, writ large on a cosmic scale). Today even so-called 'left wing' parties reveal their true commitment to democracy by their employment of grand rallies, with the leader striding majestically to the centre of an impressive arena in a way calculated to generate an aura of power and authority, just as the Nazis did before them. This has nothing to do with promoting strength, independence, or critical thought in the audience, and everything to do with promoting passive, unthinking, idolatrous obeisance to the leader. By contrast, the Dalai Lama—exiled Buddhist leader of the Tibetan people who continue to suffer oppression by the Chinese—is more likely to be found sitting cross-legged on the floor, joking with his audience. On occasions when a member of the audience asks him an important question, it is not unusual for him to think for a moment and then prick the sense of growing expectation with 'I have no idea at all', bursting into laughter. Such honesty and humility is not allowed to puncture the illusions of super-human wisdom and strength on which the authority of our 'democratic' politicians rests. As so often, it would be funny were the consequences not so tragic.

This, then, is how we can identify the true friend of humanity and freedom, as opposed to the deluded egotist. All who seek our allegiance, our obedience, our subservience, our admiring worship, are the enemies of humanity, because human beings can only be sane, healthy, happy and fully alive when they are strong, independent, critically aware, self-confident, self-directed and self-moved, as all living things essentially are and love to be. Those who try to bow before the hero will likely be greeted by a joke, to dispel the chilly ghosts of deluded idolatry—the hero hates to sap the self-belief and strength of others in this way. Indeed, one of the great qualifying characteristics of all heroes, of all the truly wise, has always been child-like foolishness. Parzival, for example, began his quest for the Grail as a spectacularly clownish fool—someone who was taken seriously by no one at all. Similarly, Zen masters—though some of the wisest and most thoughtful individuals—are not pictured sitting regally and seriously amidst a reverential hush; they are pictured with chubby, laughing faces, with the mischievous faces of incorrigible practical jokers. Dostoevsky's hero was of course The Idiot, and so on. The hero is the twinkle-eyed one—the person in whom the opposites of seriousness and foolishness, sage and clown, meet.

The stern face of the Western churchman and politician, on the other hand, is the face of power religion, of idolatry and subservience; the face not of a friend, but of a predator of humanity. While talking with a Pueblo Indian, Jung was struck by the true meaning of this Western face:

' "See," Ochwiay Biano [of the Pueblo Indians] said, "how cruel the whites look. Their lips are thin, their noses sharp, their faces furrowed and distorted by folds. Their eyes have a staring expression; they are always seeking something. What are they seeking? The whites always want something; they are always uneasy and restless. We do not know what they want. We do not understand them. We think that they are mad." I fell into a long meditation. For the first time in my life, so it seemed to me, someone had drawn for me a picture of the real white man... What we from our point of view call colonisation, missions to the heathen, spread of civilisation, etc., has another face—the face of a bird of prey seeking with cruel intentness for distant quarry—a face worthy of a race of pirates and highwaymen. All the eagles and other predatory creatures that adorn our coats of arms seem to me apt psychological representatives of our true nature.'[12]

The message of the hero is that it is not relative success (or lack of it) in our jobs and relationships that is the critical issue, but the whole definition of what true success and relationship really mean. We who have accepted the social norms of happiness and freedom can never be truly happy or free until we reject these socially-engineered 'masks' and find our true 'faces' in a version of happiness and freedom that is our own version, and not the required version of those who would have us do their bidding.

This essential message concerns the possibilities of finding happiness and sanity through freedom, and freedom through doubt and questioning. It urges each and every one of us to devote ourselves to uncovering and rejecting the lies of the socially sanctioned version of reality, by which all is reduced to the wasteland.

Through myth we can see that the concern for personal happiness and fulfilment is not at all at odds with concern for each other, the environment, and the world generally—the same solutions that can bring the self to real life and happiness, can also renew our world. From this, we can see that dedicated concern for selfish goals (as defined by society) to the exclusion of all else, actually involves a terrible sacrifice, just as the belief that we have too much on our plate to consider deeper issues guarantees that our plate will always be overloaded.

The environmental movement should ask not that people make a sacrifice through recycling this or that, but that they should stop recycling the socially supported lies of modern industrial happiness for the only truly valid cause—individual and global life, freedom and happiness. The seminal book on the history of the individual attempting this task is Joseph Campbell's *The Hero With A Thousand Faces*. With reference to this book, let us consider the difficulties and task of the doubter in more detail, so that we may be all the better equipped for that wonderful and terrible task.

Shoes for the Road Less-Travelled: The Task of the Individual

According to the heroic tales of mythology, the lot of the doubting individual is invariably a painful one. To follow that thread of thought into the forest of psychological adventure, to step onto that pollen path, to step through that magic green door, is to open our eyes to the destructive nature of modern society in an irreversible way that affects all aspects of our lives. Gradually, we begin to see everything in a new light, until even the normal becomes strange and alien; the heavy but welcome price we pay for this insight is that our old, comfortable (false) assumptions about the sensible way to live and the sensible goals to pursue, are lost forever. But what takes their place? Often, initially, very little.

The implications of this quiet revolution of consciousness are extraordinary. Suddenly, in a world single-mindedly devoted to a particular version of what is right and good, we find ourselves all but alone and bewildered. Suddenly, at an office meeting, or in the pub, or in front of the television, we may be beset by a profound internal conflict between differing ideologies. The stress and anxiety resulting may often be extreme.

There is, after all, great security to be found in the herd; we love to belong, and leaving—if only in spirit—is traumatic. A wild oscillation may ensue between our desire for truth and our desire to belong, so that, for a while, we may swing so violently between the two that we are no longer sure what we believe any more. It is almost as if the mind cannot immediately accept the shock of abandoning too rapidly our old cherished beliefs, our old guides to life; so we grow into our new view of the world bit by bit.

And how understandable this is. We might believe that the whole idea of progress is a fallacy, a process of running ever faster to stand still, that the modern version of success is in fact a desperate failure; yet we may also hold a difficult and responsible job in a company that demands maximum growth from maximum dedication to the ethos of progress and success. The conflict may be so enormous as to be almost insupportable, and time may be needed to temporarily switch off from our doubts if only to retain our sanity.

But, for the doubting, this is only the start of it. We may succeed, intellectually and theoretically, in turning against the entrenched beliefs of consumerism, but what about *us*—what are we going to *do* about it? Initially, we may well feel that we are phonies, armchair iconoclasts, prepared to criticize society, while continuing to work, play and consume in the usual way. And what a dismal prospect this is—that, perhaps, whilst we can never again go back to our earlier values, yet we may not have the courage to go forward.

Where, then, are we? In some limbo, some space between worlds? (Like Daedalus perhaps, who flew between sea and sun, or James Joyce's hero Stephen Dedalus in *A Portrait of The Artist As A Young Man*, or Wolfram Von Eschenbach's Parzival, from the French *per-ce-val*, 'through the middle'.)

In this situation, our lives may seem a hopeless confusion, a bewildering mixture of doubt, self-doubt and inaction. For all our lives, our materialist culture has insisted that a particular version of life is the good life, that we are alive and young only once, that we must make the best of it—by consuming as much as we can while we last. We consider our new ideas, our awareness of the destruction of the very life-support systems on which we depend; but then we also consider our old awareness of ourselves, of our dramatically short and troubled existence, and we feel that we owe it to ourselves to make the best of it as defined by society. We think, perhaps, of our career, our family, our standard of living, our friends, our security, and ask ourselves if it is not crazy to think that we should be prepared to radically change the way we live for the sake of a 'mere idea'. There follows, perhaps, a process of continuing doubt and re-affirmation of our ideas—and we wonder if anything will ever come of it.

This is the lot of those who have become aware of the destructive nature of the way we live, who no longer find the world view of consumerism credible or even sane. Apart from the intrinsic conflict involved, the difficulty of the situation is often exacerbated by isolation and by the absence of a clear direction in which we might proceed. We have said 'No!', but how do we say 'Yes!'—and to what, exactly, should we say 'Yes!'? Does a 'Yes!' for the world make sense as a 'Yes!' for the reality of our own lives?

This situation, as we have discussed, is the subject of myth and, as such, has for millennia been recognized as the first heroic step away from conformity and deadness to reality and life. Indeed, the message of myth for doubters everywhere is that what is truly good for people is good for nature—there is no conflict. With this realisation, the chains of doubt are released and we find a clear path, a clear direction in which to travel, where personal and global interests are unified.

Mythology never was intended as a reference to dubious historical or supernatural fact, but as a series of symbols and images which, in story form, act as metaphors to assist the individual along his or her own path of understanding. Let us take, as an indicative example, the myth of the Enlightenment of the Buddha.

Destination Unknown: The Archetypal Hero

It is impossible to reconstruct the character, life and teaching of the man who became the Buddha, for while he is supposed to have lived c. 563-483 B.C., his earliest biography was that in the Pali Canon which was set down around 80 B.C., five hundred years later. Regardless of the historical reality of the Buddha, his story is the eternally recurring archetype of the hero.

The young Prince Gautama (the future Buddha) is said to have begun his search for truth from a starting point in many ways similar to our own: he was the son of a king (society) particularly keen that he should live a privileged life (materialism), shielded as far as possible from the ills of the world (propaganda shielding reality). By all means of sensuous seduction, the well-meaning king sought to protect his son from the painful realities of life.

Despite all efforts to contain him, the future Buddha resolved to make an excursion beyond the safety of the palace walls (from conformity into doubt). Forewarned of this, his father took all precautions to ensure that his son remained protected from any unsettling sights of reality. In a golden chariot, on a road heaped with flowers, the prince set forth. The king's efforts were to no avail, for the Gods, having recognized the moment, sent forth a weak old man (painful reality) to walk along the road.

Seeing the old man, the Prince asked his charioteer what was wrong with this feeble creature, whereupon he was told that this was old age, 'the ravisher of beauty, the ruin of vigour, the cause of sorrow, destroyer of delights'[13]; he was told that it would visit him too. Understandably shocked, the young prince was greatly agitated and asked to be driven home (the oscillation between world views mentioned above).

On the next outing, however, the Gods sent another man afflicted by disease, and on the third, they sent a dead man. Thus did the future Buddha learn—despite the best efforts of his father the king (the deliberately blinkering distractions and delusions of the everyday world)—of the truth of the world. The result was traumatic:

'How can a rational being, knowing these things, remain heedless in the hour of calamity? Turn back our chariot, charioteer. This is no time or place for pleasure.'[14]

But the driver (the self clinging to its old values), in obedience to the king, continued on to a festival of women in the groves. Thus, immediately after gaining his new understanding, the prince was assailed by all manner of sweet charms to distract him. But it was too late and, even now, the prince said:

'Do these women not know that old age one day will take away their beauty? Not observing disease, they are joyous here in a world of pain. And, to judge from the way they are laughing at their play, they know nothing at all of death.'[15]

The prince had thus begun to escape from the world of everyday delusion by his understanding of old age, disease and death. Most importantly, he had begun to escape the conforming influence of society—the first step towards living an individual, authentic life. His search now is to find his own life by means of addressing the problems he perceives. The oscillations brought about by this position are reflected in the symbolic conflict between the awakened future Buddha and his father, who argues vigorously against his son's proposal to leave for the forest, but is told:

'Father, it is not right to lay hold of a person about to escape from a house that is on fire!'[16]

And so the prince left the palace for a destination unknown and, as Joseph Campbell says:

'The adventure had begun that was to shape the civilization of the larger portion of the human race. The lion roar, the sound of the solar spirit... unafraid of its own force, had broken forth in the night of stars.'[17]

The future Buddha entered the darkest part of the forest—the forest that is beyond the normal ways of men, that represents the limbo before the 'No!' to the old world is replaced by a 'Yes!' to some self-created way of living. In short, as we have discussed, the Buddha found that the cause of his and all other suffering lay in the Threefold Fire of Desire, Hate and Delusion. (*Nirvana*, from the Sanskrit *nirva*, means literally 'to blow out' the Threefold Fire, in the sense of a fire ceasing to draw: 'Deprived of fuel, the fire of life is pacified'.[18])

The similarity between this Threefold Fire of illusion and the dominant devices of modern thought control is striking. We have already discussed at some length the controlling device of persuading us to hate some threatening, demonic enemy. So too we can easily be controlled through greed: by persuading us we can achieve happiness through unrestrained consumption and luxury, we are deceived into sacrificing our freedom for the glass beads of conformity. This was well understood by earlier European exploiters of the Third World:

'To make them labour, and give them a taste for luxuries and comforts, they must be gradually taught to desire those objects which could be attained by human labour. There was a regular progress from the possession of necessaries to the desire of luxuries; and what once were luxuries, gradually came... to be necessaries. This was the sort of progress the negroes had to go through...' (Haitian Governor Charles Metcalfe in 1840).[19]

Chomsky, Herman, Fromm, Zinn and others have devoted their lives to demonstrating that we are most effectively chained not by brute force, but by delusion; for it is all too possible for us to be chained by lies while believing ourselves to be completely free, so that we have no notion of a need to resist, or escape. Here religion and politics converge. For Buddhism has one goal only—to free us from lies, from thought control, from social and individual delusions, in the understanding that the truth shall make us free, and freedom makes us happy, compassionate, sane and fully born as human beings. Chomsky's beliefs are in all essential respects the same.

Indeed, what Chomsky calls the 'tools of intellectual self-defence' are almost identical to those employed by Buddhism's 'Mindfulness', with both having the same methods and goal—the use of worldly and self-awareness, based on the principles of rational thought and argument, to bring freedom from the bondage of lies. Chomsky's writing is political Buddhism; Buddhism is psychological freedom-fighting.

The Call to Adventure

As Joseph Campbell pointed out so convincingly, in the tale of the Buddha and in an infinite number of similar heroic mythological tales, a clear pattern relevant to our modern situation can be divined.

Initially, the mythic hero can be seen to be lost in the spiritual wasteland of everyday life which, although perhaps materially comfortable, is essentially empty and desolate. Then, however, the hero experiences a 'call to adventure' from some magic visitor or experience: he or she begins to doubt, and gains a new insight into the world as he or she has known it and is drawn, inexorably, towards some new understanding of life. Thus awakened, the hero crosses the 'threshold of adventure' whereby he or she has crucially and irreversibly '…transferred his spiritual centre of gravity from within the pale of his society to a zone unknown.' [20]

Or, as James Joyce's Stephen Dedalus says in renouncing his orthodox religion and setting off on his own path to the truth:

'I will tell you what I will do and what I will not do. I will not serve that in which I no longer believe, whether it calls itself my home, my fatherland, or my church: and I will try to express myself in some [unknown] mode of life or art as freely as I can and as wholly as I can… You made me confess the fears that I have. But I will tell you also what I do not fear. I do not fear to be alone or to be spurned for another or to leave whatever I have to leave. And I am not afraid to make a mistake, even a great mistake, a lifelong mistake and perhaps as long as eternity too.' [21]

Following this leap into the dark, the hero faces all manner of dangerous tasks (challenges to the new growth towards understanding). With the help of various 'magic helpers' (insights, understanding, courage, strength), he or she sets off in search of 'the boon'—the truth, the treasure of freedom and an authentic experience of life. This boon is represented by a hoard of jewels recovered from the dragon's lair (the dragon often representing greed, duty, ego—that which stands in the way of the hero and understanding); by a golden fleece; or by a re-birth into spiritual life (the Buddha's Enlightenment from the Three-fold Fire of illusion, Christ's ascension from his physical body—repre-senting ego-desire—to the heaven of enlightenment).

The boon is found by discovering our own path to the truth—that is, the middle way between the opposing ways already set out for us. It is 'the invisible path', the way as narrow and dangerous as a 'razor's edge'.

If successful in treading this lonely and frightening path through the forest, and in meeting the challenges that inevitably occur on the way, the hero discovers his or her own answers, his or her own truth, and succeeds in living an authentic life. The lessons of this adventure are then brought back to society in the challenge of the 'return'—of communicating this new knowledge to a society in the thrall of its delusion.

The relevance of these teachings today is clear. For these mytho-logical themes are not 'fairy stories', nor are they ancient philoso-phies of only academic interest—they are incarnations of wisdom offering practical guidance, encouragement and inspiration for all today who, as Rudolf Bahro said, 'are not afraid to be insecure'.

For we, too, are living in a spiritual (and more and more literal) wasteland of desolate materialism. We, too, are protected (propagan-dized) by our own king of everyday concerns which distract us from the reality of our personal and global predicament. We, too, are distracted by our old drives and a false sense of conflict between our own good and the good of the planet. We, too, can only find a genuine experience of life in this desert through courage and independence of thought—through rejecting the normal as abnormal. So, too, around us a few brave souls are leaving for the darkest parts of their own forests to confront their own dragons, to find their own truth and live their own authentic lives. Along with Nietzsche's Zarathustra, all myth teaches us to say:

'I go new ways, a new speech has come to me; like all creators, I have grown weary of the old tongues. My spirit no longer wants to walk on worn-out soles.'[22]

Chapter 9

A CHEST OF TOOLS FOR INTELLECTUAL SELF-DEFENCE

'Nothing appears more surprising to those who consider human affairs with a philosophical eye than the easiness with which the many are governed by the few, and the implicit submission with which men resign their own sentiments and passions to those of their rulers. When we inquire by what means this wonder is effected, we shall find that, as Force is always on the side of the governed, the governors have nothing to support them but opinion. It is, therefore, on opinion only that government is founded, and this maxim extends to the most despotic and most military governments as well as to the most free and most popular.'
David Hume, *Of the First Principles of Government* (1758)

Against a Sense of Hopelessness

In this book we have examined the extent to which state and business interests stand to gain from our being bemused, confused, diverted, distracted but, above all, resigned and passive in the face of 'the way the world is'. The reason why this should be so was explained by Erich Fromm:

'This is a society which needs to make man fit in a complicated and hierarchically organised system of production with a minimum of friction. It creates the organisation man, a man without conscience or conviction, but one who is proud of being a cog, even if it is only a small one, in a big and imposing organisation. He is not to ask questions, not to think critically, not to have any passionate interests, for this would impede the smooth functioning of the organisation. But man is not made to be a thing, he is not made to shun asking questions. Hence, in spite of 'job security,' 'old-age pensions,' and the satisfaction of belonging to a large and 'nationally known' outfit, man is disquieted and not happy.'[1]

H.L. Mencken made a more general point:

'Governments, whatever their pretensions otherwise, try to

preserve themselves by holding the individual down… Government itself, indeed, may be reasonably defined as a conspiracy against him. Its one permanent aim, whatever its form, is to hobble him sufficiently to maintain itself.'[2]

When even a few people gain sufficient information and motivation to organize and protest, the illusion of popular impotence begins to be eroded. The economic costs of controlling protests are high, whilst the very act of confrontation threatens to dissolve the illusions of freedom and democracy on which the system depends. Protests of this type can lead to the identification of a 'crisis of democracy', as occurred during the 1970s when anti-war and civil rights protesters threatened to become involved in the political arena. Now, as then, politicians insist that peaceful protest is a threat to democracy. This is certainly true if by democracy we mean government by the few, for the few. Genuine freedom and democracy, however, have only ever been won by this type of collective action and protest. This is why it has always been important for those who govern us to keep us as isolated as possible, to ensure that we are imbued with a sense of impotence before our 'superiors' and 'betters' (the British class system functions as a non-stop illusion factory in this respect, spinning all manner of fictions regarding the innate superiority of the wealthiest sections of the population).

The widespread sense of apathy, hopelessness and even despair among many (particularly young) people today is not at all a reflection of the realities of what is possible, but rather of the sophistication of the system of thought control by which those possibilities have been obscured.

We need, then, to consider the possibility that even our most personal, unseen moments of resignation and despair may not be purely personal problems at all but symptoms of a challenge to our freedom, concomitants of the logic of our economic system—not as the result of anything so clumsy or obvious as a conscious plan, but as the cumulative effect of a biased system of selection.

When individuals who are acutely sensitive to their internal conflict with the outside world take their own lives, perhaps they are not so much jumping as being pushed out of the required framework. Perhaps they are victims of the requirement that we smile to survive at work even though our hearts are desolated by the irrational, isolating madness of the system in which we live, by the requirement that we be 'professional' and keep our pain, our reality, to ourselves.

Even our sense of despair and hopelessness may be yet another aspect of the efficient functioning of the system. But this knowledge surely gives us reason to doubt the validity of our despair; escape from despair may now be seen to involve escape from the limitations of thought control. This, at least, must be a cause for hope (and is certainly within our power as individuals). In this book we have seen that this rejection of hopelessness is justified. In fact, nothing could be clearer than that the success of the corporate system of domination is necessarily pyrrhic, and its future, therefore, necessarily limited.

Chomsky talks of the need to acquire the tools of intellectual self-defence. Given the enormous power of the propaganda system operating in every part of our society—our schools, work-places, political systems, advertising, entertainment, and deep within our own notions of truth, reality and sanity—we need to find ways of defending our ability to question and doubt society. With this in mind, the section that follows is intended as a sort of tool chest of assorted ideas to assist the reader in defending him- or herself from some of the more insidious devices of thought control by which we are made to control ourselves, including, above all, that most potent ally of the status quo— the false, or inadequate, 'opposition'.

Trojan Thoughts

To maintain independence of thought against the often extremely subtle manipulations of modern society is an elusive and difficult task. As discussed, mastering the arts of intellectual self defence is, in all essential respects, identical to mastering the Buddhist art of mindfulness. We need to be mindful, sensitive of how we are thinking and reacting as we encounter the world. The psychotherapist Bruno Bettelheim commented on the fact that parental praise often has the effect of angering the adolescent child on the verge of leaving home because he or she (unconsciously) recognizes the need to face the problems of early adulthood alone and understands that dependence on the praise and guidance of parents can act as a powerful hindrance to gaining the necessary self-confidence and independence. Similarly, it seems to me, if we pay close attention to our adult reactions (as Tolstoy did) we will find that, beneath the pleasure of social praise, status and 'success', lies a profound sense of dissatisfaction and emptiness, because we also unconsciously recognize the need to gain independence from society's values in order to find adequate answers to the problems of our adult lives. If we devote ourselves to being a social 'success' we may very well fail ourselves, although Bettelheim, writing of the concealed psychological wisdom with which children's fairy tales are infused, wrote:

'Maybe if more of our adolescents had been brought up on fairy tales, they would (unconsciously) remain aware of the fact that their conflict is not with the adult world, or society, but really only with their parents.'[3]

This echoes the by now familiar political naïvety of psychotherapy, and is all the more astonishing in this case given Bettelheim's own experience of the adult world and society in the concentration camps of Dachau and Buchenwald.

With mindfulness, we may notice that from one minute to the next our independent and critical stance can change to a feeling of deferential awe before some reassuring, fatherly leader, or 'expert', so that our hearts grow heavy with self-doubt (the more we believe in the authority figure, the less we believe in ourselves). We may find that our humane and rational view has suddenly been replaced by loathing for the official enemy—the Iraqis, Iranians, Koreans, Cubans (because this time those people really *do* need to be stopped). From believing we can do something about the state of the world and our own lives, we may come to find that it all suddenly seems hopeless.

To the extent to which we can become sensitive to these internal changes, we can begin to identify their causes in the influences affecting us (for example it is often enlightening to consider just who or what it was that triggered a sudden sense of hopelessness). This, in turn, may enable us to realize that what we believe is often what we have been channelled into believing by a flood of facts and ideas rooted in a very particular view of the world which reflects the interests of the dominant political and economic system. When this is achieved—when we can begin to see our own belief system more objectively, as a sort of Trojan Horse requiring wary and detailed examination—we can begin to be sceptical of our own ideas and so begin to root out the delusions of the propaganda system by which we are stifled.

The Limits of Freedom

The problem of escaping thought control is a deeply personal and emotional one. Despite any evidence to the contrary, we really do feel free. We are convinced that we are free. In fact, it is unthinkable that we might not be. And anyway we desperately want to believe we are free—we want to live peaceful lives, we do not want to become engaged in a psychological battle with our own society. We are indeed free—but only to do what is required. As soon as we try to do what is not required, to seek unsuitable answers to unsuitable questions, we find that our freedom hits an invisible boundary. As Gore Vidal has noted:

'Although AIDS can be discussed as a means of hitting out at unpopular minorities, the true epidemic can never be discussed: the fact that every fourth American now alive will die of cancer. This catastrophe is well kept from the public by the tobacco companies, the nuclear power companies (with their bungled waste disposal) and other industries that poison the earth so that corporate America may enjoy the freedom to make money without the slightest accountability to those they are killing.'[4]

Similarly, as of 1991, in Anglo-Welsh legal history there had been 'only two trials involving an indictment for corporate manslaughter, while the number of people killed at work since 1965 was 18,151.'[5] The prosecution of corporate crime in the workplace apparently falls outside the brief of the law, just as criticism of corporate activity in the Third World falls outside the brief of the corporately owned media.

Our freedom is so deceptive precisely because the illusion is so convincing, as long as we do what is required. It only begins to dissolve when we start to stray out of bounds, but most of us never do begin to stray out of bounds because we have been persuaded that there is nowhere else to go, and so we never experience the bruising reality of the invisible fence by which we are penned in (except as an ill-defined feeling of frustration and dissatisfaction). In other words, we feel free precisely because we are so well controlled. ✕

Even open-minded people will often find themselves unable to take seriously the likes of Chomsky, Herman, Zinn and George on first encountering their work; it just does not seem possible that we could be so mistaken in what we believe. The individual may assume that these writers must be somehow joking, wildly over-stating the case, paranoid, or have some sort of axe to grind. We may actually become angry with them for telling us these terrible things about our society and insist that this simply 'can't be true'. It takes real effort to keep reading, to resist the reassuring messages of the mass media and be prepared to consider the evidence again. Even when we become convinced that there is real truth in these arguments, we may well find that our ability to take them seriously fluctuates wildly—during the great consumer extravaganza of Christmas, for example, or during major nationalistic sporting events, we may think back and find that 'all that thought control stuff' seems to belong to another world. Later, in turn, it may strike us as astonishing that such trivial events could have had such a powerful effect on us.

Blaming the Victim

Because we have been persuaded to believe that we are not controlled, that our way of living is the best alternative we have, when we find our lives in crisis we usually assume there must be something wrong with us as individuals. At the other end of the scale, it is perfectly acceptable for us to become disillusioned with some abstract concept called 'life', for then 'life' can bear the sins that properly belong to corporate capitalism. Similarly, it is preferable that disasters in the Third World be attributed to terrible Acts of God, to the innately sorrowful nature of life, or to unfortunate mistakes, than that they be blamed on institutionalized systems of exploitation. In reviewing the holocaust inflicted on Indochina by the United States—with Laos alone receiving one ton of bombs for every head of its three million population—many American commentators described the US assault with such phrases as 'blundering efforts to do good'.[6]

In more general vein, it is infinitely preferable that we believe that 'Life is a tragedy wherein we sit as spectators for a while and then act out our part in it'[7], than that we perceive the less abstract truth about much of the tragedy in our world:

> 'The numerous horror stories of corporate behaviour in the Third World which have emerged in recent years show convincingly that respect for people, for nature, and for life are not part of the corporate mentality. On the contrary, large-scale corporate crime is today the most widespread and least prosecuted criminal activity.' Fritjof Capra, *The Turning Point*[8]

Given that we are living in a moral society governed by leaders passionately devoted to human rights, the people we kill in pursuit of those lofty aims *must* be to blame, as a matter of logical necessity. Hence Hegel's displeasure at:

> 'the contempt of humanity displayed by the Negroes [of Africa] who allow themselves to be shot down by thousands in war with

Europeans. Life has a value only when it has something valuable as its object.'[9]

Similarly, the *New York Times* financial correspondent Paul R. Strauss assures us:

'What we fail to realize is that corruption is a way of life in Asia.'[10]

What we also choose to fail to recognize is that very often Asian corruption is a way of life imposed by the Western requirement that the needs of the domestic population be suppressed by necessarily corrupt and vicious individuals, in deference to Western interests; this is indicated even by secret high-level planning documents:

'...we have 50% of the world's wealth, but only 6.3% of its population... In this situation, we cannot fail to be the object of envy and resentment. Our real task in the coming period is to devise a pattern of relationships which will permit us to maintain this position of disparity without positive detriment to our national security. To do so, we will have to dispense with all sentimentality and day-dreaming; and our attention will have to be concentrated everywhere on our immediate national objectives. We need not deceive ourselves that we can afford today the luxury of altruism and world-benefaction... We should cease to talk about vague and—for the Far East—unreal objectives such as human rights, the raising of the living standards, and democratisation.' George Kennan, Head of US State Department Planning Staff, 1948[11]

As Michael Parenti has said in response to this brutal truth:

'My goal is to try to get people away from saying,'Isn't it terrible how this goes on, what a strange foolish creature man is?' and point out to them that most of us aren't strange or foolish.We don't want these kinds of things to go on. These things are the product of a particular kind of social organisation and a particular use of class power.'[12]

We can take our pick between life as tragic accident and life as tragic design. The institutions responsible for much of that tragedy have an obvious preference: blame innate human aggressiveness, male hormones, Asian inscrutability, religious intractability, over-population, a flawed creator, blame anything you like; but do not seriously suggest that the real problems might lie with the institutionalisation of violence against people and planet in the economic and political systems of the West.

Opposition as Vaccine: Inoculating the Body Politic

One of the key messages of this book has been that many of the people, ideas and institutions that we imagine are on the side of humanity and freedom are false friends. Of course, if we like we can dismiss this idea as mere paranoia. Indeed, criticism of the status quo is often explained in terms of the individual psychoses of the proponents (as are obstacles to the status quo—Aristide 'the psychopath', the 'Mad Mullahs', the 'wild men on the wings' and Chomsky 'the great American crackpot'). Rarely, of course, is mental illness used to account for the arguments of those who support the status quo. No strait-jacket was requested for Lloyd George, who, when noting with approval that the British regime had ensured the 1932 disarmament convention did not forbid the bombing of civilian populations, declared:

> 'We insisted on reserving the right to bomb niggers.'[13]

Walt Whitman was not said to be 'beyond the pale of intellectual responsibility' for the direction of his questioning:

> 'What has miserable, inefficient Mexico... to do with the great mission of peopling the New World with a noble race?'[14]

No impromptu holiday was advised for Charles Darwin who, while discussing the genocide of the American Indians, suggested:

> 'There is apparently much truth in the belief that the wonderful progress of the United States, as well as the character of the people, are the results of natural selection.'[15]

Winston Churchill continued to be let loose amongst an unsuspecting public after declaring:

> 'I do not understand this squeamishness about the use of gas... I am strongly in favour of using poisoned gas against uncivilized tribes... It is not necessary to use only the most deadly gasses; gasses can be used which cause great inconvenience and would spread a lively terror and yet would leave no serious permanent effects on most of those affected.'[16]

On the other hand, the idea that profound criticism of power must be rooted in some sort of mental illness is common to all power religions.

In church-based societies the disturbance was of course seen as a symptom of demonic possession. Dissenters were hauled away by Soviet totalitarians for psychiatric 'treatment'. In our own society, the 'loony left' has long been dangerously 'infected' by the psychic 'virus' of communism. More recently, the madness of 'psycho-babble' has mutated into 'Political Correctness', manifested as an almost insane obsession with harassing our Free Press and education systems into rooting out even the hint of a suggestion of racial and sexual bias (the political manifestation of a washing compulsion).

Today, possession by devils is indicated by our failure to adequately worship the God of consumption; by a weird tendency to 'deep conversations' and serious thought. It can be seen in a bizarre concern for issues which are not the concern of the normal, fun-loving 'average man in the street'—redundant issues like politics, philosophy, and religion.

Either we are expected to discuss such matters as academic, side-issues to life, as worthy of occasional comment, or we are expected to express our cynicism about all politics, all religion, all searching for truth—this is acceptable and even applauded (as hard-nosed realism—of all things!). But if we discuss these issues in public as if they are of real concern to us, as if we feel we have an interest in doing something about them, as though we feel we can be part of a process of finding, or rediscovering, better answers to the problems of life, then we move out of bounds, 'beyond the pale' and are often met with hostile, embarrassed silence. To formulate our own arguments rather than those of the mass media, to quote ideas and statistics, to argue in an informed way about actual facts rather than loose generalizations, is to indicate our arrogance, our vanity ('Who do you think you are?'), is to manifest symptoms of neurosis. For we are challenging the religion of modern life—having fun; we are suggesting that there might be something more, something to question and perhaps resist, and this is understood to be absurd.

> 'All that matters is that nothing is too serious, that one exchanges views, and that one is ready to accept any opinion or conviction (if there is such a thing) as being as good as the other. On the market of opinions everybody is supposed to have a commodity of the same value, and it is indecent and not fair to doubt it.' Erich Fromm, *The Sane Society*[17]

But even this peer censorship by disapproval is less powerful than the self-censorship discussed earlier—we also know when we step over the line, and the tragic fact is that we also have been persuaded to judge ourselves as neurotic, as ill, when we doubt society (or as suffering from 'hormonal changes', as is the case with understandably discontented adolescents as their youthful individuality begins to feel the full weight of the propaganda system). Even a mind as independent as Nietzsche's experienced this:

> 'I sat among them disguised, ready to misunderstand *myself* so that I might endure *them*, and glad to tell myself: "You fool, you do not know men." '[18]

It takes a long and stubborn effort before we can begin to say with Thoreau's mischievous humour:

> 'Any man more right than his neighbours constitutes a majority of one.'[19]

Returning to our original subject, even a moment's independent thought demands that gaining awareness of the danger of false friends is a critical task. Beyond the easy accusations of paranoia, in the real world we can see that, from the medieval love worship of the troubadours through to socialism, the sexual revolution, the psychoanalytic movement, the environment movement, the human potential movement generally, along with ideas such as 'All you need is love!' and so on—all too often the original intention of those dedicated to human freedom has been emptied of content, and used to distract and mislead us.

How many of us believe that Orwell was a friend of free thought, a great radical master of deciphering political double-speak, or that Solzhenitsyn is a great hero of freedom? Perhaps they were, but we can also see that their efforts were readily commandeered by those eager to ensure that *our* ability to decipher political double-speak and *our* freedom were kept within permissible bounds. We have already discussed Orwell. As for Solzhenitsyn:

> 'Russian dissidents are international heroes, and their trials, personal and legal, and proclamations on all sorts of political and cultural issues, receive front page attention. Who has even heard the names of their vastly more numerous counterparts in the US client states?' Chomsky and Herman, *The Washington Connection And Third World Fascism*[20]

Like Orwell, Solzhenitsyn was used to attack the enemies of the West, to contrast the paradise of the 'free world' with the lack of freedom in the great 'slave state', so obscuring our own need to fight for our own freedom and democracy.

Similarly, it is undoubtedly true that the philosophy of love, for example, began as a genuine revolutionary movement against the tyranny of orthodox religion. Between the ages of 1170 and 1270, Henry Adams estimated that the French built eighty cathedrals and nearly five hundred churches of the cathedral class in a frenzy of religious zeal. It was against this backdrop that the French troubadours dared to defy conformity in the name of love, showing:

> '...the courage, namely, to affirm against tradition whatever knowledge stands confirmed in one's own controlled experience. For the first of such creative knowledges in the destiny of the West was of the majesty of love, against the supernatural utilitarianism of the sacramental system of the Church. And the second was of reason.'
> Joseph Campbell, *Creative Mythology* [21]

Yet what remains of this brave revolution from conformity to authenticity and life today? Rather than love being a force for human liberation, romantic love has become a central feature of the modern delusion. Many of us have been persuaded to abandon the search for true freedom and democracy in favour of the search for true love—we seek happiness in the ideal relationship as if our relationship with society was not an issue, as if personal compatibility was the only issue in determining our happiness.

All too often yesterday's revolution becomes today's controlling orthodoxy. This is only a tragedy if we fail to recognize that to follow in the footsteps of anyone, including those of the freedom-fighter, is to walk into the arms of conformity.

What is being suggested here is not that we reject these former allies of freedom, but that we seek out the heart of their fight for freedom from conformity and so reclaim the essence from those who seek to use their dead shells to contain us. Clearly, sex in the service of love is a liberating force. So, too, is love in the service of human freedom. Similarly, concern for the environment is one of the great forces for liberating thought today. But sex, love and environmental concern in the service of consumerism are very different animals; they are false friends (sex tourism, 'All you need is love!' and green capitalism being only three examples).

Thought control today does not operate by crushing an inconvenient idea. It operates by appearing to openly embrace an opposing idea and by assimilating it in an emasculated form that ensures it does not challenge the essential goals of the system, but actually supports those goals by disarming the concern that led to that opposition. Thus, we have green consumerism, sex on page three, escapist romantic fantasies, peace-loving 'doves', charity galas for the starving of Africa, Earth Summits, presidential references to 'the Almighty', and 'righteous crusades'. But, we do not for one moment have serious discussion on the deepest causes of environmental problems, on the truly revolutionary character of love as a rebellion against doing what society *says* is right for the sake of what is individually *known* to be right.

By injecting itself with tiny doses of the reality of these issues, the corporate system inoculates itself against any threat that it might be seen to be restricting freedom. Consequently, it is true that (for example) we are free to campaign against environmental degradation, but the propaganda system sees to it that we tend to do so in the same way that a child is allowed to play with 'guns' so long as they are made from harmless twigs.

What looks like progress is very often simply the immune system of the status quo defending itself: there is an explosion of genuine concern for the environment and before long we find oil company advertising filled with images of nature. We also, of course, find no sponsorship for documentaries investigating the corporate root causes of environmental crisis, and so the challenge is trivialized and contained.

The only hope, it seems to me, is to go as deeply as we can in understanding these issues. If we stay on the surface, our ideas will simply be out-manoeuvred by the banal deceptions of thought control. We need to recognize that beneath the endless variety of forms, all genuine movements for human freedom have been rooted in the same fundamental belief—that freedom consists in living authentic, individual lives, free from external control or manipulation that destroys our essence as self-directed, living human beings. The specific form that these movements take is not important. What is important is that our concern is rooted in a desire for life, in a desire to break free from what we 'should' do, to what *we want to do*.

In the last analysis, all movements for human freedom are rooted in a faith in life, in the faith that life flourishes best when it is free to live as it wants to live, rather than as others would like it to live. In a society as used to the idea of the need for 'discipline' (the doctrine that too much freedom is dangerous, that life needs to be contained and 'broken-in' to prevent it wreaking havoc) as ours is, this may strike us as a frightening idea. Yet surely the malignant destructiveness so unique to human beings is the result of our ability to *block* life, to lose life in delusion—surely it is our irrationally extreme discipline that makes us wild, our censorship that makes us perverted, our decency that makes us monstrous, our righteousness that makes us evil.

However much we might prefer 'hard' science to 'woolly' philosophy, we need to realize that when we fail to seek the roots of problems, we become extremely vulnerable to thought control. For example, if we do not understand that modern environmental problems are deeply rooted in the logic of the economic system, in the very reason for being of modern corporations, how can we avoid being fooled by the PR stunts of green consumerism and corporate responsibility? And if we are unable to appreciate that our own personal problems are rooted in the same corporate goals and the same propaganda system that supports them, how can we hope to generate the necessary motivation to respond to the wealth of information supplied by environmental groups that points to impending disaster? The three-thousand year old *I Ching* may have the key message for all dissident groups today:

'We must go down to the very foundations of life. Any merely superficial ordering of life leaves deepest needs unsatisfied. It is as ineffectual as doing nothing.' [22]

Arguably it is worse than doing nothing, because it prevents us from perceiving the need to do something; everyone already appears to be busy doing just that. And as the *I Ching* goes on to warn in its poetic way:

'The town may change but the well abides.
But if one's rope is too short,
Or if one breaks the jug,
Then one's thirst remains. Misfortune.' [23]

As long as dissident groups persevere with their shallow, dry, non-political, non-psychological, non-religious, non-philosophical, non-mythological, non-anything-fundamental-except-hard-scientific-data approach to the problems of the world, they will be playing into the hands of the propaganda system. Indeed, one of the great triumphs of that system may well be that it has managed to persuade dissident groups to restrict themselves to this ideational killing field in the belief that there they are at least on firm ground and can begin to make slow progress.

As Howard Zinn has argued in his recent book *You Can't Be Neutral On A Moving Train*, it is not bias that is the problem, but the *type* of bias (and the fact that people do not admit to their bias but feign objectivity). Any analysis of events involves bias simply because all reporting requires that we include or omit certain events on the basis of what we deem to be important. Along with Zinn, I am happy to be declared completely biased—I believe that human beings thrive to the extent to which they are free to pursue life, liberty and happiness in their preferred way. I also believe that the completely free human being would not be a greedy, vicious monster at all. I believe that these qualities are precisely traits of the human being that is *not* free (for example, it seems to me that the bloody encounter between Columbus and his murderous Spaniards on the one hand and the peaceable and kindly Indians of Hispaniola on the other, can be understood as an encounter between people who were less and more free. Real savages do not live in mud huts—they live in chains, especially psychological chains. Perhaps one day parents will castigate their children not by saying 'You're behaving like animals', which is often grossly unfair to animals, but 'You're behaving like civilized Europeans').

The issue of the false friend is a crucial one—if the doves can be a way of keeping us engaged in a murderous war, then the left can surely be a way of persuading us to reject genuine democracy, just as the greens can be a way of ensuring that we end up continuing to live for the (corporate) day and to hell with the environment.

With this in mind, we need to be critical of those we presume to be our greatest friends and allies, in the understanding that their claim to represent the 'well' of truth and goodness may be an empty, shallow one. It goes without saying that the same applies to all that has been written here; indeed, this whole book is intended, not as a declaration of truth, but a presentation of facts and ideas that *may* or may not be useful for a continued search for truth. The admirable Chomsky is not beyond criticism; nor, certainly, is the green movement, nor the left, nor any who declare their version of the truth. We surely find an urgent message in Nietzsche's warning:

> 'With whom does the greatest danger for the whole human future lie? Is it not with the good and just?—with those who say and feel in their hearts: 'We already know what is good and just, we possess it too; woe to those who are still searching for it!'[24]

Specific Problems with 'False Friends'

The Green Movement: Making the Wrong Waves

In essence, we have been concerned in this book with two very different versions of moral understanding. In the view commonly favoured by atheistic consumerism, virtue and self-interest are seen to be fundamentally in conflict. Because the incentive for not being sinful is located either in external punishment or nowhere at all, it has come to be assumed that greed, pride, hate and delusion are not, in themselves, intrinsically harmful to those dedicated to them; on the contrary, many of us believe that happiness lies in continually increasing our ability to satisfy new desires. As a consequence, we find ourselves facing apparent conflicts between, for example, the 'gains' of satiated Western greed and status and the inhuman requirement that the poor of the Third World be squeezed and suffer in order that we may achieve these ends. Having abandoned the notion of a cosmic judge, we feel free to pursue our greed with all vigour, abdicating our responsibility with easy clichés like 'That's just how the world is!', 'If I didn't do it someone else would', and so on. These arguments are of course not rooted in a serious examination of the fundamental issues involved, but are rationalizations designed to sweep such an examination out of the way.

The alternative view, presented here, suggests that there is no conflict in this situation; that this is perhaps the grandest illusion of all. The pursuit of greed, fame and status (the engines of injustice and exploitation)—being inappropriate and inadequate as a response to the human condition—is as destructive of the individual and society pursuing it, as it is of the unfortunates exploited in the course of that pursuit. In other words this lifestyle is wrong, not simply because it hurts other people, or because it is 'bad' to be selfish, but because it fundamentally 'misses the mark' of a sane human life; and when we collectively miss the mark, everyone pays a high price. Furthermore, we have argued that the reason we do not perceive the illusory nature of this conflict is because industrial consumerism and its giant propaganda system are locked into promoting greed and the pursuit of status as the way to happiness.

Earlier we discussed the ability of the propaganda system to contain thought within acceptable parameters of discussion, so that the assumed opposition becomes, itself, part of the required consensus. In this way the left, even the dissident opposition of society, may come to argue from a position manipulated and delineated to suit a corporately manufactured spectrum of necessary lies. Arguably much of the environmental movement remains caught in the required consumerist interpretation of morality in this way.

Environmentalists rightly place primary responsibility for environmental degradation and Third World suffering at the door of the wealthy countries of the North. They blame over-consumption, resulting from industrial development and rampant consumerism. However because their main focus has been on the destructive consequences of these developments in the natural environment and Third World, they assume—on the basis of the conventional, atheistic interpretation of morality—that the wealthy benefit from their exploitation. This belief is indicated by a Greenpeace leaflet which pictures the wealthy nations:

> 'gloating like brutish infants over their meteoric rise to ascendancy'.

Because environmentalists remain within the propaganda interpretation of ethical understanding they *do* see the consequences of industrial development as a rise to ascendancy that permits the wealthy to gloat. It is clear that no external force is penalising the West for its destructiveness, so environmentalists assume that the wealthy must be benefiting. Indeed, this Greenpeace statement conforms to the propaganda system by implying that consumerism *is* an adequate, ascendant answer to life for the fortunate wealthy. The implication is that the central problem is that the price is too high for the environment and the Third World, not for the wealthy. By remaining inside a propaganda-friendly framework of ethical understanding, Greenpeace unwittingly encourages industrial consumers to continue believing that industrial consumerism is not also devastating to *their* well-being and, so, actually encourages us to make the most of our lifestyles while we can before the world falls apart.

Greenpeace, like other dissident groups, relies on pleas to our conscience such as 'live simply that others might simply live', urging self-sacrifice on grounds of compassion. But these only serve to obscure the point that our motivation for living more simply is that the way we are living now is as destructive of our own happiness and mental health as it is of the environment. They serve to reinforce the modern lie that industrial consumerism is preferable to a more miserable, restrained, but 'moral' alternative. But who is willing to abandon some supposed present 'good life' because of some distant crisis? In our society, where we have been made to believe that satisfying our desires is the whole point to life, nothing is less likely to succeed than this type of call to altruism.

We should reject consumerism not in order to be good, but because a better, far more adequate life lies elsewhere; this life involves humility, compassion and simplicity, which also lead to an individually, socially and environmentally benign way of life. There is no cause for pride and anger among those who choose to live a more adequate life free from the maddening chains of obsessive greed and status. Why should we cajole and despise those living a life lost in self-destruction? From change motivated primarily by self-sacrifice and the desire to be good comes only a repression of perceived badness, a life lived as a lie and, ultimately, an explosion of badness in the destruction of people and nature in great moral crusades against 'the forces of evil'.

Probably most destructive acts are committed by people trying hard to act virtuously in some way—no doubt the SS trooper was trying to be a good and dutiful servant of his idolized Fuhrer and Fatherland. No doubt Walt Whitman, Charles Darwin and company meant well with their racist rhetoric. The aim is surely not to be good, faithful, dutiful, altruistic but to be *real*; only from this aim can virtuous lives and behaviour arise. As Emerson said so well:

'He who would gather immortal palms must not be hindered by the name of goodness, but must explore if it be goodness.'[25]

Like the Eastern sages, our society needs to grow out of its adolescent experimentation with inadequate answers to life. We should not be angry at our sin, at our missing the mark; we should not be afraid of it, we should not shy away from greed and status as infectious evils, we should *yawn* at them. We should recognize—regardless of what the propaganda system would have us believe—that we *do* yawn at them, that we are desperately bored by them because they are all unutterably superficial and inadequate answers to the question of how to live in the real world.

What we call sin only becomes dangerous when we stop calling it inadequate and start calling it wicked. Then life becomes a ridiculous war against sliding into the seductive delight of forbidden fruit which, when sampled honestly, is bland and tasteless.

Being Economical with Reality—Beyond the Left

Wherever we look in modern society, we can see the pyramid being built as the suitable people, ideas and facts find the places ascribed to them by the framing conditions which serve our corporate systems. So, too, we can see the unsuitable people, ideas and facts bouncing out—or being pushed out—and replaced. Above all, because coherent understanding of what is actually going on does not have a place in the pyramid, we are necessarily bombarded by superficiality—superficial journalism, entertainment, discussions, thoughts and ideas. A good example of why it is so important that our culture be swamped in superficial analysis is given below. In particular we can see why historical context and background vital for understanding the way the world works is absent from journalistic reporting and replaced by incoherent, disembodied snapshots and 'sound bites':

> 'During that whole period when the United States was helping build up the military and economic might of Saddam Hussein in Iraq, the issue of his human rights abuses was off the media agenda. There was this classic in the *New York Post*, a tabloid in New York. After the [Gulf] crisis began, they had a picture of Saddam Hussein patting the British kid on the head and their banner headline was 'Child Abuser'. That was very important to us and very ironic, because Amnesty International and other human rights groups had released studies in 1984 and 1985 which showed that Saddam Hussein's regime regularly tortured children to get information about their parents' views. That just didn't get the coverage. It shows one of the points that FAIR [Fairness And Accuracy In Reporting] has made constantly: that when a foreign government is in favour with the United States, with the White House, its human rights record is basically off the mainstream media agenda, and when they do something that puts them out of favour with the US government, the foreign government's human rights abuses are, all of a sudden, major news.' Jeff Cohen, Executive Director of FAIR, in conversation with David Barsamian[26]

The superficiality of modern culture and the profound confusion of the majority of people can be understood in essentially similar terms. When the ruling institutions of society depend for their very survival on the maintenance of a lie (in our case the lie that profit is subordinated to people and not the other way around), truth and understanding must be buried in a smothering blanket of half-truths, triviality and confusion. How else could the lie remain hidden?

Consequently, we may well find ourselves shocked in disbelief at the endless parade of quiz shows, sports shows, soap operas, sitcoms, holiday programmes, cookery programmes, wildlife documentaries (the perennial lioness chasing the perennial zebra), car adverts and business-biased news on the television. Even worse, when we visit our newsagents, we find hundreds of magazines all serving the needs of their all-important advertisers and (literally) only one or maybe two serving other ends. But even these essentially serve the unions, or the political left generally, who are also working for, and are supportive of, the mainstream industrial programme; whose primary concern is not at all to rid the world of this economic monster but to hang on to its tail and squeeze it that they might get a bigger share of the spoils. The problem today for the mildly reformist British Labour party is that its traditional supporters have been persuaded to believe that they can do better by voting for a party that does not restrain the beast at all but permits it to grow as fast as possible. Labour's response has been to embrace the deception and abandon any pretence of providing genuine opposition to the rule of profit. As John Pilger says:

> 'Labour has proved itself to be an enfeebled component of a rotting system, further disenfranchising those millions of people who still look to it as the constituted opposition.'[27]

And in the same way that Herman, Chomsky and Zinn insist that the US political system consists of two wings of the same business party, Pilger reports:

> 'During the election campaign, it was widely agreed that "convergence" had taken place between the principal policies of the parties. These policies reaffirmed the elevation of profit above people in almost all areas of life and derided the notion of common obligation as heresy.'[28]

This is a truth that is generally considered unfit for public consumption in Britain, as has long been the case in the United States. Gore Vidal has described the result of his attempts to transcend the confines of this type of 'convergence' in political debate.

> 'I was made aware of the iron rules in 1968, when William F. Buckley, Jr., and I had our first live chat on ABC at the Republican convention in Miami Beach... Buckley Junior's idea of a truly in-depth political discussion is precisely that of corporate America's. First,

the Democrat must say that the election of a Republican will lead to a depression. Then the Republican will joyously say, Ah Hah, but the Democrats always lead us into war! After a few minutes of this, *my* attention span snapped. I said that there was no difference at all between the two parties because the same corporations paid for both, usually with taxpayers' money, tithed, as it were, from the faithful and then given to "defense," which in turn passes it on to those candidates who will defend the faith... Although my encounters with Buckley Junior got ABC its highest ratings, I was seen no more at election times. Last year, Peter Jennings proposed to ABC that, for old times' sake, it might be a good idea to have me on. "No," he was told. "He'll just be outrageous." ' [29]

Vidal's explanation for these events?

'The corporate grip on opinion in the United States is one of the wonders of the Western world. No First World country has ever managed to eliminate so entirely from its media all objectivity— much less dissent.' [30]

Britain manages a creditable second place (although, in truth, Britain has no dissident magazines to compare with US productions like Z and LOOT).

Almost nowhere do we find discussion in magazines, newspapers, or on television, that moves beyond the parameters of those that support unrestrained business activity and those who accept the goals of business under certain mildly reformist conditions (beyond, as it were, the hawks and doves argument). Almost nowhere do the media suggest that the mainstream left might be another false friend, a false opposition that limits its concern for morality to disembodied moral imperatives like equality and social welfare; that limits its concern for change to spreading the fruits (and desolation) of our magnificent industrial programme more equably; that deals with the inherent conflict between corporate profit and human rights and environmental crisis with inaudible, embarrassed mumblings (necessarily— a party claiming to be for people and planet *and* for maximising profit *must* master the art of mumbling under its breath—this is called 'holding the middle ground').

But what we have described here is not opposition. This is not radical dissent, this is the imprisonment of thought within parameters that do not begin to embrace or deal with the depths of the problem of modern thought control and the havoc it is wreaking on the life of humanity and the wider environment.

As we have discussed, the reality is that the world is on fire, that the natural systems of life are collapsing beneath the weight of the industrial killing machine. After only fifty years of total industrial war against the needs of humanity and the natural environment, both are beginning to show signs of collapse.

In this situation, to spend our time focusing on seeking restraints on senior executive pay increases, maintaining the railways in public ownership, providing extra welfare benefits, guaranteeing a minimum wage, and so on, is simply ridiculous. The cost in terms of the health and vitality of British intellectual life, however, is unimaginably high. When the left, as it exists in Britain, is taken seriously as the opposition—as the alternative, the other pole—our capacity for thought and hope have been destroyed. When responses of this superficiality are considered adequate to the modern scale of devastation and deception, we naturally find people surrendering in droves before a sense of utter hopelessness, before the idea that all politicians are as bad as each other, that nothing can be done, that there are no answers, before the complete lack of coherent ideas that mean anything to us as real, living human beings in a decaying world. Of course improved conditions for workers, union rights, and so on, are important, but to suggest that they are primary concerns is simply a deception (albeit, in the case of some well-meaning politicians, a self-deception).

The tragedy is not that the parties of the left are completely redundant but that people continue to seek answers in them, that they somehow convince themselves that leftist superficialities are an adequate response to anything. Rather than leaving through the door on our own path to understanding and freedom from thought control, we cling to the tiny crack in the wall offered by the hope of the election of an opposition that is no opposition at all, but is an opposition painstakingly tailored to appear acceptable to the corporate system. What does it mean for a party supposedly representing the people to be elected on the condition that it follows an agenda set by corporate power? Either it is attempting to deceive that power, in which case it will soon be unseated, or it is attempting to deceive us. As John Dewey said, the inescapable reality is that 'so long as politics is the shadow cast on society by big business, the attenuation of the shadow will not change the substance.' [31]

In reality, the only true opposition lies in the individual thinking for him and herself and so perceiving the redundancy of all modern political parties.

The impression given by the current state of affairs—that the only alternative is equally useless—is an old story. The same impression is given in our schools, where the most inquisitive, curious creatures on Earth are daily convinced that all curiosity and interest are useless and doomed to failure because everything is boring and confusing. When all the conceivable alternatives are perceived to be useless, the individual human being has a tendency to assume that he or she can do no better and gives up. So, too, with politics and thinking generally.

Mainstream politics today does not even begin to deal with the reality of the human being in the human condition, and consequently strikes us (especially the admirable young prior to their being brainwashed) as utterly foolish, absurd, irrelevant and boring because we do not feel that our essential concerns are remotely catered for. Just as the neurotic individual today is relatively healthier than the 'well-adjusted' conformist, so those completely disillusioned with the modern political system demonstrate far higher political astuteness than those who take the charade seriously.

Hate as an Obstacle to Solutions

'For a holy man forms a tender estimate of the true condition of mortal beings, and how should he want to inflict further suffering on them when they are already suffering enough from disease, death, old age, and so on?' Buddhist Scriptures [32]

As we have discussed, those who seek to pacify us and to exploit others have everything to gain from the generation of hatred towards other peoples and nations. It seems likely that much racism has its roots in this type of political manipulation (though of course racism is bemoaned as a tragic fact of human nature by the same people who try to whip us into a frenzy against 'yellow perils', 'red scares', 'Muslim fundamentalists', 'floods of immigrants', and so on). Howard Zinn argues, for example, that, during the 1720s in the United States, the fear that poor whites and black slaves might join together and challenge the wealthy élite meant that racism 'was becoming more and more practical'. Zinn quotes Edward Morgan:

'The answer to the problem, obvious if unspoken and only gradually recognized, was racism, to separate dangerous free whites from dangerous black slaves by a screen of racial contempt.' [33]

A vital step in freeing ourselves from bondage to the murderous requirements of profit and power is to appreciate the real causes of our hatred for other people. All too often we respond in dependably Pavlovian fashion to the call for the destruction of some monstrous threat: Iraq, Libya, Nicaragua, Cuba, Vietnam (personalized as Saddam Hussein, Qaddafi, Ortega, Castro and Ho Chi Minh, in order to obscure the fact that it is actually men, women and children who are destroyed). The process is simplicity itself: human rights abuses are raised and pushed to the fore by the government (while those committed by us and our allies go unnoticed), 'experts' detail the awesome danger posed, other 'experts' confirm that this or that leader really is a monster capable of any amount of madness, our leaders offer to come to our rescue in the name of all that is holy and decent. Before we know it, we are cheering at the TV screens, admiring the footage of bombs curving down to their targets, and marching mindlessly off to war as part of some Just Cause, with the corpses of Third World people—and of the truth—strewn among the wreckage.

In more general terms this kind of hate, whether for foreign tyrants, domestic minorities, or individual people we know, is always rooted in a delusion, namely that it is not possible to understand another person's behaviour on the grounds that it is as incomprehensible as it is unacceptable. This has to be so because hate can exist only in the absence of understanding; where understanding is present, hate cannot exist. To take a concrete example: in the United States much public anger was recently provoked by the case of a policeman who, after a trivial argument, shot his partner dead in cold blood. As so often before, newspapers raged at the random, motiveless nature of this atrocity committed by a 'maniac' on the rampage. Later, it was revealed that the policeman was an insomniac and had been taking sleeping pills, which were shown to have psychotic side-effects (a fact revealed in pre-launch drug trials but suppressed—another story). Once off the pills, the policeman regained his peaceful personality.

Clearly hate (even, I would suggest, among the victim's family and relations) cannot exist in the presence of this kind of explanation and understanding; it dissolves and is revealed to be a symptom of a lack of understanding. Indeed, very often hate is the result of a determination *not* to understand, and this is why hate is so dangerous: it actually resists understanding. Indicative of this is the fact that when people hate they ask questions such as: 'How could anyone do a thing like that?' 'What sort of a person would do something like that?' These are purely rhetorical questions, intended to suggest that there are *no* answers, that such things could not be done by people, thereby indicating that those in question are somehow inhuman, somehow beyond understanding, that they cannot be forgiven and can therefore be hated. This bizarre attempt to prove the basic inhumanity of a human action is required as a basis for the blame on which hate depends. Ultimately it represents a temporary retreat to an irrational view of the world in deference to emotional need.

The reason why we are so vulnerable to calls to hate our demonic enemies and to choosing not to attempt to understand other people, can be explained by reference to the phenomenon known as scapegoating.

Shame Shifting—Riding the Scapegoat

As discussed, human beings are innately prone to feelings of guilt and shame. The human condition is such that we always feel we could be better able to deal with the world—we could always have tried harder, we could always be more intelligent, quicker-witted than we are. The human capacity to choose implies the capacity to fail, which implies the capacity to feel ashamed at our failure. Although we may feel keenly the pain of this shame, we will often not consciously identify the feeling as shame; we will just be angry. We will, in other words, try to avoid facing the pain of our shame.

One effective way of hiding from our shame is to secretly blame our failure on someone else. By blaming our failure on a scapegoat, we can succeed in avoiding our shame by refusing to accept responsibility for our problems—it is 'their' fault! In a sense, we deflect the shame away from our own consciousness, 'projecting it' (as psychologists say) onto someone else.

Throughout history, we find the defeated, disadvantaged and downtrodden (all of whom, perhaps unconsciously, blame themselves for being inadequate in the face of their problems), all too likely to blame a scapegoat. Thus the down-trodden Germans of the inter-war depression directed their anger at their condition onto the Jews; and as we have seen, it is often a relatively simple matter to turn poor whites against poor blacks, and so on. Always these scapegoats act as safe containers for the shame and guilt of other people. The ashamed may then unleash their self-hatred and anger against their projected selves.

If it is true that the only answer to hate is understanding, it is also true that a significant obstacle to understanding is the presence of anger and hate. Chomsky, as we have seen, uses his skill in applied wonder to prove the pervasive existence of the abuse of power, but it seems to me that even he stops short of seeking to understand why it is that politicians, industrialists and the like are so able to dismiss the sufferings of their Third World victims for the sake of profit. In his book *Deterring Democracy*, he writes:

'The problem of indoctrination is a bit different for those expected to take part in serious decision-making and control: the business, state, and cultural managers, and articulate sectors generally. They must internalize the values of the system and share the necessary illusions that permit it to function in the interests of concentrated power and privilege—or at least to be cynical enough to pretend they do, an art that not many can master. But they must also have a certain grasp of the realities of the world, or they will be unable to perform their tasks effectively. The élite media and educational systems must steer a course through these dilemmas—not an easy task, one plagued by internal contradictions. It is intriguing to see how it is faced, but *that is beyond the scope of these remarks.*' (my emphasis)[34]

But surely such an analysis *should* be within the scope of the discussion. Understanding mindless modern conformity, obedience, and human destructiveness more generally—how it is that people can be aware of the often appalling truth and yet lie and even believe the lie—is vital. Chomsky's reluctance to make such an attempt may have to do with his own personal anger (which he openly admits) at the consequences of greed and conformity. We are, after all, talking about the torture, mutilation and genocide of hundreds of thousands, even millions of innocent people as the result of the actions of individuals hell-bent on personal gain. How could we not be angry?

Agreed—and we might add that anyone who does not experience some anger at the tragedy of what is happening today is simply not able to perceive the truth of what is happening. But when we consider the scale of the problem, surely it is clear that our anger is inappropriate. We are obviously not dealing with one or two 'bad guys' who happen to have got in charge and decided to wreck the world for their own gain. We are dealing with a destructive tendency in human beings that has continuously afflicted one or other part of the human race for millennia (although admittedly not on today's scale). In other words, we are dealing with fundamental tendencies deeply embedded in the psyche of the human species and in the institutions of power.

This in turn suggests that we are in a sense addressing an extraordinarily destructive *natural phenomenon*; less destructive than the occasional crashing asteroid and ice-age, no doubt, but immensely destructive none the less. Why then do we feel so angry about human destructiveness compared to these other disasters? Because, of course, we believe that human behaviour is self-generated, that we have the power to direct ourselves, that we are responsible. This may be true, yet if this really is the basis of our anger, then Chomsky's argument makes a nonsense of it.

As Chomsky, Fromm and others have so convincingly shown, people today are subject to massive propaganda and thought control from the day they are born. It follows that we are not completely to blame for our actions. But this does not mean that we should not or cannot change; it means we must seek answers, not scapegoats.

Our response, therefore, should be not to feel anger or hate towards other people, but to attempt to understand them. Many might argue that to deny personal responsibility in this way encourages people to sit back and continue acting irresponsibly. But as we have discussed, the argument here is not based on the notion that people should be more responsible, or nice, or act out of a sense of 'moral duty', it is based on the idea that we should fight for our own reality, for our own freedom from delusion, not because this will make us good people who will be rewarded in some heaven, or so that we will be able to look at ourselves in the mirror, but because it is in all our interests to live lives free from delusions; and human beings free from delusions tend to be far more sane, healthy, happy and peaceful, than human beings lost in fantasy. Our urgent task, then, is to understand why people conform, why they so readily bow to irrational authority, why they pursue greed and status—no matter what the cost to themselves or others.

Obedience and Conformity

In the late 1940s and early 1950s, Solomon Asch conducted a series of experiments to measure the social distribution of what he termed 'independence'—the capacity for independent judgement. In his experiments, Asch brought an unsuspecting subject into a room containing a group of people instructed to falsify their answers in response to a simple perceptual test. In this test, the group was asked to assert which of three lines of varying lengths on one graph most closely corresponded in length to a single line on an adjacent graph. Unknown to the subjects of the experiments, Asch was pitting them against a pre-arranged, unanimous, yet entirely irrational, consensus.

Initially, the rigged group matched lines which were reasonably similar. Gradually, however, Asch introduced widening discrepancies so that, eventually, the group consensus matched lines of extremely different lengths, also mixing in a few disagreements amongst the group for the sake of realism. The results were extraordinary: only 20 percent of Asch's subjects proved capable of independent judgement in the face of an absurd consensus. Of these, many found the experience highly stressful. Asch concluded that:

> '…social life makes a double demand on us: to rely upon others with trust and to become individuals who can assert our own reality… We may suppose that this aim can be achieved under favourable circumstances, but even then not without struggle… But there are conditions less favourable for development which, while encouraging the individual to live in a wider and richer world than the individual can encompass alone, also injure and undermine him. This happens when social circumstances stifle the individual's impulses and deny them expression.'[35]

In another (infamous) research programme, Stanley Milgram was concerned not with conformity but with obedience. Milgram's subjects were told that they were to take part in a learning experiment. When the learner (an actor hidden behind a screen) gave an incorrect response to the subject's questions, the subject was instructed to administer an electric shock of increasing intensity to the learner who, though not actually shocked, reacted as though he was— protesting, shouting and even screaming before lapsing into feigned unconsciousness. Once again, the results were extraordinary. Only a minority of subjects refused to participate when the learner feigned protest and pain, while a considerable number were prepared to shock the learner all the way to unconsciousness at the behest of authority embodied by the white-coated 'scientist'.

The implications of these experiments are clear. Faced with a consensus—especially one endorsed by authority—modern individuals show an extreme tendency to conform; that is, to think and do as others do, or as others tell them to do, without question. It seems that the majority of people today are incapable of challenging even self-evident nonsense, while others defer to authority to the point of barbarism.

This modern susceptibility to conformity and obedience to authority indicates that the truth endorsed by authority is likely to be accepted as such by a majority of people, who are innately obedient to authority. This obedience-truth will then become a consensus-truth accepted by many individuals unable to stand alone against the majority. In this way, the truth promulgated by the propaganda system—however irrational—stands a good chance of becoming the consensus, and may come to seem self-evident common sense. History suggests that there are few, if any, limits to the level of absurdity that can be reached by such a consensus—belief in an underground cave full of sadistic devils, in the benevolence of plainly psychotic dictators, in the passionate devotion of modern states to freedom and democracy when the entire world is run (and put at risk) by the profit motive, and so on.

This kind of understanding is surely an important starting point for the creation of individual resistance to conformity and obedience. We need to approach our modern human tendency to conform and obey as human traits to be understood and dealt with, not as causes for self-hate or the hatred of others. How, after all, can we hope to solve a problem unless we understand it? Consider the alcoholic: why does he drink himself to destruction? Until we fully understand the reasons, we are unlikely to be able to offer a realistic solution. Simply accusing him of being a drunk, cajoling him for ruining the lives of others and insisting that he puts the bottle down and even punishing him whenever he takes a drink, is unlikely to result in a cure. Given that we don't know why he is drinking, our actions may well make things worse (he may even seek solace in the bottle). If, on the other hand, we discover that our alcoholic is drinking because he has extremely low self-esteem (such that he has not learnt to express himself without being drunk), then we can start experimenting with possible solutions: we can resort to self-help groups, therapy, whatever. The point is that in order to start to investigate the causes of the problem, we first have to put aside our hate.

Whenever we hate, the villain always becomes a fantasy mental projection like Greenpeace's 'gloating, brutish infants' giggling over the earth they have despoiled. In children's cartoons, the villainous wolves and cats spend much of their time merrily chortling over their spoils! This is to build us up for the hero's revenge which can only be justified if the villains are seen to benefit from their evil. In many action films of the Schwarzenegger variety, the final heroic revenge is sadistic in the extreme, a fact we fail to notice (and even delight in), because our hate has been so highly aroused. If the self-destructive truth about 'missing the mark' were revealed, the vengeful 'hero' would seem as inhuman as the villain (as is the case for anyone who understands the facts of 'Operation Desert Storm', for example). Our hate can only reach this level if we are convinced that the villains benefit from their evil, in accordance with the conventional version of moral understanding. But when we look into and discover the reason for a person's destructive behaviour, they suddenly become real, to be taken seriously as human beings and not merely fantasy projections. (Anyone who has read Ramsey Clark's book *The Fire This Time* cannot help but be struck by the reality of the Iraqi people beneath the fantasies of propaganda. These are not Arab fanatics, or Third World primitives, they are real men, women and children like us who have been slaughtered by the hundred thousand, whose entire country has been laid waste.)

With mindfulness, we will find that our hate is rooted in *a desire to hate* (we often leap to the task with great enthusiasm) and not simply in the 'wickedness' of the actions of those we choose to hate. This tells us more about the reality of ourselves than it does about the reality of the hated person—including the person distorting the media, conforming to the corporate system, pushing the B-52 bomb-release, authorising arms shipments to Indonesia, and so on.

Even Gengis Khan thought he was the Good Guy! Rationalization as an Obstacle to Truth

As we tackle the unavoidable human problem of trying to make sense of the world, we are required to constantly select or reject facts and ideas as important or irrelevant to the attainment of such an understanding. One of the human tendencies that makes this task so difficult is rationalization, the phenomenon whereby we believe something, not as a result of a rational consideration of the facts, but because we want to believe it, because it serves some pre-determined purpose.

For example an individual may be afraid of meeting someone, but unwilling to admit this fear either to themselves or to anyone else. If it is raining heavily outside, the individual may say it is raining too heavily to make the meeting. This is not a reason but a rationaliza-tion, which may be made clear by the fact that the person remains reluctant to go even when he or she is offered an umbrella, or is reminded that a taxi would be easily affordable.

Rationalization appears to be a significant factor which supports the operation of the propaganda system. This is because one of the major sources of rationalization derives from the human need to feel part of the human herd. To understand this, we need to consider the dual nature of the human being.

Herd and Individual

The human being, as we have discussed, is the great isolated animal of nature. Our relative freedom from instinct, combined with our self-awareness, make us acutely aware of ourselves as separate individuals. This gives rise to feelings of isolation and loneliness which must be resolved. For this reason, the human being is very much a herd animal. We have a powerful need to belong with, and be accepted by, other people: first by our mother and father, and later by friends and loved ones. Our worst fear from this point of view would be to be pushed away, rejected, abandoned, outcast, isolated from other people, from the herd; we must not let it happen.

But as self-aware human beings, we are also very much individuals with an urgent need to be independent and rational, so that we may solve the problems posed us by life. Simply belonging to the herd, doing as everyone else does, without developing our own ability to solve our own problems, will not be enough; there are many lessons we can only learn for ourselves. To find answers, we can only rely on our reason, on our individual ability to understand the way we, ourselves, and the world more generally, work. Only then can we hope to understand what does or does not promote—or cripple—our happiness.

Clearly these two fundamental human needs are liable to conflict with each other. It is rationalization that often intervenes to compromise our desire to be rational individuals with our desire to fit into the society around us. It is painful for us to be aware that some of our actions, which may be required if we are to 'fit in' with others, are irrational or monstrous, but it is also painful for us to feel an outsider from the herd. Because we are eager to belong, irrational or immoral aspects of herd-life will tend to be overlooked and ignored through what the psychologist H.S. Sullivan called 'selective inattention'—we prefer not to recognize truths that would make it difficult for us to accept the society to which we are eager to belong.

If the propaganda system (giving the impression that it represents the majority view) assures us that our country is peace-loving, democratic and moral, we will have powerful reasons for wanting to concur with these views, and will probably rationalize away any doubts (perhaps assuring ourselves that any violence committed by our nation has been solely in self-defence), rather than become an outsider. Sometimes this type of abuse of language by the mass media is simply a conscious lie but, equally as often, it is itself a product of rationalization—an unconscious compromise between a journalist's desire to live a rational life in touch with the real world and his or her fear of being ejected from the herd (and, indeed, from his or her job and career). To preserve our place in the herd, our job, our social hierarchy, we will invent any amount of nonsensical rationalizations for what is happening, and will often come to really believe them. This phenomenon partly accounts for the high degree of control in the mass media, although there is no conscious conspiracy. As Thoreau said:

'There is no need of a law to check the license of the press. It is law enough, and more than enough, to itself. Virtually, the community have come together and agreed what things shall be uttered, have agreed on a platform to excommunicate him who departs from it, and not one in a thousand dares utter [or even think] anything else.'[36]

Which, together with what we have said here, at least to some extent answers the interesting question posed by John Pilger's group of Russians:

'A group of Russians touring the United States before the age of *glasnost* were astonished to find, after reading the newspapers and watching television, that all the opinions on the vital issues were the same. "In our country", they said, "to get that result we have a dictatorship, we imprison people, we tear out their fingernails. Here you have none of that. So what's your secret—how do you do it?" '[37]

In 1945, an interesting piece of research was conducted which gives an example of rationalization. Two questions were put to whites in the North and South of the United States. The first question was: 'Are all men created equal?' To this question, 79% and 61% answered 'yes' respectively. The second question was: Are the Negroes equal to the whites? To this question, 21% and 4% answered 'yes'.

The explanation for such a contradiction is clear enough—these people remembered the socially approved ideal that 'all men are equal' from school and so claimed to believe it (because everyone else claimed to). But what they said they believed was very different from what they actually believed—in reality, they did not at all believe that all men were created equal.

People often claim to be socialists, democrats, environmentalists and Christians in the same way, without these beliefs playing any significant role in their lives. Notoriously, many people who believe in God as a supreme overlord are religious in this way; hence the marked capacity of the 'religious' to commit atrocities in direct contradiction to their espoused beliefs. A supreme exponent of this type of rationalization was Columbus.

Columbus declared himself to be exceedingly religious, and to have an ardent desire to convert the American Indians to Christianity. Yet one word recurs 75 times in the first two weeks of Columbus's journal subsequent to his arrival in the New World—*gold*. The extra consonant tells us all we need to know about Columbus's concern for the spiritual welfare of the Indians. Thus he wrote:

> 'They [the Indians] are the best people in the world and above all the gentlest—without knowledge of what is evil—nor do they murder or steal…'

An observation immediately followed by:

> '…They would make fine servants. With fifty men we could subjugate them all and make them do whatever we want.'[38]

Columbus's real motivation is confirmed by Las Casas, the leading Spanish chronicler of the day, who reported that the Spanish fell upon the Indians 'like ravening wild beasts… killing, terrorizing, afflicting, torturing, and destroying the native peoples' with 'the strangest and most varied new methods of cruelty, never seen or heard of before,…'[39] 'Their reason for killing and destroying… is that the Christians have an ultimate aim which is to acquire gold…'[40]

In the same way, many politicians and captains of industry today declare that they are serving the cause of humanity, in the 'developing world' perhaps, arguing that profit maximisation will lead to a golden technological age for all. In a superficial way they may even believe such nonsense. The point is that no one likes to see their own actions as monstrous or destructive; we all want to believe we are 'good guys' and so we all tend to rationalize what we do in terms of grand ideals— we are doing our duty, controlling the 'bewildered herd' for their own good, bringing God to the backward races, fulfilling our 'manifest destiny', building a great benevolent empire, administering economic medicine that will lead to a bright future for all, only doing what someone else would have done anyway so it doesn't matter, or whatever else happens to fit the bill. The important thing is to declare these things, but not look too closely at the actual facts of destruction and the real motivation behind it. (Much philosophy serves the task by allowing those who exploit others to sit back and sigh in melancholy at the inevitability of human greed and the innately tragic aspects of life. The 'hard facts of life' are often the fantasies of rationalization.) This ability to hold a view with apparent sincerity, but to actually believe it simply because it is convenient to do so and not on the basis of a reasoned consideration of the facts, is the reason psychologists are able to argue that someone is unhappy despite the fact that they claim to be happy—a counter-claim that some people find shocking. It is quite possible for us to declare that we love our jobs, our work, our country, or that we are happy, not because it is true (free association and analysis of our dreams may reveal that we hate our jobs and are deeply unhappy) but because it is 'normal', what people expect from us, and so we say these things in order to belong (Jung suggested that most people claim to be happy today simply because to not be happy is seen as a kind of failure).

Clearly, those in a position to determine what is normal in society can use the innate human desire to belong to their advantage, and this is one of the great supports of the propaganda system as a weapon of thought control. Through endless repetition the mass media determine what is normal, and rapidly manipulate the views of the populace towards the 'accepted' goal. Thus news commentators, celebrity 'experts' like Ted Koppel, are able to make the approved version of reality become social reality by matter-of-fact comments such as:

> 'Manuel Noriega belongs to that special fraternity of international villains, men like Qaddafi, Idi Amin, and the Ayatollah Khomeini, whom Americans love to hate.' [41]

No logical argument or evidence is presented, yet such sentiments, delivered in a sardonic style that flatters the public by suggesting that they are strong and stand no nonsense from the jumped-up dictators of the world, appeals to their desire to belong to a powerful herd. To go along with these beliefs is to identify ourselves as part of a formidable 'kick-ass' group of people—'Americans' (thus obscuring the fact that it is actually the majority of Americans who have their 'asses' 'kicked' by these attempts to tie them up in webs of illusion).

To bring the point closer to home—we may come across a title like *Beyond Totalitarianism: Noam Chomsky And The Propaganda Model*. We may even read the text, but because what it says is at profound odds with the declared aims, beliefs and values of the society around us, we will be faced with a powerful test of our tendency to rationalize. If we accept Chomsky's hypothesis, if we allow our reason to say 'yes, of course' to it—of course big business has a monopoly over the mass media, of course this influences what we come to see, of course there is never any discussion of this fact precisely because big business has every interest in our not becoming aware of the power it has to influence us—we will be immediately isolating ourselves from the vast majority of people around us and this, we know, may be at least painful and perhaps hugely disruptive to our lives.

On the other hand, we may reject Chomsky's hypothesis. We may decide that thought control on this scale is impossible because it implies the sort of conspiracy that could never be kept secret; or that Chomsky is just a paranoid, un-American (not to mention un-Swedish!), self-hating communist, extremist, Jew. Or we may decide that the hypothesis may be true, but there's nothing we can do about it; or that it's interesting, but it just goes too far.

Having chosen one of these rationalizations, moments later we can be settling back in our chairs in the office, or in the pub, or in front of the TV, feeling as 'comfortably' part of the 'normal' world as before. We will have avoided conflict and disruption in our individual, familial, social and career lives; we may have avoided confronting the waste of years, or decades of effort and striving for a deluded dream in a profoundly immoral and brutal system (surely one reason why it is easier for the young to doubt—the older we get the more we often stand to lose from doubting. The cliché of the transformation of young socialist into old conservative is not a change from idealism to pragmatism, but from rationality to rationalization).

The cost of surrendering our reason to rationalization is that we will tend to reject ideas that allow access to a coherent understanding of the world, including its problems, including our problems. By failing to overcome our tendency to rationalize, we are choosing irrationality and incoherence; we are missing the opportunity for truth, and so 'missing the mark'; and we have already examined the high price to be paid for this failure. Choosing rationalization is not choosing comfort and happiness, it is choosing passive suffering over active, painful—but healthful—striving for aliveness, sanity and growth.

In the previous two sections of this chapter we have been addressing the problems of hate and the capacity for self-delusion, two flames of the Buddhist Threefold Fire of Delusion which is said to be the root cause of all human suffering. Let us end, then, with a consideration of a modern example of the manipulative and destructive power of the third of these flames of delusion—Desire.

Manufacturing Discontent: Advertising Anorexia and Bulimia

Most people take it for granted that modern consumerism is about manufacturing goods and services to progressively satisfy individual needs and desires in pursuit of a more contented life. But consumerism is about much more than this. It is very much a process of creating desire, of progressively creating dissatisfaction. Indeed, today, a particularly intense seventy-year-old propaganda war continues to be waged against the women of the world. It is a war to win their money through the manufacture of discontent, at the cost of their well-being. It began in the early 1920s, around the time of women's political enfranchisement.

Following their critical contribution to the 1914-18 war effort and the related rise of feminism, women began to play an increasing role in industrial economies. From 1945 to 1984, the number of women in employment in the United States rose from 32% to 53%. In Sweden the figure rose to 77%, and in France to 55%. The real changes, however, began to take place during the sixties: between 1960 and 1990 the number of US women lawyers rose from 7,500 to 180,000; the number of doctors rose from 15,000 to 108,000 and of engineers from 7,000 to 174,000. Today, 50% of entry management positions are held by women and 25% of middle management positions.

This all points to a significant, though limited, 'liberation' of women from the nineteenth and early twentieth century role of dutiful housewife. It also indicates the explosive growth of a new, wealthier sector of the population possessing far more disposable income than before. Big business was quick to focus its attention on this new potential source of revenue.

The manufacture of discontent has long been a standard marketing ploy. The technique essentially involves suggesting an unfavourable comparison between the inevitably flawed and imperfect individual of real life and an artificially perfected ideal who, it is implied, can be emulated by buying the advertiser's service or product. Advertisers have always focused on male insecurities about being sufficiently attractive, successful, strong, intelligent, wealthy and sophisticated— thus the rugged Marlboro man, the smart set car adverts, the suave cigar adverts. Similarly, prior to women's liberation, advertisers had long focused on insecurities relating to the ideal doting mother and faithful, hygiene-obsessed housewife. But faced with a sexually-liberated, financially independent, thinking woman, advertisers were forced to find new discontents that might provide the foundation for the creation and expansion of new markets.Their answer was to latch onto the 'sexual revolution', combining it with an emphasis on female beauty.

Previously (hard though it is to believe today), appearance had been very much secondary to faithfulness in the world of advertising (the dutiful, subservient house mouse had no business being a sex kitten). With the housewife ideal revealed for the absurdity it was by feminism, businesses moved directly to the latent cultural concern for a woman's appearance, namely—that a real woman should be *beautiful*.

At the same time that real growth in women's social independence and economic affluence was taking place, the corporations went to work. Between 1968 and 1972, the number of diet-related articles in women's magazines rose by seventy percent.This escalation continued exponentially there, as elsewhere. By 1979, the number of diet-related articles in the US popular press per year had reached sixty. By January 1980, there were sixty-six in just one month. Parallel to this anti-fatness emphasis, the corporate campaign moved into overdrive against facial flaws—focusing on ageing and complexion.The results have been extraordinary. By 1990, the global dieting industry had become worth $32 billion; the cosmetics industry $20 billion and the cosmetic surgery industry $300 million.

Let us be clear that this has not been a process of satisfying women's desire for beauty products but has been a process of generating self-dissatisfaction in order to generate sales. Between 1966 and 1969, in exact correspondence to the new media emphasis on thinness, two US studies showed that the percentage of teenage girls who thought they were fat rose from 50% to 80%.A later 1984 study by the University of Cincinnati showed that 75% of all women between the ages of 18 and 35 believed themselves to be fat, of which only 25% were medically overweight, whilst 45% of women classified as underweight thought they were fat. By 1985, 90% of women said they thought they weighed too much. Again, this reflects the corporate campaign as, according to Dr C. Wayne of George Washington University, the average model used by corporate advertisers is thinner than 95% of the population. Not surprisingly, then, by 1988 the *San Francisco Chronicle* reported that 33% of all women were 'strongly dissatisfied' with their bodies.

The true cost of the growth of this multi-billion dollar manufacturing of discontent has been an explosion in physical and mental ill-health among women. At time of writing, fully 10% of all US women (and as many as 20% of all US women students) suffer from serious eating disorders. The American Anorexia and Bulimia Association reports that a million new women are stricken by these illnesses every year. Of these, 150,000 die each year (three times the total number of people who die in US car accidents). In Europe, the trends show signs of following the American path, with between 1% and 2% of all British, French and Italian women now suffering from either anorexia or bulimia. This may be only the beginning—the University of Cincinnati report also showed that whole new generations of anorexics and bulimics may be on their way—by the age of thirteen, 53% of all girls were found to be unhappy with the shape or size of their bodies. This figure rose to 78% by the age of eighteen. Meanwhile, two million Americans undergo cosmetic surgery every year, fuelling a $300 million industry growing at 10% per year. Between 200,000 and a million women have had breast implants so far, whilst every year 200,000 women have liposuctions.

We should not be surprised at the effectiveness of corporate propaganda in convincing young girls and grown women that they are sufficiently inadequate to starve themselves to death by the hundred thousand every year, just as we should not be surprised that it is able to convince children, despite all the evidence in the world as to the risks, that it is a good idea to smoke. After all, in 1991 Imperial Tobacco were found to be targeting advertisements at 'men and women' between the ages of twelve and seventeen. They invest this marketing budget not as some sort of shot in the dark, but because it works—advertisers are extremely able to change what people, and especially young people, think and do. The carrot-and-stick power of advertising revenue over the media is equally effective.

The October 1988 issue of *Harpers and Queen*, for example, carried £100,000 worth of advertisements from cosmetics companies. This is a lot of money and a lot of power. In 1956, the first 'arrangement' was made whereby a nylon manufacturer association booked $12,000 worth of advertising space in *Woman's World* on the condition that the editor agreed not to publish anything in that issue featuring natural fibres. As a consequence of this type of pressure, beauty editors are rarely able to write freely about dieting or cosmetics, especially as advertisers commonly buy editorial to support their adverts. In the case of the exploitation of women's insecurity, Naomi Woolf sums the situation up well in her book *The Beauty Myth* (see this book for further reading, and for the sources of statistics included in this section):

'Magazines, consciously or half-consciously, must project the attitude that looking one's age is bad because $650 million of their
ad revenue comes from people who would go out of business if
visible age looked good. They need, consciously or not, to promote
women's hating their bodies enough to go profitably hungry, since
the advertising budget for one third of the nation's food bill depends
on their doing so by dieting.'[42]

The effectiveness or morality of the product in question is not important. It is not important that the $20 billion cosmetics industry (four
times the size of IBM at its height) is actually selling a lie. No matter
that its creams, lotions and potions cannot at all prevent ageing or
wrinkles. Professor Albert Kligman of the University of Pennsylvania
has said:

'When they make a claim of anti-ageing, of the stuff having deep
biological effects, then they have to be stopped. It's pure bunkum...
beyond the bounds of reason and truth... [They] simply cannot
function as their backers and makers say they do, because it is physically impossible for them to get deep enough into the skin to
make any lasting difference to wrinkles. The same applies to the
removal of lines or wrinkles, or the permanent prevention of the
ageing of cells.'[43]

Although government agencies have done little to control the selling
of this lie, they have done enough to assure us of its existence. In
1987, the US Food And Drugs Administration was finally forced to
challenge the outlandish claims of cosmetics companies. Director
Daniel L. Michaels wrote to twenty-three chief cosmetics executives
asking them to account for 'magic', 'anti-ageing', 'cellular replacement' ingredients in their products, asking for immediate withdrawal
of the claims or submission for testing as drugs. Michaels added in
his demand:

'We are unaware of any substantial scientific evidence that demonstrates the safety and effectiveness of these articles.'[44]

In response, words were changed, products re-packaged and the selling
of the lie carried on as before (as with green consumerism, and so
on).

Here, then, we have a concrete example of the ability of the propaganda system to manufacture discontent, manipulate the truth and
so generate massive sales at the cost of untold human misery. Of

course, we can argue that women are free to buy or not to buy these products. But in the real world of $52 billion of diet and cosmetic industry power over our culture (not to mention the allied fashion industry), this argument is of academic interest only. The truth is that from a very early age, we are exposed to thought control of overwhelming sophistication, quantity and power. Is a young girl free to accept her normal, average, necessarily imperfect (because perfect can be forever defined as whatever we happen not to be) body and face, when the global communications networks of corporate industry imply over and over again that imperfect is unacceptable, revolting, unlovable but changeable—at a price?

How can any individual be expected to stand out against this propaganda, when self-doubt and insecurity are deep-seated human traits? We need only imagine the young sufferer of teenage spots watching the recent British advertisement for acne lotion which has a group of attractive teenagers partying happily in a cafe. On perceiving the imminent arrival of a friend, they all laugh, 'Here comes pizza-face!' Beyond the callous humour, do we really think that, having seen this advert, our young teenager is then free to look at him or herself in the mirror and feel that his or her appearance is okay, or even tolerable? Is it freedom for the young, and above all for girls and women of all ages, to be perpetually propagandized into feeling ashamed of their appearance to the point of starvation, self-mutilation and death? Is it freedom to not be able to look at ourselves in the mirror, or to dare reveal our nakedness to our loved ones? More insidiously, is it freedom to be brainwashed into judging our loved ones by the impossible standards of corporate greed? If this exploitation of human vulnerability is freedom, then freedom needs to be redefined.

Profitable Confusion, Profitable Illness

The profitable destruction wrought by corporate consumerism depends on the notion that happiness in life is a question not of being accepted as we are, imperfections and all, but of being perfect, with all imperfections painted over, surgically removed, or destroyed.

If the truth of corporate involvement in the devastation of the Third World cannot be allowed to reach the public for fear of impeding that exploitation, then how much more prohibited must be the truth that love and happiness are not about being perfect and hiding imperfection, but about being openly imperfect and accepted for what we are as real, honest, loveable, imperfect boys, girls, men and women? This realization implies a complete rejection of the whole basis of corporate consumerism and its goals, and is therefore not a matter for 'respectable' discourse.

From this we can extrapolate all the way to our modern predicament. The goals of corporate consumerism require that we accept *its* values, that we fail to seek better alternatives, that we reject the possibility of finding better alternatives ('psycho-babble'), that we fail even to see the existence of a problem to be solved, that we therefore live according to an entirely inadequate set of values, that we therefore live in complete confusion, that we therefore suffer profound and devastating psychological, physical and environmental dis-ease; that we suffer and, if necessary, die for profit.

In Conclusion: A Few Last Questions

The Need to be 'Genuinely Bewildered'

In this book we have been concerned with any number of subjects: politics, philosophy, literature, religion, psychology, human rights and the environment. But the real issue has been a simple one—*doubt*. Beyond this, the aim has not even been to supply any answers. We remarked earlier on the extraordinary contrast between our modern confusion concerning many fundamental questions of life and our certainty regarding the required beliefs of society—the value of economic growth, status as success, our attainment of freedom, our respect for human rights, and so on. This inconsistency is the clearest possible indication of the presence of thought control. The critically important task today, then, I believe, is to abandon rationalized certainty for uncertainty, doubt and wonder. By developing the capacity to be uncertain, we will have gone a long way towards loosening the chains of thought control. Erich Fromm had this to say on the role of wonder:

> 'This wondering is the most significant therapeutic factor in analysis. The patient has taken his reactions, his desires and anxieties for granted, has interpreted his troubles as the result of the actions of others, of bad luck, constitution, or what not. If the psychoanalysis is effective it is not because the patient accepts new theories about the reasons of his unhappiness but because he acquires a capacity for being *genuinely bewildered*; he marvels at the discovery of a part of himself whose existence he had never suspected.'[45]

The unknown author of *The Cloud Of Unknowing*, written around 1370 A.D., said the same thing in a different way:

'Make it your business then to see that your spirit is tied to nothing physical... Let go this 'everywhere' and this 'everything' in exchange for this 'nowhere' and this 'nothing'. Never mind if you cannot fathom this nothing, for I love it surely so much the better.'[46]

In other words, we need to seek the truth, clinging to no false certainty, to no hope of an end to questioning and learning. All we have really been suggesting in this book is that life should be a matter of extra-ordinary doubt, awe, wonder and uncertainty. How can it be that so many of us can take this existence so for granted? How much do we really understand about existence? Do we *really* know what it is all about? On what basis can we really be certain about anything? As Montaigne said, '*Que sais-je?*' 'What do I know?' Not just in terms of 'I haven't got a clue!', but in terms of 'When I think about it, what do I really know about life, and how much of it is really a complete mystery to me?' If it is not a mystery to me, then is that lack of a sense of mystery not itself a mystery? Why do we not sense the mystery in our failure to recognize our ignorance?

How much of what we consider our certainty is actually unthinking acceptance and conformity, rationalizations to lubricate our working as cogs in the economic machine? Could it be that our lack of wonder is a reflection, not of the chilling emptiness of the universe, but of the chilling emptiness of a system that sacrifices people for profit? Do the adverts want us to be uncertain as to whether we should really buy their product? Do an awful lot of people not gain from our certainty, however unrealistic, deluded and destructive it might be?

We have examined some controversial ideas in this discussion. Perhaps none of these ideas has been proven, but hopefully they have given cause for doubt; and that, arguably, is all that matters. For human beings cannot be controlled by doubt—only by false certainty; and wherever there is terrible human destructiveness, there also we are sure to find the bloody uniforms of those representing some 'final solution' in close attendance—in East Timor, Cambodia, Tibet, El Salvador, Guatemala, Bosnia, Hispaniola, My Lai, Auschwitz, and so on.

On what basis does our complacency actually rest? When do we actually ever read or hear any discussion of the deepest premises of society? How do we explain the fact that, after reading a deeply questioning book, we find that its ideas seem utterly unrelated to the 'important' issues of the day? How can we explain the fact that ideas which seem rational and important when we read them, which lift our hearts with coherence and understanding, seem to belong to an alien world to that of the mass media? Time and again we may read an utterly convincing, rational examination of a problematic aspect of the world (by a Rousseau, Fromm, Campbell, or Chomsky), and return to the quiz shows and sports specials of the media and wonder if that rational argument was not part of some strange dream. Sometimes, we may literally find ourselves returning to our newspaper clippings and books to reassure ourselves that there really was 40% ozone depletion over Scandinavia in January 1993, that the Timorese genocide is real and really has been carried out by force of US and British arms. But what has this got to do with the media version of reality by which our lives are framed, with the quiz show we are watching, with England qualifying for the World Cup? Or with the good-humoured political TV debates and their perennial underlying joke that politicians are crafty, but essentially benign, rascals, when these same 'benign rascals' make possible (and keep from public awareness) the starvation and torture of people throughout the Third World?

We can only assume from our mass media that deeper questioning, critical thinking and doubt are either irrelevant to life—with dissidents being simply paranoid neurotics, psychologists being more mad than their patients, philosophers being lost in semantics, religious thinkers draped pathetically over crutches of wishful thinking—or deeper questioning, critical thinking and doubt are somehow being discouraged by society. Chomsky's truly great contribution to the struggle for human freedom is that he has taken what we have been persuaded to believe is an insane idea, a product only of individual neurosis—the idea that society is not free and quite possibly not even sane—and shown it to be empirically, demonstrably true; he has provided the vital support for the individual to be able to declare him- and herself sane against the insanity of society, despite a million voices declaring that it is the occasional *doubter* who is mad.

To what extent would a critically thinking population be compatible with corporate consumerism? Clearly they would only be compatible if rigidly conformist, alienated, routinized, surreally boring, maddening work, and passive, unhealthy, gratuitous consumption, were the natural, best choices of humanity. The enormous efforts expended to inhibit the development of critical thought and to deceive the public more generally are answers in themselves. Similarly, even a cursory glance at human history shows that the goals of modern life are far from the norm—entire cultures through millennia have rejected gratuitous consumption and status as goals (thereby earning the title 'primitive savages'). The Zuni tribe of the South-western United States, for example, was thoroughly studied by Ruth Benedict, Margaret Mead, and others:

> 'The Zuni system can only be understood by the fact that material things are relatively little valued and the fact that the major interest in life is religious. To put it another way, the dominant value is life and living itself, not things and their possessions. Songs, prayers, rituals, and dances are the major and most important elements in this system.'[47]

Even Columbus was impressed by the communitarian values of the South American Indians he was soon to massacre. They are, he said:

> '...so naive and so free with their possessions that no one who has not witnessed them would believe it. When you ask them for something they have, they never say no. To the contrary, they offer to share with anyone...'[48]

In the 1650s, a French Jesuit priest had this to say of the Iroquois tribe:

> 'No poorhouses are needed among them, because they are neither mendicants nor paupers... Their kindness, humanity and courtesy not only makes them liberal with what they have, but causes them to possess hardly anything except in common.'[49]

A radical departure from the well-established Western assumption that human nature is ruthlessly selfish and competitive, our innate greed and brutality requiring the firm restraint of Hobbes' absolute ruler and the pacifying suckling of mass consumerism. Some Indian societies, on the other hand, rejected all government, thus effectively placing themselves in precisely Hobbes' dread 'state of nature', with interesting results:

> 'The foundation principle of Indian government had always been the rejection of government. The freedom of the individual was regarded by practically all Indians north of Mexico as a canon infinitely more precious than the individual's duty to his community or nation. This anarchistic attitude ruled all behaviour, beginning with the smallest social unit, the family. The Indian parent was constitutionally reluctant to discipline his children. Their every exhibition of self-will was accepted as a favourable indication of the development of maturing character.'[50]

A Moravian minister who lived among these Indians described the effects of this government-as-no-government:

> 'Thus has been maintained for ages, without convulsions and without civil discord, this traditional government... a government in which there are no positive laws, but only long established habits and customs, no code of jurisprudence, but the experience of former times, no magistrates, but advisers, to whom the people nevertheless, pay a willing and implicit obedience, in which age confers rank, wisdom gives power, and moral goodness secures title to universal respect.'[51]

This does not mean that all pre-industrial societies were inhabited by 'noble savages' (nor does it mean that industrial societies are inhabited by noble people who are not savage), but it does mean that our own society is quite clearly not the only feasible alternative. Despite the modern distaste for talk of a specific human nature, it is forever assumed (by capitalists) that modern capitalism, for all its flaws (actually atrocities against humanity and planet), is the only workable alternative for this innately greedy, violent human race. This is usually claimed by reference to Soviet 'communism' which, having clearly collapsed, is cited as final proof that all alternatives to capitalism are similarly doomed; indeed we are assured that 'history has ended'. That this idea can have been taken seriously by anyone is remarkable, not only because there are no rational grounds for believing that Soviet totalitarianism is the only feasible alternative to corporate capitalism, but also for the disconcerting reason that, as Chomsky has suggested, if a Salvadorean peasant living under the US 'sphere of influence' in the eighties had woken up in communist Poland, he would have thought he had died and gone to heaven (a lesson that many 'liberated' former Eastern bloc countries, including Poland, are beginning to learn the hard way, as we have seen). In reality, the ruthless crushing of any 'threat of a good example' in Nicaragua, Vietnam, Chile, Haiti, Cuba, and so on, reveals the truth: history has not 'ended' at all; it has been stopped by force, and the 'masters of self-adulation', despite their bragging, know full well that it threatens to start up again at any moment.

When we contrast it with many earlier societies, our society gives every appearance of being far less adequate, indeed far less sane. According to June McKerrow, director of The Mental Health Foundation, for example:

'Mental illness affects 1 in 4 of the UK adult population at any point in time and kills four times as many as road accidents. It is as prevalent as heart trouble and three times more common than cancer.'[52]

Returning to our original question, it seems reasonable to assume that independently minded, critically thinking, self-confident individuals are in fact a threat to the corporate monoculture (just as independently minded governments like the Nicaraguan Sandinistas were a threat to the global economic monoculture). Critical thought threatens to raise the spectre of more sane ways of living. On the basis of this awareness, our task is surely to seek to understand, and thereby extricate ourselves from the mechanisms that prevent us from developing the capacity for critical thought. Above all, we need to keep asking questions.

Why does the US President talk of his hope that the 'peace process' in the Middle East will be guided by the 'wisdom and compassion of the Almighty', when few people believe in this type of God any more, when the system he fronts has no regard whatsoever for Christian ideals, when those managing that system would advise psychiatric help for anyone who actually believed the observance of such ideals was a guiding principle of policy? Why are leaders who speak in this way not roundly denounced for attempting to deceive the public? Why is the historical and documentary record not raised to demonstrate the deceit? Why are such banal lies allowed to become axiomatic truths through the silence of journalists, religious leaders, teachers and the rest? Why do intellectuals merely sit and laugh cynically at such lies when they are not irrelevant, not a joke, when they have a powerful effect on what people come to believe, when history shows that such deceptions are a cornerstone of exploitative power?

Why do we never discuss or understand anything in depth? Why does nobody understand why the United States, rather than the United Nations, is 'mediating' in the Middle East and Haiti? Why the West furiously railed against 'the New Hitler' Saddam Hussein's destruction of the Iraqi Kurds (although only when it served our purpose), while Yeltsin's assault on the people of Chechnya, with the barbaric cluster-bombing of civilian populations, is met with barely a murmur of disapproval, with US Secretary of State Warren Christopher describing the Russian assault as merely 'ill-conceived and ill-executed'? When UN condemnation of Indonesia's invasion of East Timor was vetoed by the West? When the United States itself invaded

Panama, killing 3,000 civilians to arrest one man?

Why are we so obsessed with keeping up with current events but not with understanding those events? Why does no one discuss the fact that it is often literally impossible to make sense of what is happening on the basis of the reports we see on the news (certainly the case with regards to Haiti)? Why is this not a source of outrage in democracies whose life-blood is supposed to be the free flow of information, when our representatives are acting and even killing other human beings in our name, but we have no understanding of what they are doing or why? Is this all a way of making us feel we are seeing the truth, when all we are seeing is a stream of useless, meaningless facts?

Why can we not vote on the issues we want to see investigated in the news, when the fate of places like Haiti, Iraq, Panama, Grenada and Chechnya show such a marked tendency to be 'disappeared' from the news? Why can we not vote for the commentators we would like to see giving their perspective on the news, when Fairness In Accuracy And Reporting found that of 1,530 guests interviewed on the prestigious US Nightline public affairs programme, 92% were white, 89% were male and 80% were professionals, government officials, or corporate representatives, with the issues covered 'closely aligned with the agenda of the US government'?

Why do governments and companies justify their actions on the basis of the need to 'create jobs', as if profit was a secondary issue, as if everyone gained equally, as if the quantity and not the quality of jobs was the only issue? Why does not everyone who has ever worked for a corporation, who knows the truth, not expose such nonsense, such complete reversals of the truth, for the transparent deceptions they are? Why are jobs 'created' but never 'destroyed'—only 'lost'? Why are politicians protected from the public, from all genuinely awkward questions, when it is we who are *their* leaders? Why are our political representatives treated with such reverence and awe in a democracy that is supposed to place 'the people' in highest regard? Why can we not see that people like John Major, Bill Clinton and George Bush are just men, just individual people like you and I (regardless of the podium they stand on and the cut of their suits) who need to give account of themselves, who need to convince us that they are worthy of our attention, let alone our respect?

Why are so many of our artists so bleakly world-weary, so convinced of the hopelessness and tragedy of life when, each and every night, we look up to behold a self-evident mystery that is your mystery, my mystery? Why is the search for truth deemed neurotic, but the acceptance of superficial platitudes deemed practical? Why is it considered realistic to dismiss human life as absurd, but naive to dismiss our social system as absurd? Why is it considered realistic to deem people innately wicked, but simple-minded to deem our political and economic system innately wicked? Is realism what is real, or what is *required* to be real?

Why is our society still not in love with (or even tolerant of) that wonderful menagerie of 'asses', 'Neptunians' and assorted 'wild men [and women] on the wings' who, over the years, have sought the truth motivated, not by financial or political power, but by a sincere desire to understand the world? Why can we not see the obvious parallels between the burning of Giordano Bruno at the stake, the denouncement of the writings of the great humanist Spinoza as monstrosities 'forged in hell by a renegade Jew and the Devil', the dismissal of that braying 'ass' Copernicus before Luther, and the abuse meted out to Chomsky—that 'liar', 'crackpot', purveyor of 'absolute rubbish', that 'self-hating Jew'? Why, with the spectacle of all history before us, do we not automatically suspect absolutely everyone declared respectable, unbiased and praiseworthy by those who have power over us?

Why does our society find it unworthy of discussion that we and our precious, impressionable children are continuously hounded by advertisers with the same set of interests (profit from mass consumption) propounding the same essential view of the world (happiness and status through unrestrained consumption)? Why does it not occur to us that this continuous flood of propaganda might be a threat to our view of reality, might be a threat to our independence and sanity? Why does that not send even the tiniest chill up our spines?

Is it because our political and economic systems are rooted in a great system of necessary lies? And when we find ourselves so convinced by those lies that our hearts sink to see how irrelevant our search for truth suddenly seems, then what damage must that system of lies be doing inside us?

How could we ever hope to find contentment when we are required to live lives based on profitable illusions? When the most important issues to which we devote ourselves have become getting that new car, moving to that new house, getting that extra promotion for the extra money; when these really have become the central concerns in our lives, though we don't really know why, or what anything is really all about—how can we hope to be happy, or sane?

How can we hope to build relationships, to find love, on these foundations?

People talk of the emptiness of life, which may sound nebulous and other-worldly. But let us put it another way: how can we be happy when we have a complete lack of understanding as to why we are doing what we are doing? How can we feel good about life when it makes no sense to us? Is that what we mean when we call life meaningless? And if we are not able to interpret that sense of meaninglessness in terms of failure to understand, because the system has trained us not to think that way, then is that why we interpret our sense of meaninglessness in terms of life not leading to some goal?

We are required to misinterpret our own problems because, like this book, the alternatives seem to make no sense in the 'real' world that continuously assaults our senses. The world tells us that 'of course this is the right way to live—there is no other way', so the problem must lie outside the political and economic system.

Everyone wants to find answers to life. Everyone needs genuine relationship with other people, peace of mind, fulfilment, a sense of community and belonging. Everyone wants to be free from crippling stress and dullness and boredom. Everyone wants life to continue on this planet.

Let us, then, put a last question as simply as possible—how on earth can we ever hope to answer these questions adequately, if we are not free to consider or answer them in ways that do not suit the requirements of corporate consumerism?

REFERENCES

CHAPTER ONE

1. Erich Fromm, *The Art of Being*, Continuum, New York, 1992, p.25.
2. Paul Robinson, *New York Times Weekly Book Review*, 25th February 1979, p.3.
3. Noam Chomsky and Edward S. Herman, *Manufacturing Consent: The Political Economy of The Mass Media*, Pantheon Books, New York, 1988, p.XI.
4. Ibid., p.XII.
5. Ibid., p.8.
6. David Barsamian, *Stenographers To Power (Media And Propaganda)*, Common Courage Press, 1992, pp.134-5.
7. Chomsky and Herman, *Manufacturing Consent*, p.15.
8. James Curran (ed.), *The British Press: A Manifesto*, Macmillan, London, 1978, pp.252-5.
9. Quoted in Bagdikian, *Media Monopoly*, 2nd edition, Beacon Press, 1987, p.160.
10. Chomsky and Herman, op. cit., pp.17-18.
11. Quoted in Naomi Woolf, *The Beauty Myth*, Vintage, 1991, p.78.
12. Chomsky and Herman, op. cit., pp.21-22.
13. Ibid., p.29.
14. Quoted in *Wall Street Journal*, January 5, 1990.
15. Noam Chomsky, *Deterring Democracy*, Hill and Wang, 1992, p.182.
16. David Barsamian and Noam Chomsky, *Chronicles of Dissent*, AK Press, 1992, p.203.
17. Ibid., p.194.
18. Ibid., p.70.
19. John Pilger, *Distant Voices*, Vintage, 1994, pp.297-298.
20. Quoted in Noam Chomsky, *Year 501: The Conquest Continues*, Verso, 1993, pp. 133-134.
21. *The Age*, Melbourne, December 8, 1975. Quoted in John Pilger, op. cit., p.235.
22. Quoted in Mark Achbar (ed.) *Manufacturing Consent: Noam Chomsky And The Media*, Black Rose Books, 1994, pp.115-116.
23. Quoted in *Amnesty* magazine (British Section), September/October 1994, p.5.

24. *Wall Street Journal*, April 25, 1989. Quoted in Chomsky, *Year 501*, p.130.
25. *Wall Street Journal*, June 8, 1992. Quoted in Chomsky, *Year 501*.
26. *Economist*, August 5, 1987. Quoted in Chomsky, *Year 501*, p.130.
27. *Sydney Morning Herald*, December 10, 1991. Quoted in John Pilger, op. cit., p.249.
28. *The Australian*, March 18, 1994. Quoted in John Pilger, op. cit., p.318.
29. Quoted in *Amnesty* magazine, op. cit., p.5.
30. Ibid., p.5.
31. Quoted in Mark Curtis, *The New Internationalist*, March 1994.
32. Quoted in John Pilger, op. cit., p.311.
33. Quoted in Chomsky, *Year 501*, p.135.
34. Topol Backgrounder, *Indonesia: The British Perspective*, 1993. Quoted in John Pilger, op. cit., p.306.
35. Quoted in John Pilger, op. cit., p.309.
36. Quoted in Noam Chomsky and Edward S. Herman, *The Washington Connection and Third World Fascism*, Volume One of 'The Political Economy of Human Rights', South End Press, 1979, p.137.
37. Quoted Mark Achbar (ed.), op. cit., p.99.
38. In an interview with John Pilger, quoted in Pilger op. cit., pp.319–20.
39. Strategic Studies Institute of the U.S. Army War College, 1990 quoted in Ramsey Clark, *The Fire This Time: US War Crimes In The Gulf*, Thunder's Mouth Press, 1994, p.12.
40. *New York Newsday*, January 21, 1991. Quoted in Ramsey Clark, op.cit., p.15.
41. *San Francisco Chronicle*, March 13, 1991. Quoted in Ramsey Clark, op. cit., p.15.
42. *The New Yorker*, September 30, 1991. Quoted in Ramsey Clark, op. cit., p.15.
43. 'The Glaspie Transcript', in *The Gulf War Reader*, Sifry and Cerf, quoted in Ramsey Clark, op. cit., p.23.
44. *New York Times*, July 17, 1991, quoted in Ramsey Clark, op. cit., p.23.
45. Ramsey Clark, op.cit., p.37.
46. Ibid., p.12.
47. *The Nation*, quoted in Ramsey Clark, op. cit., p.33.
48. Quoted in Ramsey Clark, op. cit., p.171.

49. Ibid., p.59.
50. Quoted in Ramsey Clark, op. cit., p.xii
51. Ibid., p.129.
52. Ibid., pp.127-8.
53. Ibid., p.147.
54. *Science*, August 3, 1990.
55. Ibid.
56. Quoted in Tom Athanasiou, *US Politics & Global Warming*, Open Magazine Pamphlet Series, Pamphlet #14, 1991, p. 4.
57. Ibid., p.8.
58. Quoted in Joseph Campbell, *Creative Mythology* (The Masks of God, Volume IV), Penguin, 1976, p.596.

CHAPTER TWO

1. Noam Chomsky, *Necessary Illusions: Thought Control in Democratic Societies*, Pluto, London, 1991, p.19.
2. Erich Fromm, *Beyond The Chains of Illusion*, Abacus, 1989, pp.157-158.
3. David Barsamian and Noam Chomsky, *Chronicles of Dissent*, p.69.
4. Rachel Sharp, *Knowledge, Ideology and The Politics of Schooling*, p.109. Quoted in Dollimore and Sinfield (eds.), *Political Shakespeare*, Manchester University Press, 1985, p.138.
5. Leo Tolstoy, *Shakespeare And The Drama*, 1903. Quoted in George Orwell, *Inside The Whale And Other Essays*, Penguin, 1962, p.104.
6. Ibid., p.101.
7. Howard Zinn, *Failure To Quit: Reflections of An Optimistic Historian*, Common Courage Press, 1993, p.154.
8. Ibid., pp.155-156.
9. Noam Chomsky, *Deterring Democracy*, Hill And Wang, 1992, p.372.
10. George Orwell, op. cit., p.106.
11. Ibid., pp.110-111.
12. Ibid., p.116.
13. Noam Chomsky and Edward S. Herman, *The Washington Connection And Third World Fascism*, Volume One of 'The Political Economy of Human Rights', South End Press, 1979, p.XIV.
14. Quoted in *Chicago Tribune*, January 1, 1994.
15. Noam Chomsky, *Media Control: The Spectacular Achievements of Propaganda*, Open Pamphlet Series.

16. Erich Fromm, *Beyond The Chains of Illusion*, Abacus, 1989, pp.131-132.

17. Erich Fromm, *The Fear of Freedom*, Ark, 1989, p.229.

18. James Hillman and Michael Ventura, *We've Had A Hundred Years of Psychotherapy (And The World's Getting Worse)*, Harper, San Francisco, 1992, pp.3-4.

19. Ibid., p.6.

20. Noam Chomsky, *Deterring Democracy*, p.369.

21. Quoted in Noam Chomsky, *Necessary Illusions*, p.17 and p.18.

22. Quoted in March Achbar (ed), *Manufacturing Consent: Noam Chomsky And The Media*, Black Rose Books, 1994.

23. Quoted in Noam Chomsky, *Necessary Illusions*, p.132.

24. Hillman and Ventura, op. cit., p.12.

25. C.G. Jung, *Memories, Dreams, Reflections*, Flamingo, 1983, p.170.

26. Erich Fromm, *The Sane Society*, p.77.

27. Erich Fromm, *The Revision of Psychoanalysis*, Westview Press, 1992, p.84.

28. David Burston, *The Legacy of Erich Fromm*, Harvard University Press, 1991, p.185.

29. Ibid., p.185.

30. Henry David Thoreau, *Walden*, Penguin, 1983, p.49.

31. R.D. Laing, *The Politics of Experience*, Penguin, 1990, p.24.

32. E.F. Schumacher, 'Insane Work Cannot Produce A Sane Society', in John Button (ed.), *The Best of Resurgence*, Green Books, 1991, p.54.

33. Ibid., p.54.

CHAPTER THREE

1. Chomsky and Barsamian, *Chronicles of Dissent*, p.11.

2. Nietzsche, *Thus Spoke Zarathustra*, Penguin, 1969, p.76.

3. Bertrand Russell, 'A Free Man's Worship', in Robert Egner (ed.), *Basic Writings of Bertrand Russell*, Touchstone Books, 1961, p.72.

4. Joseph Campbell, *The Hero With A Thousand Faces*, Paladin, 1968, p.3.

5. Joseph Campbell, *Occidental Mythology* (The Masks of God, Volume III), p.312.

6. W.B. Yeats, *The Tower*, 1928, quoted in John Gross (ed.), *The Oxford Book of Aphorisms*, Oxford University Press, 1983, p.347.

7. Socrates, *Symposium*, 210a-212a, quoted in Joseph Campbell, *Occidental Mythology*, pp.230-232.

8. Arian, *The Discourses of Epictetus*, iii, 22.45-46, quoted in Joseph Campbell, Occidental Mythology, p.249.
9. Nietzsche, op. cit., p.71.
10. Noam Chomsky, *Necessary Illusions*, Pluto Press, 1991, p.18.
11. James Joyce, *Portrait of The Artist As A Young Man*, in *The Essential James Joyce*, Triad Grafton, 1977, p.266.
12. Quoted in Noam Chomsky, *Deterring Democracy*, Hill and Wang, 1992, p.93.
13. Lyndon B. Johnson, Congressional Record, March 15, 1948. Quoted in Noam Chomsky, *On Power And Ideology* (The Managua Lectures), South End Press, 1987, p.34.
14. Quoted in Noam Chomsky, *On Power And Ideology*, p.34.
15. Erich Fromm, *Psychoanalysis And Religion*, Yale University Press, 1978, p.85.

CHAPTER FOUR

1. Edward Conze, *Buddhist Scriptures*, Penguin, 1959, p.30.
2. Ibid., p.108.
3. Richard Wilhelm, *The Pocket I Ching*, Arkana, 1984, p.117.
4. Leo Tolstoy, *A Confession (And Other Religious Writings)*, Penguin, 1987, p.29.
5. Edward Conze, op. cit., p.84.
6. Erich Fromm, *The Art of Being*, Continuum, New York, 1992, p.77.
7. Richard Wilhelm, op. cit., p.49.
8. Edward Conze, op. cit., pp.38-39.

CHAPTER FIVE

1. Joseph Campbell, *The Hero With A Thousand Faces*, Paladin, 1988, p.59.
2. The Pentagon Papers, quoted in Chomsky, *Turning the Tide*, Pluto, 1985, p.252.
3. Sigmund Freud, *Civilization and its Discontents*, W.W. Norton, 1962, p.91.
4. Ibid.
5. A.R. Heron, quoted in Erich Fromm, *The Sane Society*, Rinehart & Company, 1955, p.223.
6. Erich Fromm, *The Sane Society*, p.204 .
7. Ibid., p.144.
8. C.G. Jung, *Memories, Dreams, Reflections*, Flamingo, 1983, p.261.

9. From the song 'Train Runnin' Low On Soul Coal', by Andy Partridge, XTC, on the album 'The Big Express'.

10. R.D. Laing, *The Politics Of Experience*, Penguin, 1990, p.58.

11. Vauvenargues, quoted in *The Oxford Book Of Aphorisms*, Oxford University Press, 1983, p.181.

12. Paulo Freire, *Pedagogy of The Oppressed*, Penguin, 1972, p.45.

13. Ibid., p.47.

14. Ibid., p.47.

CHAPTER SIX

1. Quoted by Jane Kentish in her introduction to Leo Tolstoy's *A Confession (And Other Religious Writings)*, Penguin, 1987, p.7.

2. Ibid., p.22.

3. Ibid., p.24.

4. Ibid., p.24.

5. Ibid., p.23.

6. Ibid., p. 27.

7. Erich Fromm, *The Sane Society*, Rinehart & Co., 1955, p.205.

8. Tolstoy, op. cit., p.28.

9. Ibid., p.28.

10. Ovid, *Metamorphoses*, I, 504-557, quoted in Joseph Campbell, *The Hero With A Thousand Faces*, Paladin, 1988, p.61.

11. Proverbs 1:24-27, 32.

12. Tolstoy, op. cit. pp.28-29.

13. Ibid., p.29.

14. Ibid., p.30.

15. Ibid. pp.30-31.

16. *Vishnu Purana*, translated by Heinrich Zimmer, quoted in Joseph Campbell, *The Hero With A Thousand Faces*, p. 195.

17. Tolstoy, op.cit., p.31.

18. Ibid., p.63.

19. Ibid., p.67.

20. Ibid., p.71

21. Quoted in *The Oxford Book of Aphorisms*, John Gross (ed.), Oxford University Press, 1983, p.350.

22. Tolstoy, op. cit., p.60.

23. Ibid., p.65.

24. Ibid., p.59.

25. Joseph Campbell, *The Hero With A Thousand Faces*, pp.52-53.

CHAPTER SEVEN

1. Quoted in Noam Chomsky, *On Power And Ideology* (The Mangua Lectures), South End Press, 1987, p.18.
2. Quoted in *The Oxford Book of Aphorisms*, Oxford University Press, 1983, p.109.
3. Quoted *Independent On Sunday*, November 11, 1991.
4. Quoted in Noam Chomsky, *On Power And Ideology* (The Managua Lectures), South End Press, 1987, p.14.
5. Susan George, *How The Other Half Dies*, Penguin, 1991, p.16 & 17.
6. David Pepper, *Eco-Socialism*, Routledge, 1993, p.107
7. Susan George, op. cit., p.18.
8. Ibid., p.19.
9. Susan George, *Ill Fares The Land*, Penguin, 1985, revised and expanded edition 1990, p.238.
10. Ibid., pp.225-226
11. Aldous Huxley, *Brave New World*, Grafton, 1977, p.53.

CHAPTER EIGHT

1. Joseph Campbell, *Creative Mythology* (The Masks of God, Volume IV), Penguin, 1976, pp.5-6.
2. Thoreau, *Walden*, Penguin, 1983, p.113.
3. Quoted in Noam Chomsky, *Year 501*, Verso, 1993, p.18.
4. Erich Fromm, *The Fear of Freedom*, Ark, 1989, p.102.
5. Ovid, *Metamorphoses*, quoted in Joseph Campbell, *The Hero With A Thousand Faces*, Paladin, 1988, p.61.
6. Lyrics from the song "The Ballad of Peter Pumpkinhead" by Andy Partridge of XTC, on the album Nonsuch, Virgin records, 1992. This song is a wonderful sketch of the life and fate of the archetypal hero—half-fool, half-sage.
7. Joseph Campbell, *Creative Mythology*, op. cit., p.388.
8. Ibid., pp.36-37.
9. Quoted in Erich Fromm, *Man For Himself*, Ark edition, 1986, p.v.
10. Quoted in *The Buddhist Bible*, Ed. Dwight Goddard, Beacon, 1970, p.418.
11. Quoted in *Chicago Tribune*, article 'Strong Words', 1 January 1993.
12. C.G. Jung, *Memories, Dreams, Reflections*, Flamingo, 1983, pp.276-277.

13. Quoted in Joseph Campbell, *Oriental Mythology* (The Masks of God, Volume II), Penguin, 1976, p.260.
14. Ibid., p.261.
15. Ibid., p.262.
16. Ibid., p.264.
17. Ibid., p.265.
18. Quoted in Joseph Campbell, *The Hero With A Thousand Faces*, Paladin, 1968, p.163.
19. Quoted in Noam Chomsky, *Year 501*, op. cit., p.227.
20. Joseph Campbell, *The Hero With A Thousand Faces*, op cit., p.58.
21. James Joyce, *Portrait of The Artist As A Young Man*, in *The Essential James Joyce*, Triad Grafton, 1977, p.361.
22. Nietzsche, *Thus Spoke Zarathustra*, Penguin, 1969, p.108.

CHAPTER NINE

1. Erich Fromm, *Beyond The Chains Of Illusion*, Abacus, 1989, pp.131-132.
2. *The Impossible H.L. Mencken: A Selection of His Best Newspaper Stories*, edited by Marion Rodgers, Doubleday/Anchor, 1991.
3. Bruno Bettelheim, *The Uses of Enchantment: The Meaning And Importance of Fairy Tales*, Penguin, 1991, p.98).
4. Gore Vidal, *United States*, Random House, 1993, p.1032.
5. Gary Slapper, senior lecturer in law, Staffordshire Polytechnic, in a letter to *The Independent*, 16 December 1991.
6. Anthony Lewis, *New York Times*, April 1975.
7. Quoted in *The Oxford Book of Aphorisms*, Oxford University Press, 1983, p.29.
8. Fritjof Capra, *The Turning Point*, Flamingo, 1982, p.235.
9. Hegel, *Philosophy*, 96, quoted in Noam Chomsky, *Year 501*, Verso, 1993, p.119.
10. Paul R. Strauss, *New York Times*, 24 February 1977, quoted in Noam Chomsky and Edward S. Herman, *The Washington Connection And Third World Fascism*, p.63.
11. Quoted in Noam Chomsky, *Turning The Tide: US Intervention In Central America And The Struggle For Peace*, Pluto Press, 1985, p.48.
12. Michael Parenti, in David Barsamian, *Stenographers To Power (Media And propaganda)*, Common Courage Press, 1992, p.59.
13. Kiernan, *European Empires*, p.200, quoted in Noam Chomsky, *Year 501*, p.23.
14. Quoted in Noam Chomsky, *Year 501*, p.26.

15. Charles Darwin, *Descent of Man*, Part 1, p.70, quoted in Noam Chomsky, *Deterring Democracy*, Hill and Wang, 1992, p36.
16. Winston Churchill, quoted in Chomsky, *Deterring Democracy*, p.182.
17. Erich Fromm, *The Sane Society*, pp.156-157.
18. Nietzsche, *Thus Spoke Zarathustra*, Penguin, 1969, p.204.
19. Thoreau, *Walden*.
20. Noam Chomsky and Edward S. Herman, 'The Washington Connection And Third World Fascism' in *The Political Economy of Human Rights*, Volume 1, South End Press, 1979, p.12.
21. Joseph Campbell, *Creative Mythology* (The Masks of God, Volume IV), Penguin, 1976, pp.54-55.
22. *The Pocket I Ching*, Richard Wilhelm (trans.), Arkana, 1984, p.96.
23. Ibid., p.96.
24. Nietzsche, *Thus Spoke Zarathustra*, Penguin, 1969, p.229.
25. Ralph Waldo Emerson, *Essays and Poems*, selected by Tony Tanner, Everyman Library, 1992, p.26.
26. David Barsamian, *Stenographers To Power*, p.142.
27. John Pilger, *Distant Voices*, Vintage, 1994, p.107.
28. Ibid., pp.97-98.
29. Gore Vidal, *United States*, Random House, 1992, p.1033.
30. Ibid., p.1031.
31. John Dewey, quoted in Noam Chomsky & David Barsamian, *Keeping The Rabble In Line*, AK Press, 1994, p.246.
32. Edward Conze, ed., *Buddhist Scriptures*, Penguin Classics, 1959, p.109.
33. Quoted Howard Zinn, *A People's History of the United States*, 1980, Harper Perennial, p.56.
34. Noam Chomsky, *Deterring Democracy*, p.370.
35. Quoted in David Burston, *The Legacy of Erich Fromm*, Harvard University Press, 1991, p.153.
36. Henry David Thoreau, *Journal*, 2 March, 1858.
37. John Pilger, *Distant Voices*, Vintage, 1994, p.13.
38. Howard Zinn, *Failure To Quit: Reflections of An Optimistic Historian*, Common Courage Press, 1992, p.123.
39. Quoted in Noam Chomsky, *Year 501*, op. cit., p.198.
40. Howard Zinn, op. cit., p.125.
41. Quoted from ABC TV in *The Progressive*, February 1990.
42. Naomi Woolf, *The Beauty Myth*, Vintage, 1991, p.84.
43. Ibid., p.111.
44. Ibid., p.112.

45. Erich Fromm, *Psychoanalysis And Religion*, Yale University Press, 1978, p.96.
46. *The Cloud of Unknowing*, Penguin, 1978, pp.142-143.
47. Erich Fromm, *The Anatomy of Human Destructiveness*, Pelican, 1982, p.233.
48. Quoted in Howard Zinn, *A People's History of The United States*, Harper Perennial, 1990, p.3.
49. Ibid., p.20.
50. Ibid., p.136.
51. Ibid., p.136.
52. The Mental Health Foundation, promotional pamphlet, 1994.

BIBLIOGRAPHY

Mark Achbar (editor) *Manufacturing Consent - Noam Chomsky And The Media* (Black Rose Books, 1994)

Anon *The Cloud of Unknowing And Other Works* (Penguin, 1978)

Tom Athanasiou *US Politics & Global Warming* (Open Magazine Pamphlet Series, Pamphlet #14, 1991)

Ben Bagdikian *Media Monopoly* (Beacon Press, 1987)

David Barsamian *Stenographers To Power - Media And Propaganda* (Common Courage Press, 1992)

David Barsamian and Noam Chomsky *Chronicles of Dissent* (AK Press, 1992)
Keeping the Rabble in Line (AK Press, 1994)

Bruno Bettelheim *The Uses of Enchantment: the Meaning and Importance of Fairy Tales* (Penguin, 1991)

John Button (editor) *The Best of Resurgence* (Green Books, 1991)

David Burston *The Legacy of Erich Fromm* (Harvard University Press, 1991)

Joseph Campbell *The Hero With A Thousand Faces* (Paladin, 1968)
Primitive Mythology (The Masks of God Volume I, Penguin, 1976)
Oriental Mythology (The Masks of God Volume II, Penguin, 1976)
Occidental Mythology (The Masks of God Volume III, Penguin, 1976)
Creative Mythology (The Masks of God Volume IV, Penguin, 1976)

Fritjof Capra *The Turning Point* (Flamingo, 1982)

Noam Chomsky *American Power and the New Mandarins* (Pantheon, 1969)
At War with Asia (Pantheon, 1970)
For Reasons of State (Pantheon, 1973)
Radical Priorities, edited by C.P. Otero (Black Rose Books, 1981)
Turning The Tide: US Intervention In Central America And The Struggle For Peace (Pluto Press, 1985)
Pirates And Emperors: International Terrorism and the Real World (Black Rose Books, 1987)
On Power And Ideology: The Managua Lectures (South End Press, 1987)
The Chomsky Reader, edited by James Peck (Serpent's Tail, 1987)
The Culture of Terrorism (South End Press, 1988)
Language And Politics, edited by C.P. Otero (Black Rose Books, 1988)
Manufacturing Consent (1988) – see Edward S. Herman and Noam Chomsky
Necessary Illusions: Thought Control In Democratic Societies (Pluto, 1991)
Deterring Democracy (Verso, 1991; updated edition, Hill & Wang, 1992)
Year 501: The Conquest Continues (South End Press, 1993)
Letters From Lexington: Reflections on Propaganda (Common Courage Press, 1993)
Rethinking Camelot: JFK, the Vietnam War, and US Political Culture (South End Press, 1993)
World Orders, Old and New (Pluto Press, 1994)

Noam Chomsky and Edward S. Herman *The Washington Connection and Third World Fascism*, The Political Economy of Human Rights, Volume One (South End Press, 1979)
After The Cataclysm, The Political Economy of Human Rights, Volume Two (South End Press, 1979)

Ramsey Clark *The Fire This Time: US War Crimes In The Gulf* (Thunder's Mouth Press, 1994)

Edward Conze (editor) *Buddhist Scriptures* (Penguin Classics, 1959)

James Curran (editor) *The British Press: A Manifesto* (Macmillan, London, 1978)

Jonathan Dollimore and Alan Sinfield (editors) *Political Shakespeare* (Manchester University Press, 1985)

Ralph Waldo Emerson *Essays and Poems*, selected by Tony Tanner, (Everyman Library, 1992)

Paulo Freire *Pedagogy of The Oppressed* (Penguin, 1972)

Sigmund Freud *Civilization and its Discontents* (W W Norton, 1962)

Erich Fromm *Fear of Freedom* (Farrar and Rinehart, 1941)
   Man For Himself: An Inquiry into the Psychology of Ethics (Rinehart, 1947)
   The Sane Society (Rinehart and Winston, 1955)
   The Art of Loving (Harper and Row, 1956)
   Psychoanalysis and Zen Buddhism (George Allen and Unwin, 1960)
   Beyond The Chains of Illusion - My Encounter With Marx and Freud (1962. Reprinted Abacus, 1989)
   The Anatomy of Human Destructiveness (Holt, Rinehart and Winston, 1973)
   To Have or to Be? (Harper and Row, 1976)
   Psychoanalysis and Religion (Yale University Press, 1978)
   The Revision of Psychoanalysis (Westview Press, 1992)
   The Art of Being, edited by Rainer Funk (Continuum, New York, 1992)
   The Erich Fromm Reader, edited by Rainer Funk (Humanities Press International, 1994)
   The Art of Listening, edited by Rainer Funk (Constable, 1994)

Susan George *How The Other Half Dies: The Real Reasons For World Hunger* (Pelican, 1976. Reprinted Penguin, 1991)
   A Fate Worse Than Debt (Pelican Books, 1988. Reprinted Penguin, 1990)
   Ill Fares the Land (Penguin, 1985)

Dwight Goddard (editor) *The Buddhist Bible* (Beacon, 1970)

Edward S. Herman and Noam Chomsky *Manufacturing Consent, The Political Economy of the Mass Media* (Pantheon Books, 1988)

Edward S. Herman *Beyond Hypocrisy - Decoding the News in an Age of Propaganda* (South End Press, 1992)

James Hillman and Michael Ventura *We've Had A Hundred Years of Psychotherapy - And The World's Getting Worse* (Harper, San Francisco, 1992)

Aldous Huxley *Brave New World* (Grafton, 1977)
James Joyce *Portrait of The Artist As A Young Man*, in The Essential James Joyce (Triad Grafton, 1977)

C.G. Jung *Memories, Dreams, Reflections* (Flamingo, 1983)

Sheldon Kopp *If You Meet the Buddha on the Road, Kill Him!* (Sheldon Press, 1991)

R.D. Laing *The Politics of Experience and the Bird of Paradise* (Penguin, 1990)

Friedrich Nietzsche *Thus Spoke Zarathustra* (Penguin, 1969)

George Orwell *Inside the Whale and other Essays* (Penguin, 1962)

M. Scott Peck *The Road Less Travelled* (Simon & Schuster, 1978)
The Different Drum (Arrow, 1990)

David Pepper *Eco-Socialism - From Deep Ecology to Social Justice* (Routledge, 1993)

John Pilger *Distant Voices* (Vintage, 1994)

Jonathon Porritt *Seeing Green* (Blackwell, 1990)

Paul Reps *Zen Flesh, Zen Bones* (Arkana, 1991)

Henry David Thoreau *Walden* (Penguin, 1983)

Leo Tolstoy *A Confession, And Other Religious Writings* (Penguin, 1987)

Gore Vidal, *United States* (Random House, 1993)

Alan Watts *The Way of Zen* (Pelican, 1987)
The Wisdom of Insecurity (Rider, London, 1989)

Richard Wilhelm (translator) *The Pocket I Ching* (Arkana, 1984)

Naomi Woolf *The Beauty Myth* (Vintage, 1991)

Howard Zinn *A People's History of the United States* (Harper Colophon, 1980)
Failure To Quit: Reflections of an Optimistic Historian (Common Courage Press, 1993)

SOME SUGGESTED MAGAZINES

The Environment Digest
11-21 Sturton Street
Cambridge CB1 2SN, UK

Extra!
Fairness And Accuracy In Reporting
130 W. 25th Street
New York City, NY 10001, USA

The New Internationalist
55 Rectory Road
Oxford OX4 1BW, UK

Resurgence Magazine
Ford House
Hartland, Bideford
Devon EX39 6EE, UK

Z Magazine
116 St. Botolph Street
Boston, MA 02115, USA

BOOK AND MAGAZINE CATALOGUES

AK Press
22 Lutton Place
Edinburgh
Scotland EH8 9PE, UK

Common Courage Press
PO Box 702
Monroe, ME 04951, USA

WEBSITE (co-edited by the author)

www.medialens.org

INDEX